A YEAR OF PRACTICULTURE

For Berry

A YEAR OF PRACTICULTURE

Rohan Anderson

hardie grant books

Contents

Practiculture

prak-ti-kul-cha *noun*

1. a lifestyle choice of practical living:
His life has improved since he embraced practiculture.

In my effort to live the simple life, I inadvertently stumbled across practiculture. It's a way of living where daily choices are made based on their practical outcome. You see, moving away from the conventional approach of earning my livelihood behind a desk, to a lifestyle of DIY (almost everything), has meant having to focus my energy on what will deliver tangible results. For example, I used to earn money from my full-time job that I would use to buy food, or pay someone to deliver my firewood or mow my lawns. Now I don't have that income, I have no option but to do those practical tasks myself. It may not be everyone's cup of tea, but it sure works for me. I spend my days performing tasks, completing chores or setting off on adventures that will provide some useful, practical result. It's been a way of life for ancient cultures around the world for aeons. And it still works. Even in this modern age.

This book is an account of a year living in practiculture. It's a collection of observations, victories and failures, a collection of questions and of opinions, and a record of the reality of living a practical life.

This is a lifestyle choice. I don't think it's an option for everyone. I don't believe this way of life will eliminate the world's problems. It's what works for me and my little family. It works in my world. I'm sharing it in the hope that you may find certain elements of some use, be they practical, humorous or philosophical.

Science stuff

I am an animal. You are an animal. Before you read any further I'm going to ask you a favour. I want you to really clear your mind and consider something very important. And don't panic – just because I mentioned that I'm an animal doesn't mean I've converted to the trend of Paleo living. The very notion is absurd.

Consider that our animal bodies have evolved over thousands of years to run on a specific fuel of certain food. It's food that's derived from natural sources. You don't need to be a scientist to comprehend this rudimentary principle. Over thousands of years, we humans have evolved to run effectively by consuming, in some way, shape or form, a mixture of plant and animal material. Scientists call this being an omnivore.

The human body can easily process and extract the goodness from this type of food, but as soon as you start putting the wrong fuel in a human body – for example, processed modern food – crappy things start to happen. It may not be overnight, but it will happen.

Consider the way a car works. You fuel it with petrol, right? Imagine, though, that one morning on the way to work you're feeling a little adventurous so you decide to fill the tank with yoghurt, or maybe some freshly cut grass. It wouldn't work so well, right? This very same principle applies to our bodies. If we put the wrong type of fuel in, our bodies don't seem to run as well, or they start to break down. This is what happened to me. Years ago, I consumed the wrong fuel and as a result my body began to break down. From this experience I was fortunate enough to figure out the abovementioned biological principle, which, thankfully, has put me on the right track regarding my health.

I also really like eating tasty food, so a marriage of the two elements of delicious food and the right fuel seemed like a good idea. So I'm a bloke who grows most of his food, hunts for meat and sneaks around in the bush looking for free tucker. Then I cook it. Eat it. Then I loosen my belt.

Like many forward-thinking people around the world, I just happen to be concerned about the health of the natural world and its complex mechanisms. I understand the basic principle that we need the natural world to be healthy if we want to be healthy. I wish for this principle to be more widely understood – if it were, I'm sure more care would be given to our daily choices, all of which have some impact on the health of our shared natural environment.

Hard pill to swallow

There's a reality about the Western way of living that's based on cause and effect. It's a reality we can argue about until the cows come home. It's a reality that none of our opinions and arguments can change. This reality is that as long as we continue to consume food that has been tampered with (i.e. during agricultural production and industrial processing), we'll continue to see the rise of modern Western illnesses. We might not be able to cure ourselves once a disease has taken hold, but we sure can dramatically reduce our chances of getting it. I used to suffer from loss of breath (respiratory inflammation) after consuming food and beverages that contained preservative sulfites. Now that I've removed those processed foods from my diet, I no longer suffer that ailment. That's a very obvious example, but consider the less obvious ones. My old life involved consumption of lots of highly processed, high-fat,

high-sugar food, which eventually caught up with me. I found myself clinically obese and a basket case of health issues, from hypertension to anxiety, depression and more. Being in this poor state of health increased my chances of diabetes, heart disease, stroke and cancer.

The point I'm making is that we're all presented with a chance to be proactive. Eating foods that are chemical-free, unprocessed and nutritionally valuable will have a positive impact on our health. As a side benefit, the way much of this type of food is produced is kinder on the natural environment. It makes complete sense to me to state that a life with real food, food that has been produced via natural means, will service your body and our natural world as they should be, resulting in a better chance of a healthy, more enjoyable life. I'm telling you this because I've experienced it. I'm not saying I'm an expert, I'm just sharing my thoughts based on personal experience. And by the way, this is not a self-help book. You have to find the answers that are right for you. Living off the land like a wild mountain man is not for everyone, but it sure beats filing TPS reports.

Practiculture calendar

My year starts in spring and ends in winter. No, I haven't joined some weird cult where we believe the alien lords once told us that each year shall begin in spring. Although secretly, between you and me, I think there is someone out there … watching us.

My calendar is based around seasonal and natural productivity. You see, it's all about surviving the winter. In my previous life this wasn't such an issue. In winter I'd simply drive to the supermarket and buy whatever food I wanted (regardless

of whether it was out of season). But I simply can't do that now, because I'm committed to living with the seasons, the life choice I've made to survive on what I can grow, hunt and squirrel away.

This way of living makes winter slightly more challenging. But again, I've looked to the past for my answer. Many cultures had a solution for this challenge, which is to work your butt off for three seasons in order to provide your family with enough resources to get through the winter. And that's what I do. Okay, so you're scratching your head and asking, 'Why the hell would you embrace something like that in this day and age?'

By living with the seasons, by eating food that I've worked for, by cooking meat I've hunted or killed myself, I'm personally addressing a whole bunch of issues that concern me. With this approach, my food travels far less (equating to almost zero carbon emissions – except when I eat too many beans). My food is fresh and still maintains nutrient integrity. My food is free of added chemicals. My wild meat is always free-range and organic.

My backyard animals that I slaughter have lived good lives. There's no packaging for my food, which means fewer natural resources are required.

These are all good outcomes for my world. These are all ethical elements I'm concerned about, so I've embraced a way of living where the seasons dictate my daily activities. The same way the villagers from an ancient Roman village would have survived, only I don't get around in a toga. But you get the idea, right?

The yearly cycle is full of challenges. It's loaded with really happy moments and downright dirty and depressing moments. Sometimes you win and sometimes you lose. But over the length of a year there's balance. Maybe the balance comes about because it's a system that works closely with nature's will. I don't know, to be honest, but it just works. Personally speaking, it's a lifestyle that's brought me a great sense of accomplishment, joy and pride – feelings I hadn't experienced much since I was a kid. I take pride in feeding my family. I find joy in the success of a hunt, a good harvest or the roar and warmth of the woodfire heater. I relish the sense of purpose and accomplishment from starting a practical project and

seeing it to completion. I love the sense of being a lifelong student of practical things, of learning to figure things out, of trying new skills and adventures. I like that this life has once again made me brave.

Disclaimer

I'm not professing to be an amazing groundbreaking chef. I'm not a chef. This book is more a set of real-food recipes I've cooked over the period of a year, food I feed my family. What's special about this food is that it's come from my hands. I've toiled in some way for it. Well, it's special for me. The idea is that if I share it with you, you may enjoy some of the same types of food from ingredients you've toiled for, too.

I'm not a big fan of strict rules, and I think my cooking reflects this. I'm a big believer in experimentation and going with the flow in the kitchen. A glug of oil is a measurement in my world. It's either a little glug or a big glug. I've put more 'precise' measurements in most recipes, but really it's up to you and your palate. Cook, taste, then make changes before you serve. Seems to work well for me. Enjoy!

Spring

Spring

The mornings have been rather crisp, the air is fresh and pure. Through the windows to the east, bright rays of sun sneak in a little earlier each day, waking me, taunting me to get up and do something useful. I wish I could lie in bed, listening to the warbling of magpies, the chirping of fairy wrens, but there's always something that nags at me to be done. Something to be planted, repaired, chopped, stacked, shot, built, dispatched, preserved, harvested or cooked. You couldn't ask for a fuller and busier life. There's little room for idle time now – that will have to wait until the following winter. And I like it that way. There's something new for me to discover with each passing day, and every season the same chores come and go to be replaced by some other task that demands attention. There's no doubt in my mind that my life is now dictated by the seasons.

It's been a cold winter that's just passed, and I have to admit that I've formed a bit of a naughty habit. I do linger in bed a little longer than I should. I'm reluctant to be anywhere other than under those cosy warm blankets. Unavoidable parental duties are what usually force me up. Normally they arrive in the form of a small child jumping on me asking to be fed or clothed. These rats are so damn needy, and they appear to be getting smarter and smarter! My attempts to feign unconsciousness are often futile – I must create some new avoidance techniques. It's a pity the children don't feed themselves. I wish they would – though, actually, scrap that idea. If kids fed themselves we all know what shit they'd choose to eat.

Even with sleepy eyes, I sometimes enjoy the morning routine. It provides that level of consistency, which I'm sure helps maintain sanity. And don't be fooled by appearances; as much as it may appear that I'm happy to simply go with the flow, I do in fact relish a splash of order. Chaos has always been a very dear adversary. There's order in a cycle, and it's at this time of year that the fresh cycle begins – and I'm referring to the many and varied facets of nature. The circle of life, *The Lion King* and all that. Birds are busy building nests or feeding new chicks, minuscule tadpoles wiggle in the dams, and darling little rabbits pop their heads out from dark and dusty warrens. Nature is very active.

For the sheep grazier, this time of year is all about new lambs, born in late winter through to spring. Like insects to a porch light, they come seemingly from nowhere. And like the night-time buzzers, the new lambs arrive in big numbers. The paddocks of the Central Highlands are soon filled with clumsy, leggy lambs. Often I'll pull the car over on the way to school, so the kids and I can admire and wonder at the beauty of new life. The kids love it. I'm hoping one day for my kids to see a lamb being born from a ewe. It's a beautiful sight to witness.

One Sunday when I was a kid, we were in the family car on the way home from town when we spotted a cow calving. Dad pulled the car over, and like a horde of gawking tourists we leaned on the fence and watched the proceedings. I remember feeling goosebumps with the beauty of it all. Maybe I got a tad teary – so what, I was a young teen, I had hormonal issues. Anyway, it's remained a clear memory ever since. Quite momentous, you might say. I guess I didn't realise the significance of the experience, but now as an adult, with no semblance of innocence remaining, I look back at it with 'wiser' eyes. The paradox of life, that it cannot exist without death, is a frustrating reality. But without a birth, that very life would not exist. So as bloodied and gross as a birth may appear, it is in fact one of the most beautiful sights on the planet. And that's something to celebrate.

I remember a farmer once saying to me, 'If you got livestock, you got dead stock.' And lambing season involves a great deal of death. Death seems to sit comfortably beside life out here. Even though fresh lambs frolic in the paddocks, you'll also see plenty of dead lambs. They may have been attacked by a fox, frozen to death or had their eyes pecked out by a raven – any which way, like newborn turtles on a sandy beach, a lot of them simply don't make it.

After nights of extreme cold, wind and rain, the sight in the morning is something to see. Sometimes the losses are so great, there seem to be more dead lambs than live ones. The carrion-feeders, like the raven and the wedge-tailed eagle, feed greedily. I often wonder how the sheep farmers feel about this. I wonder if they get emotional about the loss or whether they simply account for it in their percentage estimates for annual production. It's nature, I guess. We can't really call the shots. Or can we? Don't think I'm anti sheep farmers. I know a few. They seem like nice folk. I'm merely observing a reality of food production, something most of us don't get to see.

I see those dead lambs on the drive to town and I wonder how many more dead lambs there are across this country. The loss must be staggering. I mean, if Australians ate 21.5 million lambs in 2012, how many more died along the way? I wonder how many lambs weren't even lucky enough to make it to maturity. I guess it's either die on a cold night or be killed at the abattoir, but it seems like such a senseless waste. If we manipulate nature by servicing ewes with a ram to

impregnate them, then shouldn't we take the responsibility to ensure the new life we've brought into the world gets to survive more than a few weeks? Something worth pondering. No wonder so many people turn vegan.

For so many years now I've thought that by not eating supermarket meat I'd be making a difference. I figure that if we all bought meat knowing how it was raised, where it was raised and even better if we knew who raised it, we'd all make a difference. We'd definitely reduce our food miles by buying meat raised as close to us as possible, and by knowing who raised it we'd be supporting someone who cares about the animals' welfare. This spring I've tried this approach, purchasing an entire lamb from a local farmer.

After being on a self-imposed supermarket-meat 'black ban' for so many years, I have to admit I was fairly intimidated by all this lamb meat, not having cooked with lamb for so long. Over the years I'd been given a few lamb goodies – some sausages here, chops there, and if I was lucky a roasting cut – but this was a whole lamb! The farmer had the lamb butchered into all the standard cuts, but I reckon there were a lot more missing that I could have used. I'm not complaining, though, as I now have a freezer full of potentially delicious lamb. I'm sure a lamb-cooking fiesta will begin soon, and with gusto! There are a lot of chops from the loin, which to my mind are kind of boring on their own, so I'm going to try to make the most of the cut, not by cooking it by itself on the 'barbie' but by using it as an ingredient in a dish. It seems a good approach to me to eke out the meat as much as possible by adding it to other ingredients, such as beans or veg. I'm not comfortable with the idea of meat and three, where the meat is the hero. In any case, I'm simply not rich enough to purchase a lamb every few months, although I'm happy to partake in this experiment.

Cooking wild meats has got me into a rhythm of slow and low cooking. When it comes to farmed meat, I find myself drawn to the commercially less desirable cuts, as they usually demand the same cooking approach as wild meat. With

a dwindling supply of my dried summer beans, I've come up with (totally stumbled across) the most delicious bean meal. The peasant cook has a knack of transforming humble ingredients into food so divine that it's fit for a king.

Over the last few years I've fallen head over heels for the beautiful little French flageolet. It's a white bean similar to the larger white Spanish bean or Italian cannellini. There are many varieties of the flageolet, but the one I grew last summer was simply labelled French flageolet. When I first saw these pure white beans I'd purchased, I thought little of them. It was just a new bean for me to try growing. I'd been experimenting with planting different varieties to find those best suited to our challenging climate. I planted all the white beans I had last summer, every last one. Most of them germinated, which is always a relief, and after a summer of growing, the beans appeared, plump and pretty. I dried them out in their pods, and now it was time to cook them. My normal approach to cooking with dried beans is to soak them overnight, to reintroduce moisture to them before boiling them for

roughly an hour until they've softened. This time, however, I cooked them for quite a bit longer – a few hours on a low simmer, in fact. On their own they had a lovely creamy texture, but I discovered something that's made a big change in my bean-cooking approach.

That evening I slow-roasted a few cuts of lamb for about six hours. The lamb was so tender, it fell off the bone when introduced to a blunt spoon, and mastication was optional. I pulled the meat off the bone, added the beans to the pot with all the roasty lamb juices, and soon entered bean and lamb heaven. (For the full recipe see Lamb & French Flageolet Beans, page 16.) The roasted lamb provided a beautiful stock, the meat was sublime and the beans were buttery. Here I had stumbled across a meal that used one of the cheapest cuts of lamb with the humblest of vegetables and they had formed a union that made a simple man very happy. The best bit? Leftovers. The following morning's breakfast was even better than the previous night's dinner.

Lamb & French Flageolet Beans

What you need

400 g (14 oz/2 cups) dried French flageolet beans, soaked in water overnight

1–2 tablespoons olive oil

2 celery stalks, sliced

2 onions, sliced

2 carrots, sliced

4 garlic cloves, finely chopped

500 g (1 lb 2 oz) lamb chops

725 g (1 lb 10 oz/2¾ cups) tomato passata (puréed tomatoes)

40 g (1½ oz/2 cups) parsley, finely chopped

salt and pepper, to taste

goat's feta, to serve

crusty bread, to serve

If NME did a top 10 cheap meals, this one would be in it. It's a union of thrifty ingredients – one from the paddock, most of the rest from the garden – and so tasty it's bound to be made over and over again. Well, it is in my kitchen!

I feel some guilt cooking with lamb and I've avoided it for a good few years. My initial concern was that lamb could be raised in one part of the state, transported to an abattoir, packaged and then transported to a supermarket. Seemed like a lot of road miles to me. Lamb is a free-range animal in Australia, so I wasn't concerned about that, but unfortunately they're often treated with a good deal of inorganic chemicals and medications to deal with parasites such as worms, pathogens and so on. It's simply unnatural, and buying lamb has always felt like a gamble because of that.

When I stumbled across a sign down the road offering whole lambs for sale, butchered and packed, I thought I'd give that a try. It ticked a few boxes – reduced food miles, if not necessarily organic. I guess it's better to tick at least a few boxes, even if we can't manage them all, although I wish we could.

I'm not sure if I'll do it again – I think I've grown too accustomed to hunting. But for now, I have a supply of lamb, and this meal is one I enjoy. It's far more enjoyable than simply cooking chops on the barbecue.

How to make it

Bring 2 litres (68 fl oz/8 cups) salted water to the boil. Add the drained beans and simmer for 2 hours, or until soft. Drain when cooked and set aside.

Preheat the oven to a measly 130°C (270°F).

Meanwhile, in a large flameproof casserole dish, heat a generous glug of olive oil over medium heat on the stove top. Gently sweat the celery, onion and carrot for 15 minutes, stirring regularly. Add the garlic, then add the chops, sealing them on all sides. Pour over the passata and add water if necessary to ensure the meat is covered. Stir through half the parsley, and season with salt and pepper.

Pop the lid on the casserole dish and transfer to the oven. Cook for 3 hours, or until the meat falls from the bone, ensuring optional mastication ;-). Return the dish to the stove top, and cook to reduce the sauce if necessary. Stir through the cooked beans and the remaining parsley, and adjust the seasoning if necessary.

Crumble over some feta and serve with crusty bread.

It's exciting in spring when the first goose eggs start showing up. The egg lull over winter is frustrating – as there isn't much happening in the garden, any fresh eggs become mighty valuable. We've been fortunate that a mate keeps geese and shares some eggs with us. We have our own geese now, so fingers crossed we'll get our own supply of eggs next year. To be honest, I can't really tell the difference between the taste of a duck, chicken or goose egg. They're all pretty similar, with only very subtle differences. In a meal like a shakshuka, you'd be hard pressed to tell the difference. The thing I like about using goose eggs is that it's fun. They're massive and we always get a laugh out of it. Yes, my family laughs at egg sizes. Living with no TV can make the simplest of things more interesting. Go figure.

Goose Egg Shakshuka

SERVES 2

What you need

1–2 tablespoons olive oil	1 tablespoon ground cumin
6 garlic cloves, finely chopped	1 tablespoon chilli powder
2 carrots, finely chopped	handful of chives, snipped
2 onions, finely chopped	2 goose eggs
100 g (3½ oz) chorizo (page 49), sliced	shaved Parmigiano Reggiano, to serve
725 g (1 lb 10 oz/ 2¾ cups) tomato passata (puréed tomatoes)	

How to make it

Heat a generous glug of olive oil in a large frying pan (one with a lid) over low heat. Gently sweat the garlic, carrot and onion for 10–15 minutes, or until browned and soft. Add the chorizo and cook for a few minutes.

Now add the passata, cumin, chilli powder and chives (reserving some as a garnish), and simmer, uncovered, for about 10 minutes to reduce and thicken the sauce.

Crack the eggs into the sauce and pop the lid on. Simmer gently for 5 minutes, or until the eggs are cooked to your liking.

Garnish with the parmesan and reserved chives, then serve.

Mountain gold

There's one wild food I happily put more energy into acquiring than I get in return. It's one of those really hard-to-find wild foods that has the ability either to make or totally ruin your day. Hours of hard graft with little produce in return can leave you pulling your hair out and crying tears of frustration. It's elusive, it's fussy, and it often looks like kangaroo poo. The upside is that it's tantalisingly delicious (unlike kangaroo poo … apparently). Morels have been on my food radar for a few seasons now, thanks to a friend who was kind enough not only to introduce me to their very existence, but also to give away his foraging spot. Tim, you fool!

My life pre-morel seems bland now. I might be going a little overboard there, but you get the idea – they're balls of bloody amazement. For such a small mushroom they offer so much flavour. Describing their flavour is a hard nail to hit, so I won't even try. In any case, I think they're more exciting than dirt-tasting truffles. Okay, so I've obviously failed 'foodie' school.

Last season I had a few lucky days. My basket was never overflowing, but I got enough morels to keep me marginally content knowing I had to wait another year for my next mouthful. Yes, that's right, it's a yearly treat. When the first break of warm weather comes in late winter to early spring, the morels wake up and sprout from the soil. They have particularly fussy requirements when it comes to soil type, aspect and temperature. You'll only ever find them in places where the perfect combination of these elements exists. And I'm not going to tell you where that might be. You'll have to figure that out for yourself. Luckily for me, my friend was kinder/stupider when he took me right to his special spot. He taught me what to look for and to check everything, even if it looks suspiciously like kangaroo poo. Everything must be investigated, because if it's a morel, dinner shall be grand.

This spring I eagerly awaited the call from my morel mate. When the call came, I headed straight out, basket and sharp knife at the ready. Two visits garnered nothing but heartache. I clambered over boulders, searched through wet grass, checked anything that hinted at being a morel, but I came away empty-handed. I decided that my third trip would be my last. If I came home with no morels, then it was a sign that this year was to be devoid of these delicious fungi. On the final trip I had extra servings of enthusiasm. I felt the need to give it a red-hot go. Nature may have fooled me so far, but I was determined to work harder and have a win. It would be good for my morale ;-). I waited for the weather to turn, I waited for the telephone to ring. I couldn't go up too early, I couldn't venture out on a whim. I had to wait for confirmation from my mushroom man. When the message came through, my inner voice gave a prepubescent squeal of excitement. My outside appearance, however, was as cool as a cucumber: 'Like, whatever, man … If I find some, rad … if not … whatever.' I set aside the good part of an entire day. I wanted to make this trip count, so I needed to allow as much search time as possible. I packed a few provisions and headed to the spot where my friend had plucked a basket of beauties just a day earlier.

Out in the bush alone is one of my favourite places to be. There's no one talking at me and no one expecting me to talk, just the sounds of the bush and whatever adventure I'm on. I find such peace in the bush. Everything around me seems so much more important. Everything out here is very real. When I'm looking for wild food or hunting, my senses are on high alert. It's nothing at all like walking the aisles of a supermarket – like I said, this is the real thing out here. Thankfully, this time of year is pretty clear with regard to snakes. I think most of them are still curled up in bed, waiting for the real hot weather to turn up. I don't blame them. This final day of searching was a typical spring day – morning drizzle, then warm sun followed by sun showers and more sun. No wonder plants grow with vigour at this time of year – the conditions are ideal.

I'd spent a while walking aimlessly around before I stumbled upon the first little beauty. Sitting in a valley among the lush grass, in a bed of clover and soursop, was a cluster of morels. I lay on the ground with my eyes as low to the earth as possible so I could spot any others, and this approach paid dividends. I found a few more on the outskirts of the cluster and added them to my basket. Not much of a feed so far, but what a start! My heart was racing with excitement. How can this wild-food thing be so powerful? Why does it affect me so much? Does this happen to other people? Is this the way we're supposed to live?

It's interesting how excited I can get when I see food I haven't set eyes on for more than year. I was never like this at the supermarket. I guess it was because I'd become accustomed to getting whatever food I wanted, whenever I wanted it. Maybe it was too easy and thus I didn't appreciate that kind of food. But this wild stuff gets me hyper-excited.

There in my basket sat a once-a-year treat. Food that has had no human intervention – that is, until the moment my sharp blade slices their base, and my fingers gently place the treasured fungi in my basket for safekeeping. What joy these funny little things can bring a man, and how they've made me think and reassess the way I view different foods. But I needed to put my thinking aside, for surely there were more fungi-filled valleys and gullies to explore, more patches of wet grass to investigate, more morels to lay in my almost-bare basket. I spent the next few hours following every lead, picking more morels and considering all my options for the evening meal.

After much lone-man-on-a-hillside conversation with myself, I decided to cook the morels with as little interference as possible. Why manipulate those unique flavours when I could just appreciate them for what they offered? In early autumn I do a similar thing with pine mushrooms: I cook them just with butter, olive juice and sage. Minimal effort, maximum return. Wild food has so much to offer.

It often amazes me that people are literally afraid (yes, literally, not figuratively) of eating something taken from the wild, such as a mushroom, yet have absolutely zero fear of eating highly processed foods loaded with sulfites, high in sodium, and often treated with pesticides and herbicides. How did we get to this point, where the way we view food is skewed towards accepting fake food that's been manipulated and is likely no good for our health?

I often find myself having to convince people that it's safe to eat meat from a wild animal, chomp on a weed or devour a wild mushroom. I've had people refuse this food. It's that individual's choice to do so, but the irony is frustrating at times. I've even had the odd person turn their nose up at vegetables pulled straight from the garden covered in dirt. Have we become too sanitised? The most interesting situation is when someone who eats a great deal of meat turns down my offer to teach them how to kill an animal (with disgust, I might add). It's a paradox for us to consider. Maybe it's human nature to prefer a world where we remain in the dark about where our food comes from and the processes involved in its production.

Is it important that we should be prepared to deal with dirt-covered vegetables? To contend with blood and guts in order to eat meat? Or is the system we have in place – of not needing or wanting to know about the reality of food processes and origins – totally acceptable? Will it make a difference to humanity if the Western world embraces what most developing countries see as totally normal? Or do we simply continue to eat what's provided to us in the aisles of our local supermarket, and remain blind to the realities of how our food is produced? Maybe I should just eat the damn mushrooms and stop thinking.

Rabbit Backstrap with Spring Morel & Sage

SERVES 2

What you need

4 backstraps from young wild spring rabbits
60 ml (2 fl oz/¼ cup) olive oil
2 garlic cloves, finely chopped
handful of sage
60 ml (2 fl oz/¼ cup) white wine
50 g (1¾ oz) butter
10–15 morel mushrooms, halved lengthways
salt and pepper, to taste
crusty bread, lightly toasted, to serve

In early spring there arrive two delicious treats from the bush: baby rabbits and morel mushrooms. If the conditions are right, then I'll make this meal a few times. There's not much to it and, to be honest, that's the way I like it. The morel has a unique delicious taste, and the rabbit is a simple white meat that really just acts as the delivery system for the mushroom. Add some garlic and sage, maybe a splash of wine and a generous amount of melted butter, and you have yourself an enjoyable feed. I once fed this to a lovely older lady, and I'm sure she made some of those noises. You know the noises I'm talking about. It was slightly awkward, but I was glad I'd made someone happy with food. Let's not discuss this again.

Shoot the smaller rabbits. They're the most tender.

How to make it

Using a sharp knife, cut the gristle and sinew out of each backstrap, then wrap it in plastic wrap and give it a hearty tap with a rolling pin to tenderise it – more good cop than bad cop.

Heat half the olive oil (a glug) in a heavy-based frying pan over low heat, then add the garlic and the sage (keeping a sprig as a garnish) – this will create a nice flavoured base for the rabbit to cook in.

Add the tenderised (unwrapped, naturally) rabbit and cook on both sides for a few minutes each. Splash over the white wine and cook until the liquid has evaporated.

Continue cooking the rabbit, but you can overcook it so be mindful. I reckon flip them over a few times, and they should be done within 5 minutes.

Remove the rabbit from the pan and wrap in aluminium foil.

Add the butter and the rest of the olive oil (another glug) to the same frying pan, then fry the mushrooms until they soften.

Garnish the rabbit and mushrooms with the reserved sage and season the lot to taste. Serve with crusty bread.

Cold comfort

A few days of warm weather in spring and I slide into feverish pottering mode in the veggie patch. Each year it happens, almost on cue. The clouds part, some warm sun visits my epidermal layer, and I get rather excited by the slight hint that the summer and its growing season might just be upon us. It's the potential for fresh, delicious, home-grown food that gives me spring fever. Once it's firmly set in, I get to work weeding beds, sowing crops and planting seedlings. I check the watering system is up to scratch and I dig over beds that have rested over winter.

But I'm fooled. I'm a gullible gardener. Invariably, that warm spell doesn't hang around for long – it's pushed back a few weeks, maybe another month. It's those frigid winds that do it every time. They make their way to our hill, freezing everything in their path. I'm sure they come all the way from the iced continent Antarctica. I'm quickly reminded that spring hasn't yet fully arrived. The weather is merely toying with us, like a cat with a ball of hipster string.

It's no time to complain, though. Instead, it can be viewed as the firecracker up the proverbial I often need to get the place in order. It pays big dividends to be prepared for the coming season. If I don't get the plants in the ground at the right moment, many crops just won't have enough growing time over the summer and I'll get a poor yield. It's like a plane landing on a shortened strip.

Winter is harsh here, and the garden gets minimal love over the cold months. Not much grows, so I find myself hunting more than gardening at this time of year. It actually makes a lot of sense to hunt in winter. The wild animals have fed well from summer to autumn and are at their peak, and mixing hunted animals with winter veg makes for some pretty hearty meals.

So even though early spring has fooled me once again, I'll take this opportunity to sneak in a few more heart-warming meals before the kitchen becomes dominated by the salads and vegetables of summer. One tool in the kitchen gets some heavy use at this time of year – 'Big Blue', my cast-iron Chasseur pot. People often talk about what's essential in a kitchen, and for me this guy is a no-brainer. It sure cost me a pretty penny, but it's dished out plenty of hearty meals in return. Dished out. Get it?

What value do you put on items that are well built, reliable, practical and last you a lifetime? They're priceless, right? Few things in our lives fill these boots. Most mechanical gadgets eventually break down. Most 'state of the art' implements fade, wear and give up the ghost. But cast iron lasts. I treat Big Blue with respect. I use wood to stir his contents; I soak and wash him clean after use. He's something one of my daughters will get use from, long after I'm gone. He's a provider of memories. A creator of joy. A curator of pleasure.

The meals I've slow-cooked over the years have brought smiles of joy and groans of contentment to those who sit at my table. It's drastically different from my old days of opening up packets of frozen processed meat, placing it on a baking tray and cooking it as directed on the back of the cardboard packet. Slow-cooked meals with Big Blue are a far cry from those pre-cooked TV-dinner-type meals. I had no idea what was in that 'food' and I didn't care. I just wanted my belly filled. The contrast often amazes me. How can I have turned my back on this easy-to-prepare/reheat food? It said clearly on the packet that it was a 'healthy choice'. That alone should have been enough to convince me, yes? I mean, the packaging doesn't lie, right? Instead it plainly states the facts. What the hell was wrong with me? Why did I consume such garbage? Here's the honest truth: I knew it wasn't right. I knew that highly processed food wasn't rad. I knew it was loaded with shit. I ate it because I was lazy. I didn't care about my health. I guess I thought it was the best option for me at the time.

It was simply a mindset. It took a great deal of thinking to persuade me to make changes. I actually had to convince myself that it wasn't good for me. Thankfully for my health, a few events, a few reality-check moments opened my eyes to the realities of food. In my previous life, I used to walk the supermarket aisles impressed with the choice of 'food'. Now I walk the aisles and view only a small percentage of the 'food' on offer as real food.

Imagine showing someone from the 1940s one of those 'on the run' breakfast meals – you know, those thick drinks in a small cask with a little feed straw to suck the contents out? It's like astronaut food, but we're not astronauts. What would these people from seventy-five years ago think of our modern food? How would they react to instant microwave risotto? Scrambled eggs in a carton? Instant noodles with sachet flavour? They'd probably be impressed with the convenience, but I wonder if they'd view it as real food.

Convenience is a killer. It's the best excuse we use. I know, because I used it as an excuse for many years. Anything that would make my life easier. I'd use gravy powder to make gravy. I'd use a premixed stewing powder to flavour a casserole. I'd use a pre-made marinade mix to coat meat before barbecuing it. Can you believe I had no idea what was

in any of these packets of flavouring? Yet I used them without a thought. How can we do this to ourselves? How can we eat food when we don't even know what's in it? There's a simple answer – a combination of laziness, clever marketing and deceptive packaging.

Marketers and advertisers take advantage of the fact that we live 'busy lives'. They market products to us that 'save us time', products that are supposed to make our lives easier, more convenient. But there's always a price to pay for this alluring convenience. What we consume affects our health, and that's not new information. Marry that with our stressful (often unfulfilling) lifestyle, and you get unhealthy, unhappy people. Take me as an example. My busy existence meant I ate busy-person food. That food, highly processed and loaded with rubbish, compounded with a high-stress lifestyle, resulted in very poor health. It gave me off-the-scale high blood pressure, I was carrying too much weight and I had high cholesterol. I suffered from debilitating anxiety and exhausting depression. If I'd continued, I would, as my GP warned me, have finished up just another statistic, beaten by the preventable health problems of the modern Westerner. That was enough for me to take stock, look at how I was living, what I was eating, and decide that I needed to make changes. Hell yes, it made me change!

Not only is our personal health important, but the health of our natural world should be high on our list of priorities. The energy required to make these processed 'food' products has a very clear detrimental effect on our environment. Broad-acre farming takes from the earth more than it returns. Much of the food that feeds the Western world relies on chemical treatment, either in the paddock or in the processing factory. These chemicals require loads of natural resources to be produced, and let's not forget the damage they do as residuals in waterways and soils, and as drift. The packaging of said food requires a massive amount of resources to produce, and inevitably ends up as trash and landfill. It's one hell of a problem to consider. It's unfortunate that this modern dilemma is in no way communicated to us in the aisles or at the checkout. It's not a conspiracy, it's just a shit situation. But the most frustrating reality is that even after all this effort to make food to feed the world, most of it ends up being thrown out. Work a week at the back end of a supermarket or at a restaurant and you'll know what I'm talking about.

Imagine for a minute that we cut a lot of this type of food out of our system. Imagine a cultural shift where people made a

cont.

concerted effort to source as much of their food as locally as possible. Imagine if more of us supported organic producers. Imagine if we returned to mostly cooking with wholefood ingredients. Imagine if we all cooked instead of reheated. Imagine. Would it have any impact? Would fewer resources be squandered if we all made that fundamental shift in how we acquire food? Would we as a Western population reduce our chances of preventable diseases? I reckon so.

The way I cook now is really basic and honest cooking. It's about using real ingredients. I start everything from scratch. Now this doesn't make me better than anyone else, I'm just telling you how it is. The result of this approach is worth the effort involved, which really is minimal in the scheme of things. The amount of time I'd save by using pre-made food is absolutely negligible, especially when compared to the benefits. To make a slow-cooked stew is now a real joy. I start off making a base of vegetables plucked from the patch. Typically, I then braise the meat. Next I add the liquid, then set the heat to low and let it run its course. The result is food that's full of flavour, unique in taste and texture every time. And it makes life more interesting. It's lighter on the environment, and nutritionally speaking it's packed with real-food goodness. This is an 'old-world' approach to cooking. It's what we as humans have been doing for thousands of years. It's just unfortunate that in the last seventy-five years or so, this way of living has slipped from our grasp. I intend to hold onto it. Tightly.

Putting my old-world view of cooking into action, I once again pulled out Big Blue, my oven pot. I still had plenty of lamb. So many barbecued chops to get through, and a lamb neck. What the hell was I to do with a lamb neck? I ended up making a slow-cooked lamb madras (page 29). Sometimes I wish this cold weather would stick around forever.

I love cooking this spicy hot curry on cold winter days, but then again, I love to cook it on hot and spicy days. Mad? Yes, most probably. Hence the mad-ass/madras curry was born.

I'm a big fan of offcuts, which are often overlooked. Most of the meat available to us is the prime cuts, which is a pity. A lot of each animal ends up as secondary cuts, even wasted. Lamb neck isn't something most people would ask for at the butcher's, but it's worth trying. We'd organised a whole lamb from a local farmer, so we got a lot of cuts we'd not been used to. It wasn't a matter of choice, it was a matter of working with what we'd been given. It makes you slightly more creative. Having organised a whole lamb, we also had a freezer stacked with a generous serve of chops. I'm not a big fan of a slab of meat for dinner – I like my meat in things, coated with things and full of flavour. (That sounds a little wrong if you say it out loud.) I've been using lamb chops in slow-cooked meals. I think it actually turns out a better result – well, compared to those chewy chops straight off the barbecue.

Next season I think I'll take up the offer of some orphaned (poddy) lambs and raise them in the backyard. But for now I'm happy for the opportunity to get a lamb locally and experiment with meat I don't usually cook with.

Madras Lamb Neck

SERVES 4

What you need

1–2 tablespoons olive oil

4 large onions, sliced

1 tablespoon brown sugar

700 g (1 lb 9 oz) barbecued lamb chops, cut into chunks

500 g (1 lb 2 oz) lamb neck, cut into chunks

725 g (1 lb 10 oz/2¾ cups) tomato passata (puréed tomatoes)

salt, to taste

cooked rice, to serve

coriander (cilantro) leaves, to garnish

goat's yoghurt, to serve (optional)

The madras paste

10 garlic cloves, chopped

4 chillies, seeds in

4 kaffir lime leaves

4 curry branches, leaves picked

100 g (3½ oz/½ cup) freshly grated ginger

1 tablespoon smoked pimentón (Spanish paprika)

1 tablespoon cayenne pepper

1 tablespoon ground coriander

1 tablespoon garam masala

1 tablespoon ground cumin

1 tablespoon ground turmeric

5 cardamom pods

1 cinnamon stick

1–2 tablespoons olive oil

How to make it

To make the madras paste, crush the garlic, chillies, lime leaves, curry leaves and ginger in a mortar and pestle until a smooth paste forms. Heat the pimentón, cayenne, coriander, garam masala, cumin, turmeric, cardamom and cinnamon in a dry frying pan until aromatic, then grind to an even powder in a mortar and pestle. Add the garlic mixture and enough olive oil to bind the lot.

Start preparing the curry by heating a glug of olive oil in a large saucepan over low–medium heat. Add the onion and cook slowly, stirring often, and make sure it doesn't burn. After 10 minutes it will have changed colour and the pan may be dry, so add a splash of water and stir it through until it evaporates. Continue this process for another 10 minutes.

The onion will now be soft, mushy and almost brown. Add the curry paste you made and stir it through. Add the brown sugar and stir through for a few minutes.

Add the lamb to the pan, stirring it around for a few minutes to seal it slightly. Add the passata and stir until well mixed.

Pop on the lid and simmer over low heat for a few hours, or until the meat falls off the bone.

Season with salt and serve on rice, garnished with coriander leaves and maybe a dollop of cheeky goat's yoghurt.

Big pig

Each year I see those trashy magazines with headlines like '10 steps for a bikini body' or 'Get hot for summer now'. These articles are immensely irritating – in fact, they're downright offensive to common sense and reality. Magazines present a body image that's unachievable for most of us (which makes us feel like crap), and every human body is different. We can't all look as hot as the people in the magazines; they fit criteria of physical features that just aren't present in the entire human population. The real whale of a problem I have is the knowledge that I'll never have a bikini body. It's devastating.

It's this time of year, in spring, that I realise that I've had a few too many evening stews accompanied by too many glasses of vino. My bikini body seems months away! I do, however, think it's perfectly natural to eat stodgier meals during winter – it suits the season. In late spring, summer and through to autumn we tend to be more active, and the food that's in season during the warmer weather allows us to favour lighter meals, such as salads, grilled veg and fish. So for now, while the cool season lingers, I'll enjoy this stodgy grub while I can. The truth is that I have limited vegetables at hand. I do, however, have a great deal of meat, which is contrary to the norm for me. Not only is there lamb in my freezer (for which I'm very grateful), but there'll soon be pork, too.

I gave up buying pork from the supermarket when I learned of the shitty conditions in which the sows are housed to raise their young. They're often in large, overcrowded commercial pig farms that are really just massive sheds with caged pigs inside. It's amazing how we humans can be so brutal to animals. It's all driven by the lure of a cheap buck.

When you understand that there are pigs in small cages and they never see the light of day and never get proper exercise, it's likely to influence how you view the 'end product'. Robotic piglet producers don't make pork very appealing. It's like eating huge amounts of guilt and sorrow. It's not appetising in any way.

But when I see pigs out in the paddocks, happy being pigs, rolling in mud, making little piggy grunts, well that kinda makes sense to me. I black-banned supermarket pork because I couldn't be assured of its origins, so I've been sourcing pork from a handful of good farmers who do it right. They farm pigs free-range and keep the farm organic. They normally sell their produce at farmers' markets or via those great grassroots email newsletters, along the lines of, 'Guys, we've butchered some pigs … place an order.' That is until now. This year things

stepped up a notch with my pork supplies. Some lovely lady offered us a pair of two-year-old sows. They'd started off as her parents' pets, but like all pigs they'd grown into megatronic-sized livestock, and to be honest I think her mum and dad were sick of feeding the hungry girls! I should inform you that I'd never actually handled a live pig. I'd never raised pigs and never intended to raise pigs. It's just that when someone presents me with an amazing opportunity like this, I simply can't pass it up. The idea of a freezer full of pork seemed like a wish granted from a Lady Gaga–style bacon-clad genie. It would surely cover the current shortfall of veg supply in my newly established veg garden. The only deal was that I had to pick the pigs up, and then I had to find a place to house them. And eventually, I'd need to organise the mobile butcher to kill them and break the animals down. Sounds easy enough, right?

I've always been fond of the idea of having a menagerie of farm animals. I guess growing up on a farm has something to do with it. After many years living in a city, I'd lost my connection with animals. They just never appeared on the train to work, in the office and especially not at the supermarket. Animals, in particular farm animals – the ones you can get up close to, smell, touch and hear – are the closest most of us get to experiencing living nature. If you're a meat eater, the reality is that animals are your living future food, food that's alive, food that we raise in order to fill our bodies with protein. For thousands of years, raising animals for food seemed to occur relatively ethically. Animals were permitted to be animals, roaming paddocks, scratching in the soil, generally being what they're supposed to be. Then we outgrew the Old World, invaded the New World, plundered and grew until our population was such that we had to invent horrible ways to mass-produce meat, leading to a system that now treats animals like – hmmm, let's say, animals. You know what I mean, right?

But why care about how animals are treated? They're just animals and we're going to kill them anyway! What's the difference between eating an intensively farmed animal and a wild animal? They both end up dead, don't they?

Consider that wild animals are introduced to this world by nature, whereas farmed animals are introduced to this world by our arrangement. We force it. We force and manipulate nature to our advantage. And forcing nature, twisting its outcomes to our advantage, comes with a responsibility. We arranged for that newborn piglet, chick, duckling and calf to come into the world, so it's our responsibility to take good care of it, to provide it with a good life. It sure is food for thought.

Let's consider, for example, the methods used to mass-produce pork. Most of it (like chicken) is done behind closed doors, in large tin sheds. The smell is ridiculous, similar to a three-day camping trip sans shower. The animals are kept in cramped cages. They're so physically restricted they get little or no exercise. They're fed types of food that encourage speedy growth and the production of plenty of saleable meat. It's nothing like how a pig is supposed to live. And once again, because there are so many of us, all wanting meat, the process is accepted. It's definitely not publicised in the mainstream media.

Imagine an advert for Christmas hams that graphically showed the living conditions in which the pigs were housed. No one would buy them! Instead, as for most things in the Western world, we're lied to purely because that's what makes things sell. Instead of the reality, a perfectly sliced Christmas ham is pictured on the advertising billboard, with a few added seasonal accompaniments to make the setting look totally appealing and desirable. The reality, though, is pig shit, stench, antibiotic injections, robotic butchering and short lives to promote tender meat. Would you buy that Christmas ham?

This gift of these two plump pigs was a real coup. I wasn't prepared for it – in fact, I'd only just been on the telephone to our closest free-range pig farmer to order half a pig for the coming year's pork supply. We ended up housing the pigs at a nearby farm, where they had a better set-up. We made an agreement to give them one of the pigs in return for housing. Keeping pigs turns out to be very enjoyable. The pigs make sweet grunting noises and they're a constant source of entertainment with their antics. They're intelligent animals, which makes them easy enough to fence in. Since they were piglets, these girls had been housed with one line of fluorescently coloured electric fencing line. Even though they were now big girls housed in a well-built cattle race, it was the fluorescent battery-powered electric line that kept them in order. They ate anything and everything. We sourced bags of juicing carrots, offcuts from the fruit and veg shop, and supplementary grain from the livestock feed store. After just one week they'd dug up, turned and eaten whatever vegetation was in the lot, giving me the idea of using them in future to dig over new garden beds while fertilising them with their poo. They had plenty of space to roll in, lounge on, and generally snout about in. They were as happy as pigs in shit.

Much as I considered them handy in the garden, the truth is that I'd accepted them as future food. I was eager to learn

cont.

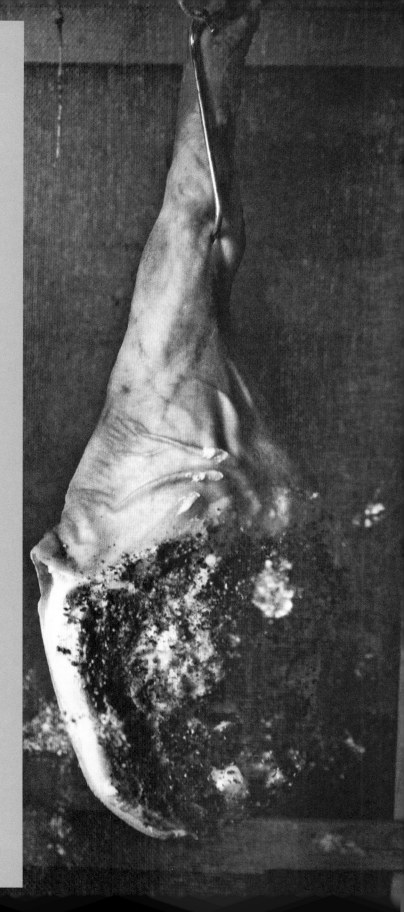

the process from beginning to end. I could have taken them to an abattoir, but I would have dropped them off and then picked them up all butchered and bagged, having learned nothing of the process. My other option was to use a mobile butcher, alongside whom I could work and pick up some new skills. I called the mobile butcher and spent a good half-hour explaining what I wanted done with the pigs. I planned to use as much of the offal as I could – I guess the 'nose to tail' approach sits well with me, as I don't have as much money as I once did, so everything now has added value. I especially wanted the skin for crackling, but I also wanted to use the head to make pâté de tête, the trotters for a Spanish tapas dish, the ears for the dog – I wanted it all. There was so much value in this pig; the potential for future food for my family was immense. When the time came for the butcher to perform his craft, unfortunately for me I was double-booked, so I missed the big day.

It was a pity I missed it, not only because I wanted to learn the method

of processing such a large animal, but also because it didn't get done the way I wanted it to. It's not normal for a pig in Australia to be used to the nth degree. Offal isn't used much these days – well, not for human consumption anyway. I'm sure most of it ends up as pet food. Due to the large size of the pig, the mobile butcher decided it would be easier to skin it, which meant no skin, no crackling! Nooooo! And no skin meant no moisture-sealing skin for my jamon. Instead, the skin, insides and head were left in the paddock for a day or so, and by the time I arrived for the butchery day the offal was covered in flies. It weighed a ton, and maggots had already appeared, but I had no choice but to lift it into the skip. To rub salt into the wound, the stench was just plain nasty. It was the waste that frustrated me most. I'd organised to kill this animal; I wanted to make the best use of it. I felt guilty.

I did, however, have a whole carcass of pork that needed to be broken down. On butchery day we moved the quartered pig from the mobile coolroom to the cutting

room, where the butcher and I set to work. He was a nice bloke, this butcher, and I wasn't angry with him for the mix-up. I guessed he wouldn't be asked very often to keep the offal. And given it was a month since I'd explained what I wanted done, it was my responsibility to remind him closer to the date. These things happen. I'd learned a valuable lesson – next time things would be different.

But for now he and I had an hour's butchery to perform. We set out his mobile saw, workbench and bagging table. We lifted the heavy, fat-laden pig onto the bench, one quarter at a time. Sliced, trimmed and bagged. Each cut he'd tell me if it was suited to stewing, roasting or frying. We filled a huge tub with the trimmed fat and meat to make sausages. We cut out the loin and belly for me to make green bacon and pancetta. The bags of meat kept piling up. I felt like I had money in the bank – we'd be set for pork for at least half a year! My freezer would be overflowing. In fact, I started to think it might not all fit in there!

Easy-as Bacon (Green Bacon)

MAKES 2–3 KG (4 LB 6 OZ–6 LB 10 OZ)

What you need

2–3 kg (4 lb 6 oz–6 lb 10 oz) side of pork loin

260 g (9 oz/2 cups) salt

100–200 g (3½–7 oz/½–1 cup) brown sugar

Who doesn't love bacon? Well, as amazing as it may seem, there are actually a lot of non-bacon-lovers out there – studies show that four out of five people love bacon (study consisted of five of my mates). Whether it's cooked over the morning campfire or in the kitchen at home, the smell of frying bacon gets me going. I used to buy the dodgy stuff from the supermarket, then my inquisitive mind totally ruined that when I researched the conditions of factory-farmed pigs, so I had a spell without bacon. It didn't last long. I had to find a way to get back on the porky bandwagon, so I decided to start making my own. Having an entire pig's carcass in your freezer is also good motivation to make bacon.

The pig butchered this year was massive, weighing in at well over 120 kilograms (265 pounds)! Not ideal for standard butchery cuts, the oversized sow was better suited to making salami. But I wasn't to be put off: I had bacon brain and nothing was going to stand in my way. Seriously, it didn't take much research to find out how easy it is to make bacon at home. And there are so many variations, which tells me there's plenty of room for mistakes. Let's keep everyone happy here and remind the reader about the importance of hygiene and safety when curing any meat. This recipe is but one approach to curing bacon. There are plenty more ways to do it, but this is what works for me.

How to make it

Keep the skin on the loin but trim off any loose bits.

Mix the salt and sugar in a bowl and then rub the mixture all over the meat, ensuring an even spread.

Place the loin in an airtight plastic container and refrigerate for 7–9 days. Each day, flip the bacon over so the liquid drains from the meat.

Once the meat has hardened (because the salt has drawn out the moisture) wash the salt and sugar off. (I then slice off the skin because it's annoyingly hard to cut through without an electric slicer.)

Slice some up and fry it! I love it with an egg and sliced chilli.

Pancetta

MAKES 2–3 KG (4 LB 6 OZ–6 LB 10 OZ)

What you need

2–3 kg (4 lb 6 oz–6 lb 10 oz) pork belly

260 g (9 oz/2 cups) salt

handful of freshly cracked black pepper

butcher's twine

This little gem is the Italian bacon (on the far left in the photo opposite). I'd been buying it for years and using it in cooking, but when I moved away from pork products due to the factory-farming issue I missed it too much. So when I got my own pigs, I started making it myself. As for anything, there's a bunch of different ways to make it, and there always seems to be someone saying their way is best, blah, blah, blah. That really puts me off being a foodie. The very thought of competition in food is a bit of a wank, really.

I don't overdo the spice and herb mix. I've added fennel, dill and other dried herbs in the past, and it's turned out well each time, but then I was limited as to how I could use it in cooking, as those herby flavours would be present. Savvy? I prefer to keep the pancetta simple, so that it's just dry-cured belly – and that has a distinctive taste of its own anyway. I use basically the same curing process as I do for bacon, but I do add black pepper to the belly when I roll it.

How to make it

Carefully cut the skin off the pork belly and trim off any loose bits. Coat the pork belly in the salt, rubbing it all over for an even covering.

Place the salted belly in an airtight plastic container and refrigerate for 7–9 days. Each day, flip the meat over so the liquid drains from the meat.

Once the meat has hardened (because the salt has drawn out the moisture), wash the salt off.

At this stage, I cut off a small slice and fry it to check its salt content. If it's way too salty, I pop the meat in a pot of cold water for a few hours, which reduces some of the saltiness. Drain and allow to dry completely before continuing.

Lay the belly down on what was the skin side. Evenly sprinkle the pepper over the meat.

Cut a 1 metre (1 yard) length of twine, then roll that belly up nice and tight. Strongly tie one end of the rolled belly with the twine, then make a loose loop in the long end of the twine, pull it down over the roll to just below the first tie and pull tight. Continue this process until you get to the end of the rolled log of meat.

Take another long length of twine and thread it through those loops from one end of the log to the other. Repeat this step four or five times, making lengthways threads that will provide some support to the pancetta as it cures hanging up.

Hang in a non-draughty, fly-proof meat safe for 8–10 weeks, then treat as you would a bought pancetta.

Imagine you're in Paris. It's spring. The sun is out, a light warm breeze drifts down the Seine and the smell of French cuisine is in the air. You're feeling adventurous – let's face it, you're not in Paris every day. You sip your pinot as you peruse the French menu, searching for familiarity. Escargot catches your eye. You tell yourself, 'When in Paris!' So you order a bowl of snails and enjoy the moment.

So why is it that when I eat brown snails from my garden people turn their noses up at the very thought? I've never understood it, but it does mean that I benefit from having the snails all to myself. There are some things to know about snails and their edibility. In my backyard there are brown garden snails (Cornu aspersum). They're one of the edible species but they do need to be prepared correctly before cooking. I catch mine, pop them in a breathable container and feed them fresh lettuce for a week. This will purge any crappy toxins and such, and then they're okay to eat.

This isn't really a main meal. It's more a tapas dish.

Important safety message: Snails need to be purged for a week on clean food such as fresh organic lettuce. They then need to be thoroughly rinsed under cold water before cooking.

Snails & Bacon in Boozy Sauce

SERVES 2

What you need

50–60 brown garden snails

1–2 tablespoons olive oil

1 large onion, cut in half and sliced

4 garlic cloves, finely chopped

4 rashers (slices) smoky bacon (page 189), chopped

250 ml (8½ fl oz/1 cup) white wine

handful of parsley, finely chopped

1 teaspoon smoked pimentón (Spanish paprika)

1 chilli, finely chopped

freshly cracked black pepper, to taste

50 g (1¾ oz) butter

dollop of thickened (whipping) cream

crusty bread, to serve

How to make it

Cook the snails in boiling water for 1 hour, then strain and set aside.

Heat a generous glug of olive oil in a frying pan over low heat and gently cook the onion and garlic for 10 minutes. Add the bacon and cook for a further 5 minutes. Add the cooked snails then splash in the wine.

Add the parsley, pimentón and chilli, and crack over a generous amount of black pepper.

Add the butter and stir through until melted. Add the cream, then cook until the sauce reduces and thickens.

Serve with crusty bread.

I never really got pork. I mean, I've always loved bacon – who doesn't? – but I'd rarely make the choice to buy a pork cut for roasting. That is until I started this DIY food lifestyle. I was offered two large pigs that had become unwanted pets, and I suddenly had a whole lot of pork meat to deal with. Since then, pork and I have developed quite the relationship. Every year one whole pig will be raised for our family at my friend's pig farm and we'll get our pork on while it lasts. To be honest, I use one leg for curing, most of the shoulder for chorizo, and the belly and loin make bacon or pancetta. There's only a little bit of leg and shoulder left for roasting, and I try to stretch the meat as far as possible. I love this spiced-up slow roast because it provides us with a few meals instead of just one pork fest. And the best part is that the meat tends to taste better after a few days in the fridge, especially when it's fried and dropped into a taco. But for now, let us eat it in buns.

Lazy & Slow Pork 'n' Slaw Buns

SERVES 6

What you need

2–3 kg (4 lb 6 oz–6 lb 10 oz) pork shoulder

2–3 tablespoons olive oil, plus extra for drizzling

pinch of salt

brioche buns or chewy sourdough, to serve

fresh jalapeño chillies or Pickled jalapeño (page 293), to serve

The dry rub

10 garlic cloves, crushed

1 tablespoon smoked pimentón (Spanish paprika)

1 tablespoon piri piri spice blend (you can invent your own version of this Portuguese mix)

2 teaspoons ground cumin

1 teaspoon ground cinnamon

2 teaspoons dried oregano

1–3 tablespoons olive oil

The slaw

¼ large cabbage

1 red onion, finely chopped

60 ml (2 fl oz/¼ cup) Red wine vinegar (page 293)

juice of 1 lemon

100 g (3½ oz) sour cream

freshly cracked black pepper, to taste

125–250 g (4½–9 oz/½–1 cup) Mayo (page 292)

How to make it

Preheat the oven to 220°C (430°F).

Score the pork skin all over with a sharp knife.

To make the dry rub, crush the garlic in a large mortar and pestle, then add the spices, oregano and enough olive oil to make a wet spice rub. Now rub the shoulder with the spice mix – fun, isn't it?

In a large flameproof casserole dish over medium heat on the stove top, heat a big ol' glug of olive oil and brown the pork on all sides. Sprinkle the salt over the scored skin and drizzle with olive oil.

Pop in the oven with no lid for 30 minutes, then add 250 ml (8½ fl oz/ 1 cup) water, put the lid on, turn the heat down to 120°C (250°F) and cook for 5–6 hours, or until seriously melty.

Meanwhile, make the slaw. Shred the cabbage finely and transfer to a mixing bowl. Add the remaining ingredients and toss well to coat the cabbage evenly.

Serve slices of the pork on buns or sourdough with the slaw and a few slices of chilli or some pickled chilli.

Twice-cooked Pork Tacos

What you need

60 ml (2 fl oz/¼ cup) olive oil

8 onions, chopped

about 1 kg (2 lb 3 oz) left-over pork meat (page 41), roughly chopped

50 g (1¾ oz) butter

at least 15 corn tacos

cheddar cheese, grated, to serve

Chipotle sauce (page 187), to serve

spring onions (scallions), sliced, to serve

sour cream, to serve

If you're a busy person, time poor and stressed, you can find it difficult to allocate your precious time to cook a decent meal. I know, I've been there. That used to be my life. I ended up using my time-poor situation as an excuse to eat shit food. It eventually made me fat and burdened me with a bunch of physical ailments. I then learned to be slightly more cunning with how I spend time in the kitchen. This meal is one of those answers to being successfully frugal: it's a celebration of leftovers, and there's nothing wrong with that. In fact, I actually go out of my way to cook too much of some dishes because it's the leftovers I'm more interested in – arancini is a good example, which I make from left-over risotto or paella. Tacos are also a good way to mop up leftovers. Often when I roast a large cut of meat, there's too much for the family to eat for dinner so the leftovers end up in tacos the following night.

This pork meat is a leftover from the Lazy & slow pork 'n' slaw buns (page 41). I purposely cook the large pork cut with these two meals in mind. You can use left-over slaw from the pork buns or use the sweet onion suggestion below.

How to make it

Heat a little more than half the olive oil (a generous glug) in a heavy-based saucepan over low–medium heat and gently cook the onions for 20 minutes. Try not to burn them, but instead sweat them gently to release their sweetness. Add a splash of water occasionally if the pan begins to dry out. When cooked, set aside in a bowl.

If you're using left-over slow pork, it will be well coated in spices and will simply need reheating. Otherwise, season the pork if you feel it needs it.

Melt the butter with the remaining olive oil (a small glug) in a heavy-based frying pan over medium heat. Throw in the pork and stir well.

At the same time, heat another frying pan over high heat, and toast the tacos – 30 seconds for each side should do.

When the tacos are cooked, place them on a serving platter on the kitchen table.

Transfer the twice-cooked pork to a serving platter and arrange on the table with a bowl of grated cheddar, the slow-cooked onions, the chipotle sauce, the spring onions and the sour cream, then watch it all disappear before your very eyes.

Meat my sausage

I've been using chorizo in cooking a great deal over the years. It's become so important and I use it so often that I had two options: either cut back on it because of its expense, or start making my own. I opted for the latter. Who wouldn't? Being an opportunist and deciding to have the pig killed in spring was a little risky in terms of making dry-cured meats. Usually I'd have the meat hanging in the depths of winter – the conditions are prime when it's bloody cold. In cooler weather the moisture in the meat doesn't seem to exit so fast, so the process is slower and the product you're trying to cure doesn't sweat so much. Making dry-cured sausage in spring can be chancy, especially if we encounter a spell of warm days. Luckily for me, that's a rarity on this hill.

If you ever want to experience one of those super-rewarding chores of the good life, I can tell you that making sausages is a sure bet. The first time I made sausages was surreal. I kept mumbling to myself, 'Look, a sausage! I just made a sausage!' If I can do it – me, a total sausage novice – then surely anyone can. If we don't at least try things, we'll never know, eh? And by the way, I don't have any majorly specialist equipment. In fact, I'm pretty sure I have the cheapest, crappiest and smallest hand-cranked sausage-maker ever produced. I bought mine in this crowded 'food DIY' place run by a family of Italians. I looked at a heap of different machines, too many to choose from. I couldn't see the difference, nor could I see a reason to pay a large sum of money for something I might only use three or four times a year. I also wanted to steer clear of electric sausage-makers, as I plan to be off-grid one day. I finally asked for some help, and a beautiful Italian nonna talked me through the pros and cons of each machine. I found myself continually asking, 'Do you have anything cheaper?' as most contraptions seemed to be over the $400 mark. That's an expensive sausage, I thought. I ended up investing in a little Italian number that she assured me was good value for money. 'So it makes sausages, right?' That's all I really wanted. Nothing fancy, just something practical and functional. I still ended up forking out a few hundred dollars and I felt pretty guilty even spending that much. It seemed like a frivolous purchase as I walked out the door with a cheerful 'Ciao, ciao!' I've changed my mind now, though, as it's a machine that's served me well and will continue to do so for years to come. It makes my sausages – my chorizo, the sausage that's so important to my cooking. I can't put a price on that now, can I?

Chorizo is like salami, not in flavour but in that there are so many recipes – each household, butcher, aunty or uncle will have a different one. Some frown upon putting chilli in, some don't use wine, some put in less garlic, some more. It doesn't really matter. What matters is that it tastes good and it makes you happy. What matters is that you enjoy sharing it and you enjoy eating it. That's the goal, really, to get someone to eat and enjoy my sausage.

My final task as the butcher's assistant was to mince (grind) the remaining meat from the shoulder and all the trimmed fat we'd been collecting. At the end of the butchery session we had a large rectangular bucket of meat to process. I was a bit amazed how much mince I was going to receive. I could see a lot of chorizo in that bucket! With the belt-driven mincer we processed all the meat into a mass of white and pink.

My freezer literally overflowing with pork, I went to work immediately on curing and sausage-making. I've learned some very valuable lessons from curing meat at home, the most important being to respect the power of salt. Too much salt and it's like a fever you just can't shake – and once that salt's in the mix you can't take it out. Too much salt and the meat is ruined. If you've transcribed a recipe and, let's say, accidentally added a zero to the end of a salt quantity, you might find out the true definition of frustration in defeat. This, my friends, is how I acquired, through first-hand experience, my knowledge of torture by salt. My first batch of chorizo had great flavours, the spice mix just right, but the salt … OMG, the salt! I fucked up on the salt. It was inedible. In an effort to save the situation, my only option was to add more meat. Thankfully, I had no shortage of pork mince. Into the mixing bowl went double the amount of mince. I saved it to some extent, but it was still salty. It was a painful lesson, albeit one I won't forget in a hurry. It's like the first time you successfully figure out how to undo a girlfriend's bra. Get it right and memories are made. Get it wrong and you look like a dick.

I'd like to share a few tips about the process of making a chorizo using a hand-cranked machine similar to mine. I'll tell you what I've learned from my experiences in the hope you may in turn be brave enough to attempt it yourself. You'll be armed with a few pointers, learned by a novice sausage-maker like me. So here's my process from beginning to end.

How I make chorizo

I mix all the ingredients into the mince, ensuring the spices, herbs and wine are all worked into it thoroughly (see My Chorizo recipe on page 49 for ingredients). I fry up a small amount to taste. If the salt–spice balance is okay, then I transfer that mixture to the fridge overnight, to allow the flavours to mingle and get well acquainted with the pork. I use natural casings, which I source with ease from a commercial butchers' supplier in town. The casings come in a plastic bag and are covered in salt to preserve them. This salt needs to be rinsed off, so I pull out the number of casings I need and soak them in a tub of cold water for about half an hour. I then fill them with water and rinse out any remaining salt inside the casings. I rinse twice. To be sure, to be sure.

Next step is to fill the meat reservoir in the sausage machine with the pork mince. I attach the nozzle – I use the larger of the two sizes to allow for sausage shrinkage. (Warning, from here on in there may be a few penis puns.) I crank the handle until meat begins to cometh from the spout. Then I load the rinsed casing over the shaft of the nozzle. Ensuring there is no trapped air, I tie a double knot at the end of the casing. Now I'm ready to go. The meat is in the reservoir, the nozzle is attached and the casing is mounted and sealed with a strong double knot to withstand the pressure that will come down the shaft.

When I work with sausage, sometimes I like to work alone and sometimes I like to work with someone else. One person can crank and one can feed the meat into the casing. Crank, feed! Crank, feed! Either way, you need to find your own rhythm. If you crank too fast the pressure of the meat may split the casing. If you don't crank hard and fast enough you may end up with less meat in your casing, allowing air pockets that are a perfect breeding ground for bacteria and bad penis jokes. I recommend playing some Al Green to ease any tension during sausage production.

The idea is to fill the casing tightly with meat. This will give you a harder sausage, and let's face it we all want that. As I crank away, a large sausage forms. It naturally wants to curve into a circle like a snake coiled in the grass. I tend to move the large sausage, turning it around and around as new meat fills the casing. You end up with a big ol' pile of sausage, all twirled up in a heap. To finish off I normally pull a bit out to leave a length

cont.

of empty casing, enough to allow a tight knot with plenty of casing remaining, as I'll need to tie on the string for hanging. I also recommend that you finish off with a cuddle.

Using butcher's twine (not blue-dyed nylon twine) I then make incremental tight knots separating the long sausage into smaller sausage-sized sausages. Get it? You can make the sausages as big or little as you want. I tie in around 10–15 centimetre (4–6 inch) increments, as it helps push the meat either side of the knot, making the sausage even tighter. Don't worry about the unsightly twine. Once the chorizo is cured you can discard it.

You can eat the chorizo fresh (and freeze it to eat 'fresh' later), or you can dry-cure it. If you're planning on hanging the chorizo to dry-cure it, pop it in the fridge for a few hours to let it settle, which will help it hold its shape when it hangs. When you're ready to hang, use a sterilised pin to prick each chorizo ten to twenty times – just enough to allow exit points to assist the shrinkage process. Hang the chorizo in a place that's ideally got a low temperature, high humidity and isn't too draughty. If the sausages hang in warm, dry conditions (even worse with a draught), they tend to go rock-hard and are difficult to cut. You can hang the chorizo in the fridge for a week, then vacuum-seal them in bags and they'll keep for a very long time. You can also hang them in your larder for six to twelve weeks and enjoy them later. I use both methods with equally good results.

Commercial producers commonly use sodium nitrate as a curing additive. If you're concerned about adding it yourself, do some research and make an informed decision. I stopped using it a few years ago, but that's not to say it's not a dumb thing to do. It does work well to limit the chance of botulism, but a sodium nitrate serve of 22 grams (¾ oz) is enough to kill a man. I don't like it in the house, so I cure without it. I use all of my chorizo in cooking – I never eat it raw. If you don't want to take the chance of botulism, I guess a smart person would opt for sodium nitrate. It's your choice.

Now, go back over those instructions and count how many penis and sex innuendos I inserted.

Look, it's not really my chorizo, it's practically a recipe someone gave me and I think I just added more heat and – surprise, surprise – more smoked pimentón (Spanish paprika). That's pretty much how I roll. I simply add more heat and smoky flavour to everything – although this approach is not recommended for baking a cake. I've tried a few other chorizo recipes and found them not chorizo-y enough or too salty or too something else that made me less than excited, so I've been using this recipe over and over again. If you haven't noticed by now, I have a bit of a thing for good chorizo. And I'm talking Spanish chorizo not Mexican. Although they both have their place, this recipe is for the cured Spanish version. And it's the porky pearl of my chorizo dreams.

I've shared it with heaps of people – the finished product, not the recipe – and everyone's said it tastes like Spanish chorizo. I guess that's because it stays true to the formula of keeping it simple and honest.

One highlight for me recently was handing a chorizo to a pig-farming salami-making guru friend of mine, Tammi, and her saying I've nailed it. I guess now she might understand my lack of interest in her salami recipes.

The first time I made a batch of chorizo, the butcher made the mix too fatty. Tammi and I recommend 25 per cent pork fat to meat.

My Chorizo

MAKES 3 KG (6 LB 10 OZ)

What you need

2 garlic bulbs, cloves separated and peeled	1 tablespoon ground cumin
750 ml (25½ fl oz/3 cups) red wine	⅓ cup dried oregano
3 kg (6 lb 10 oz) pork sausage mix (25% fat, 75% meat)	¼ cup black peppercorns, crushed
½ cup smoked pimentón (Spanish paprika)	100 g (3½ oz/¾ cup) salt
⅓ cup sweet pimentón (Spanish paprika)	natural sausage casings (intestines; see notes on page 45)
¼–⅓ cup cayenne pepper	butcher's twine

How to make it

Steep the garlic in the wine in a saucepan over low heat for 20 minutes. Strain out the garlic and pour the wine into a large mixing bowl.

Add all the remaining ingredients except the casings and twine (!) and mix well with clean hands until everything is evenly spread. Take your time with this and mix it well – it's actually important.

Rinse the salted casings in cold running water.

Fill your sausage-stuffer with your mixture and load a casing on the nozzle. Don't forget to tie a knot at the end!

Basically, I recommend you follow the instructions for your sausage press, as they're all different. The general idea, though, is to get an even stuffing – you don't want big gaps in the meat, because it's a place for nasties to grow and spoil your chorizo.

When you've pressed out all the mix into the casings and sealed the end with a knot, use butcher's twine to tie off each chorizo to your desired length. Pop in the fridge for a few hours.

Use a sterilised pin to prick each sausage ten to twenty times, then hang them in a meat safe for 9 weeks.

(See pages 44–46 for more detailed instructions.)

If you buy a packet of natural sausage casings, prepare a small batch initially, then get more ready if you have left-over sausage mix.

Disclaimer: *I don't use sodium nitrate in any of my cured meats, but it's recommended that you do. Do your research and make up your own mind.*

Tip: *If your chorizo forms white mould, don't panic – it's okay. If it bothers you, dip a cloth in a bowl of vinegar and wash the mould off before you eat the chorizo.*

I made this for lunch one day and giggled when I served it up. It bore an uncanny resemblance to a campfire. The funny thing is, I'd just returned from a few days' camping and fishing and, for some reason, I was still in autopilot mode of setting up a campfire – in this case with anything!

I've found that if I crumb food and fry it, my kids will eat it without hesitation. Seriously! My kids have had two versions of the one dad. The first version (draft model only) was happy for them to eat processed chicken nuggets. The second (full production model) does not approve of chicken nuggets, so version 2 dad sometimes makes food look like food from version 1 dad. The kids appear to be dumbfounded as they crunch through the fried-nugget-like meal. I guess they're wondering if it's some sort of trick. But it's not. We butchered our pig, I made the breadcrumbs from my sourdough, the mayonnaise with eggs and garlic from my backyard, and the lemon is from Mum's tree. So no trips to see the Kentucky chicken man with the beard. Instead they eat tucker from the Victorian bearded man with pork butt and a sneaky plan to get his kids to eat real honest food.

Campfire Crumbed Pork Butt with Piri Piri Mayonnaise

SERVES 4

What you need

The piri piri mayonnaise

3 egg yolks
250 ml (8½ fl oz/1 cup) sunflower oil
juice of 1 lemon
1 tablespoon piri piri spice blend
2 teaspoons cayenne pepper (optional, but totally do it)
5 garlic cloves, crushed
salt and pepper, to taste

The pork schnitzels

1–2 kg (2 lb 3 oz–4 lb 6 oz) pork butt
plain (all-purpose) flour, for dusting
4–5 eggs, lightly beaten
Toasted sourdough breadcrumbs (page 293), for coating
oil, for shallow-frying
3–4 jalapeño chillies, thinly sliced
2 lemons, halved, to serve
salt and pepper, to serve

How to make it

To make the piri piri mayonnaise, whisk the egg yolks in a medium bowl while slowly adding the oil. Take your time and whisk well. A mayonnaise-like substance will form. That's because it's mayonnaise. Continue whisking until you've added all the oil. Mix in the lemon juice, piri piri blend, cayenne, if using, and garlic. Mix well and season to taste. You've just made a kick-arse mayonnaise!

To prepare the schnitzels, cut thin slabs of meat off the pork butt. Using a meat tenderiser or a rolling pin, give each slab a tap to tenderise it.

Line up three bowls on the bench: one with the flour, one with the beaten egg and one with the breadcrumbs. Dip each schnitzel in the flour, then the egg, then the breadcrumbs, and set aside on a tray.

Heat some oil in a frying pan deep enough to cook one side of the pork at a time. Pop in a small test piece as a temperature gauge. When it starts to snap and crackle, you can start cooking the schnitzels. Cook each schnitzel until golden brown, laying it on paper towel to drain off any excess oil while you cook the next schnitzel. Slice each schnitzel into chip-sized (fry-sized) slices.

Make a little campfire on each plate, with the mayonnaise as the flames and the chilli on top. Serve with a lemon half, and salt and pepper for people to help themselves.

Note: *To make plain mayonnaise, prepare as for the piri piri mayonnaise, but omit the spices, garlic and seasoning.*

That time I delivered hundreds of green babies

When the green peas and broad (fava) beans appear it's the garden's way of hollering, 'Spring is here!' They're two mega-easy garden gems that most people like to eat. Well, broad beans can be tricky for some people, but I've managed to convert a few by cooking broadies in a 'palatable' manner.

For me, green peas were in the same castaway raft as pears – for years they existed adrift in the ocean of 'clean food' I didn't like. In an effort to expand my fruit intake (in my previous life), I often tried pears from the supermarket, and every time I'd spit them out in disgust. My pea memories aren't much better. My nan overcooked tinned peas and they came out bland and tasteless. My ex-mother-in-law used to laugh at me when I'd separate the more palatable corn kernels from the peas when she served me one of those frozen pea–corn combos. It wasn't until I tasted real green peas from a friend's garden that I had one of those moments of exciting pop-in-the-mouth freshness that got me hooked! Broad beans soon followed suit. It's all down to freshness and realness. If only we could all access such real food! Well, if you have a bit of soil, some sunlight and water, you're one of the privileged few who can. You just have to grow it yourself. But don't panic, bugger all effort is required. Trust me.

Sometime in winter I'll dig the soil over with a long-handled shovel. The soil is normally moist, and chock-full of wriggling worms. If the soil was used pretty intensively over the previous summer, I'll replace some of the goodness with manure or compost. You see, with nature, it's important to remember that if we take we should also return. So in goes some seasoned manure, usually sheep, cow or chicken. If I don't have a cache of manure, I'll shandy in some well-seasoned compost and, as a final option, I'll use an organic mix of 'rock dust', which will boost some of the mineral levels in the soil for the next crop. A little rake-over to flatten out the soil and it's ready to plant the peas and beans. I'll then make some rows using the end of the rake, a stick or my hand – it doesn't really matter what you use, as long as a little trench has been formed. I'll drop the seeds in, spacing them well to allow for future growth, then I'll fold the soil over the seeds. It's that simple. The rest of my effort goes into waiting and seeing what happens.

In a week or so the seeds germinate and it's like delivering a new baby. These little plants are beautiful living organisms that you've assisted in having their turn at life. When a few little leaves stretch out from the soil, there's nothing more exciting – well, there was losing my virginity, but let's just say it's a rewarding and exciting moment. Especially the first time. Neat(ish) rows of tiny green shoots, they're my babies! As the season progresses, I check on the baby greens, often like a fussing helicopter parent. Every little bit of growth is exciting to observe. Even better is the knowledge that eventually they'll flower, and when pollination occurs those flowers will turn into pods that will burst with springtime freshness!

Raising a crop of either of these two beauties is a great introduction to growing your own food. Being able to observe the process from seed in the soil all the way to harvest time is so rewarding, and will no doubt encourage anyone to do it again year after year. That's what happened to me, and I'm addicted. This spring is no exception. Again I've watched the plants from the beginning. I got excited when they germinated and formed those sweet green rows of promise. I kept an eye on them as they advanced into tall, healthy bean bushes and climbing pea plants. Finally, the flowers appeared, pretty as any ornamental flower. The pods arrived and, like every other year, I found myself enjoying fresh raw beans and peas straight from the garden! It's the taste of spring, exploding in your mouth. This is how food is supposed to be, mega-fresh, simply grown in soil. No additives, no preservatives, no pesticides, nothing but real. It amazes me that I even find myself writing this. It's so illogical to add all those nasties to our crops and our food when for centuries the human race has survived so prolifically with the very basic process of growing food naturally. There seems to be a fear now that we as a civilisation cannot survive without the interference in our food that we've become so comfortably used to. But growing these little beauties is the way for me. It may not be everyone's medicine, but I'll take a serve, thanks. It's a pretty easy process, and the practical outcome is fresh real food – and plenty of it!

Now, what to do with all this produce? There are plenty of options for both green gems, and the best part is that even if you have more produce than you can eat in season, both the beans and the peas can be frozen for future food. I've found peas freeze well plucked straight from the pod but broad beans are better blanched first to retain that unique flavour and soft texture.

The spring darling that is the broad bean! I still can't believe I used to simply dig this in as a mulching crop. What a turkey! Now I'm happy to say I've been a convert for many years, and it's all thanks to the double-peel. Yes, so sue me, I'm a proud double-peeler. It takes the bitterness out of the bean and turns it into a fresh green burst of spring goodness. Each year in late autumn I plant a big crop of broad beans hoping for a good spring harvest. Coming out of the winter veg-growing lull, anything that's fresh and green is more appealing than a meat dish! Broad beans mark our impending semi-vegetarian summer and that puts a smile on my dial. Having said that, this little bean number goes great with meat. Oh, the irony! I serve it as a side to all sorts of stuff, from pork to rabbit. It just brings a freshness and awesomeness to the plate. And that's scientific.

Mushy Broad Beans

SERVES 4 AS A SIDE

What you need

350 g (12½ oz/2 cups) podded broad (fava) beans

handful of mint, finely chopped, a few leaves reserved to garnish

45 g (1½ oz/½ cup) grated pecorino

juice of 1 lemon

salt and pepper, to taste

olive oil, for drizzling

goat's feta, to serve

How to make it

Boil the beans for a few minutes then strain them and allow them to cool. Peel off the outer layer and drop them into a mixing bowl. Stir in the mint, pecorino and lemon juice. Mash with a potato masher to achieve your desired consistency – I like mine mashed well. Season with salt and transfer to a serving bowl.

Drizzle with olive oil, top with a generous scoop of goat's feta, garnish with the reserved mint, grind over some black pepper, and serve.

You can cook a paella over the gas hob in the kitchen, but cooking paella over the flames – well, it's a whole different story. It's more fun – or that's my take on it anyway. If you asked a Spaniard how to cook paella, I'm sure they'd insist it's a fireplace process and gas is a no-no. I'm not really fussed – I reckon these beliefs about how food should be cooked develop into rules, and I deplore rules. I've cooked paella both ways and I prefer cooking it outside over the hot flames and coals, but it's just a personal thing. Sure, it may give the meal a little smoky flavour and the rice on the bottom, if cooked right, develops a nice even crust. But really, who's going to tell the difference? You'd have to be a real purist to tell one from the other.

The way I cook paella over a fire is to get the heat up for at least an hour before I cook. This makes a good base of hot coals and constant heat, and it allows for a bit of vino refuelling. You won't find a 'paella' pan at your local camping store, but you probably will find a tripod frying pan for cooking eggs and bacon over a fire. It's practically the same deal.

Broad Bean & Chorizo Paella

SERVES 6

What you need

1–2 tablespoons olive oil

3 onions, sliced

2 leeks, sliced

5 garlic cloves, sliced

300 g (10½ oz) fresh chorizo (page 49), sliced

725 g (1 lb 10 oz/2¾ cups) tomato passata (puréed tomatoes)

500–800 g (1 lb 2 oz–1 lb 12 oz) broad (fava) beans, boiled and peeled

handful of parsley, roughly chopped

2 tablespoons smoked pimentón (Spanish paprika)

1.5 litres (51 fl oz/6 cups) Home-made meat or veg stock (page 294)

400 g (14 oz) bomba paella rice

135 g (5 oz/1½ cups) grated manchego

goat's feta, to serve

½ lemon, to serve

How to make it

When the fire has died down and the frying pan is at medium heat, add a generous glug of olive oil and sweat the onion, leek and garlic for 10 minutes. You don't want these to cook too hot and fast. A slower, gentler cook seems to get the sweetness out of the onions. If it's looking too hot, splash over some water to cool it.

Add the chorizo, passata, broad beans, parsley, pimentón and stock, and add a little bit of wood to the flames to bring the paella to a gentle simmer. Add the rice and stir evenly through the liquid.

Finally, spread over the manchego then sit back and wait. It normally takes about 30 minutes, but every fire is different, so it's a good idea to check a little bit of rice. If it's too crunchy it needs more time, if soft it may well be ready. Oh, and if you think your fire is too hot, you can just add a bit of water to the brew, which will also help cook the rice.

Serve with feta crumbled over the top and a squeeze of lemon.

Black fingernails

After many months of relatively lame garden activity, it's great to see some action in the patch once again. It doesn't matter if it's a cool spring; the thought alone that the garden will once again be active is good enough for me. The shift in the season can defrost the human spirit. Even though mornings and evenings are still cool and the fire remains stoked, the odd balmy spring day can really lift your spirits. Never in my life have I cared more about the weather than when I've been a grower of food. I check rainfall measurements, I keep an eye on forecasts and any mention of oncoming frosts, and I lament the insanity of the wind on our hill.

In my experience, the more I connect with nature (by working with her in such activities as growing food), the more I feel rightly human. It makes sense to work with nature, to be aware of her quirks. It's not so much about forcing yourself to understand her completely as it is a matter of simply getting to know her better. She's a fickle beast, one that I'm sure still has some surprises in store for us yet.

The slight change in weather is a call to arms. Sure, there's some food in the veg patch, but truth be told, it offers anything but great diversity. The future is bright, though. In a few months' time we'll be grilling zucchini (courgettes) and eggplants (aubergines), tossing fresh tomatoes and basil and munching on raw corn. Summer, the most critically important season in the calendar, is upon us. The earlier I can prepare for it the better, so I can grow as much food as possible. It's that food I'll store away just as a squirrel does. The cold season we've just endured was full of food I grew the previous summer. Year in, year out, the cycle repeats, just like a broken hipster record.

I bring the seeds I saved the previous year out from the dusty seed case. I select from my cache of hardened DNA-delivery casings (i.e. seeds) and I list everything I wish to grow. It usually happens over a cuppa or an evening wine. Kate and I talk about what we loved last year, the species and the varieties we ate the most of. We reminisce about that beautiful variety of tomato we discovered last summer, or groan about the fact that we planted too much of a food we didn't appreciate so much. The discussion is really a way for us to brainstorm for our future food – it's like a shopping list for the future, minus a DeLorean and a white lab coat.

With a list in hand (usually scribbled on whatever paper is around, dotted with coffee stains or wine rings), I head to the shed to rummage through my seed collection. I believe my seed box to be as good as a bank. In fact, if the world as we know it collapsed in some apocalyptic event, my box of seeds would carry more value than paper money. But even now, before the zombie alien attack, those seeds, if only just in my eyes, are valuable to no end.

Florets aplenty

There's a hint of blue in the garden. Well, I really should get that checked – it could be a shade of green. Yep, it's green. But let's say it's a bluey green (I'm colourblind). At the height of spring my garden is full of green, notably the supply of broad beans and peas. If it weren't for the rainbow chard mixing things up a bit, the place would appear to be a monoculture. There is, however, a little row of broccoli, which to me looks blue. Whatever! A lot of men are colourblind!

Visual disabilities (enhancements) aside, I need to tell you how much I love broccoli. I've not always liked the stuff. In fact, I used to go out of my way *not* to eat it. In my previous life I'd set it aside on my plate and just focus on eating the other more palatable bits of the meal.

What was wrong with me? Broccoli is delicious, right? Well, as for most other whole foods, I'd been jibbed for years. That broccoli that I didn't like all those years ago was commercially grown broccoli. And as for most things I eat now that I hated eating in my past, I owe my change of heart to freshness. This time of year, broccoli is the master of spring freshness. If I grow a sprouting variety I tend to break off mini florets in the garden and eat them raw. What the fuck has happened to me? Raw broccoli? Enjoyable? Yes, and I'm deadly serious.

Even better, though, is celebrating the fresh feeling of spring by cooking with broccoli. After a few hard months in winter, where a lack of freshness can drive a man mad, it's a refreshing change to have that crunch of a broccoli for dinner. I've found a heap of different ways to play with it, too. Not in an awkward fetishistic kind of way, but just in the kitchen. Fully clothed.

With almost every vegetable ingredient, I've tried to make a pasta dish, and broccoli did not escape this brilliant approach. A simple pasta with broccoli, egg and cheese, and I'm in brassica heaven. When I tuck into this food I cannot understand for the life of me why I ate bad food for so many years. Did I get struck by lightning like John Travolta in *Phenomenon* and suddenly have some sort of awakening? In a way, I guess, but who cares? Here's proof that real food can triumph over rubbish. Isn't that enough in itself to be worthy of celebrating?

Broccoli Pappardelle

What you need

1–2 teaspoons olive oil, plus extra to serve
5 large garlic cloves, finely chopped
500 g (1 lb 2 oz) Pasta, cut into pappardelle (page 295)
at least 120 g (4½ oz/2 cups) chopped broccoli florets
180 g (6½ oz/2 cups) grated pecorino, plus extra to serve
55 g (2 oz/¼ cup) mascarpone or cream
1 egg
salt and pepper, to taste

It seems like forever until the first florets of broccoli are ready in spring. And all that time I could have bought out-of-season broccoli from a supermarket. What an idiot to wait, but the wait is worth it! I love having to go without an ingredient until it comes back into season. It brings an extra element of excitement into our lives. We don't own a TV any more. Does that explain things? Seriously, though, this is yet another no-brainer meal – nothing fancy, a weeknight meal the kids will eat. It has cheese in it. Pecorino, too – they love the pecorino. You can make this with any pasta you want. I like the pappardelle because it's easy to make and it's massive and fun to eat. As simple as that.

How to make it

Bring a large saucepan of water with a pinch of salt to the boil.

While the water is warming up, heat a little olive oil in a frying pan over medium heat and fry the garlic until golden brown. Set aside.

Pop the pasta in the boiling water; fresh pasta should only take 8–10 minutes. Around the 5-minute mark, add the broccoli to the pasta pan. When the pasta is al dente, drain with the broccoli and return to the pasta pan.

Stir through the fried garlic, pecorino, mascarpone and egg, then season to taste.

Serve with extra pecorino and a drizzle of your finest olive juice.

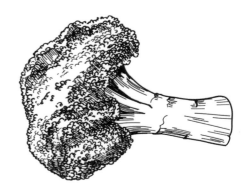

Broccoli Fritters

SERVES 4

What you need

3 broccoli heads

110 g (4 oz/¾ cup) plain (all-purpose) flour

150 g (5½ oz/1½ cups) grated Grana Padano

2 eggs

olive oil, for shallow-frying

goat's feta, to serve

Pickled jalapeño (page 293), to serve

It's only since I've made 'the change' that broccoli has come onto the menu at home. In my 'previous life' I never would have imagined cooking with it, let alone growing it. How much a man can change! Now, I'm not saying I'm a better man, I'm just different. Until recently, I'd never heard of a broccoli fritter, a corn fritter or a zucchini fritter, for that matter. All three recipes are loved in our house. They're like our version of fast food, a go-to option when I'm in a rush to cook dinner for the kids.

The idea of cooking veg this way was completely foreign to me, and I don't mind that it was either. I've very much enjoyed the journey I've been on at the home-cooking school. I enjoy the process of sharing ideas with other people, and the idea of veg as a fritter was shared with me by Kate.

I'm also glad that I no longer tear open packets of the processed food that was making my family and me unhealthy. Instead I cook our food from scratch, no matter how simple it may be. Case in point: broccoli fritters.

When it comes to frying them, you can use sunflower or canola oil, as they have a higher burning point, but apparently those oils have been found to be a bit toxic for humans in the old digestive process, so I stick to the ever-reliable olive juice. Use whatever oil you like. I'm no doctor or nutritionist.

PS: If you have kids, make a bigger batch and have some ready for school lunches in the morning.

How to make it

Cut the stems off the broccoli. Use a potato peeler to peel some of the larger stalks – the 'meat' underneath that hard skin is really yum. Blanch the broccoli for at least 5 minutes. I like to cook mine a little longer to really soften them. Strain and transfer to a mixing bowl.

Add the flour, cheese and eggs, and mash together with a potato masher.

Heat some olive oil in a frying pan. Working in batches, cook flattened handfuls of the broccoli mixture until golden brown. Lay on paper towel to drain off any excess oil while you cook the next batch.

Serve with melty goat's feta and pickled chillies.

My winters are thick with meaty stews and casseroles. During winter I feel more like a carnivore than an omnivore, but that's all part of the yearly cycle, I guess. There aren't many fresh vegetables in my garden over winter, so when they start appearing in spring I get more than excited. Never in my wildest dreams would I have imagined me, broccoli and excitement being used in the one sentence, but that's my life now and it has been for a while. It's a real no-bullshit appreciation of seasonality. It's about eating what nature allows me to grow at any given point in time. Broccoli is ready to eat in early spring in my poly tunnel and late spring outside. I like to grow two varieties, one a non-sprouting broccoli that gives large single heads, and one a sprouting variety that allows you to pick small florets continuously over a period of a few weeks. I've had a few challenges with seed saving for both varieties, so I just buy seeds now. In any case, the large broccoli plants take up too much room when left to go to seed, and at this time of year I need all available garden real estate for the oncoming summer crops, which are crucial for my future food.

Grilled Broccoli & Sriracha Salad

SERVES 2

What you need

2–3 broccoli heads, stems removed

1–2 tablespoons olive oil

5 large garlic cloves, sliced

100 g (3½ oz) soft goat's cheese or feta

50–100 g (1¾–3½ oz) slivered almonds

Green sriracha (page 199), for drizzling

salt and pepper, to taste

How to make it

Blanch the broccoli for 2 minutes in boiling water then drain.

Heat a chargrill pan or barbecue hotplate to high and start to grill the broccoli – you may need to work in batches, depending on the size of your pan. The idea is to give the broccoli a bit of a burnt, charred feel. When the broccoli is cooked, transfer it to a large mixing bowl.

Meanwhile, heat some olive oil in a frying pan over low heat and fry the garlic until golden.

Add the fried garlic, goat's cheese and almonds to the broccoli, drizzle over some sriracha, season to taste, and toss well.

Grab a fork and tuck in!

You can make this salad as a side, but quite frankly, after eating meaty stews served with a carb base like couscous or rice, I'm happy to eat a whole bowl of this wonderful plant. It's light and fresh, and sets a benchmark for more light vegetable meals in the summer ahead.

Sriracha is a fermented chilli sauce you'll find at Asian grocery stores – or you can have a go at making your own (page 199).

Tunnel of love

Spring leads to summer, and the peak growing season ends in autumn. It's a beautiful cycle, one into which I've been happily dragged. I think I should get these three seasons tattooed on me one day. The thing is, though, that as the growing season ramps up in spring, it's not only what I can grow in that season that's important – it's more important for me to make sure that the summer and autumn growing seasons are totally prepared for. When I grew my vegetables in a city backyard I had the benefit of the city's thermal mass. An array of buildings, roads and concrete all helped keep the nasty weather away. The buildings blocked the cold wind, the brick houses and roads harnessed the sun's rays, warming the soil and keeping away the hard frosts, and the drainage systems kept the yard from becoming waterlogged. When I moved further out to the land, I revisited the challenges my parents would have faced when they were growing vegetables back on the farm. The wind off the hill where I have my patch can be like an iceberg. The rain can collect and make drainage challenging, especially for those plants that aren't keen on having wet feet.

A friend of mine, Jack, had built a few small poly tunnels using a technique of interlinking PVC conduit. The results he was getting were unbelievable. He was totally putting my garden to shame. Now it's not a competition, but if it were I was definitely the sore loser. Every time he dropped over, he'd offer me excess produce from his overabundant poly-tunnel supply and I'd cringe in failure. I felt like a fake at times. Why couldn't I get my veg to grow as fast, as furious (could be a movie in that)? It was all due to that controlled environment his poly tunnel offered. These small structures have an amazing ability to harness any sunlight, even on a dull day in winter, especially if they're built as airtight as possible. So after receiving yet another batch of poly-tunnel broccoli I decided to construct my own. I really had no idea what I was in for, and for a long time I'd been fighting the idea of a large blanket of plastic camping in my backyard. But the proof was there for me. It came in the form of fresh delicious vegetables from my mate Jack.

After a few visits to look over the original structures, I drew up plans for my own love tunnel. It was to be larger, grander and more opulent than Jack's. No, just kidding! Just bigger. Instead of having two small tunnels I decided to make one large one (much to Jack's disgust). He was genuinely concerned that I was pushing the friendship with regard to the 'structural integrity' of my planned tunnel. Its footprint was around 4 by 8 metres (13 by 26 feet), almost double the size of the original and proven formula. But you know, I can't just do the same

thing. Life isn't a blueprint we must all follow. I incorporated some extra support with concreted-in masts and hardwood ends, also concreted deep within the soil of my garden. With my plans in mind I started to scavenge the local tip and bonfire piles for the wood I needed. Over a few weeks of being as opportunistic as buggery, I had the timber I needed and started to construct the lower frame. In the back of my mind, doubt suddenly grew about my plans for a larger construction. I could just see the whole damn thing blowing off in the wind, flapping away like a superhero's cape. Unfortunately for me I'm stubborn as a mule, so I persevered with the frame construction … nervously.

The next stage of the build was cutting, slicing and setting in the PVC conduit. The PVC frame was a fairly simple concept: loops would be supported by a cross member, which would slide into a larger PVC pole via a hole cut using a hole-saw drill bit – a clever way of using the thicker conduit to support the thinner. With all the materials now sourced for stage two, I started the drilling, cutting and joining. Before long, there in front of me was the framework of the tunnel. A tear welled up in the corner of my eye, probably from PVC dust. Even though the end product was still a long way off, there I was, looking at something I'd been too intimidated to build for ages. But I'd done it by myself. The reward was visual and a little overwhelming.

The next stage required me to make framed walls at either end of the tunnel. One end would have a swinging door and the other would have two windows to allow the hot air to escape. I'm not much of a builder – I'm more comfortable playing in dirt, hunting or fishing – but this job wasn't going to do itself, and I sure as hell didn't have the finances to employ someone to make it for me. So to work I went. My first job was to pull out all the nails, hinges and whatnot from the timber I'd scavenged. I figured it made sense to use this second-hand timber for a few reasons, the most obvious being that I'd be saving a few extra trees from being cut down. It was probably a romantic notion but it made sense at the time. Secondly, my budget really only covered the PVC, the plastic and the fittings. So it was off with the nails and into a bucket they landed. Must have been thousands of the bastards! I'd already worked a few days on removing metal from the timber I used on the framework so my bucket of used nails was getting rather heavy.

Setting up the end frames was relatively simple. Two large pieces of structural hardwood were cemented into deep holes and allowed to set; this formed the door or window frame. The rest of the frame was an upright fastened to the lower frame, holding a cross member to the doorframe, all held together with screws and taking a lot less time to construct than I initially thought. At the other end I copied the design, but added two square wooden frames, hinged to cross members hanging on the frame – a super-simple approach, but effective. I hung the door, which I'd bought from a house-wrecker for the measly sum of $5. My frame and walled ends were now complete. More bloody tears ensued.

It took a few weeks before Jack and I were both free and we could roll the plastic over the framework. One night after he finished work, he and his wife, Al, joined Kate and me, and over the frame the plastic went. We stapled it to the timber frame, nice and tight. The only remaining task was for me to cover the door and windows with the remaining plastic. And there she stood. My very own poly tunnel of love. I'd put so much love into its construction, and she would return the love with oodles of produce. Not a bad relationship, I reckon. Over the next few months I planted more and more inside her, until there was no room remaining. This poly tunnel was now ready for summer.

Hipster's Kale Pizza

SERVES 2

What you need

1–2 tablespoons olive oil, plus extra for drizzling

50 g (1¾ oz) butter

4 garlic cloves, finely chopped

2–3 cups chopped, stalks-removed, just-picked kale

1 Pizza base (page 295)

plain (all-purpose) flour, for dusting

90–125 g (3–4½ oz/⅓–½ cup) rich tomato paste (concentrated purée)

250 g (9 oz/1⅔ cups) grated mozzarella

8–10 rashers (slices) smoky bacon (page 189; or use non-smoked bacon if you want it to be lame)

semolina, for dusting

100 g (3½ oz) blue cheese, sliced

Kale is, like, so hot right now! I've never tried a kale smoothie, but they appear to be all the rage this season. So much so that there's a kale shortage! I'm not really about to eat a grassy smoothie, but I do like to come up with creative ways to eat this vegetable, as it's one of a handful dumb enough to grow in our freezing winter conditions. One of my go-to kale (or silverbeet/Swiss chard) meals is a breakfast with smoky chorizo and egg, smothered in plenty of hot chilli sauce and maybe some cheese. It's a brilliant start to the day, but my kids turn up their noses at the vey thought. So I make them a kale pizza instead. Not so much for breakfast, more a lunch or dinner arrangement. And because I'm eating it too, I add two of humanity's greatest culinary inventions: blue cheese and bacon.

The key with kale is to cook it down well enough to soften it. Some people like it crunchy and woody, I do not. I like it soft and delicate, like my women. I love women. I love kale. A kale woman?

How to make it

Preheat the oven to its highest temperature (around 250°C/480°F).

Heat a generous glug of olive oil with the butter in a large frying pan over low heat, then gently cook the garlic. Add the kale and cook until wilted, then continue to cook, adding a splash of water (or white wine) if it starts to dry out a bit. It will take 5–10 minutes to soften the kale, so test it as you cook it.

Roll out the pizza base on a floured bench. Smother it with the tomato paste, spoon over as much of the kale as seems reasonable (see note), then scatter over the mozzarella.

Lay out the bacon strips on top then drizzle the pizza with olive oil.

Dust a pizza stone or baking tray with semolina and heat in the hot oven. Add the pizza and cook for 10–15 minutes, or until the pizza is golden brown and the bacon is crispy.

Throw the blue cheese in top as soon as the pizza comes out of the oven. It will get all melty and delicious.

Note: *There should be enough kale for two pizzas, but none left for a smoothie.*

In my backyard and surrounding paddocks grows a healthy population of stinging nettles. It's a weed, and it's an invasive species, but it's one of those rare problem plants that you can eat away at, literally. It's loaded with healthy antioxidants and minerals and stuff that I know nothing about but heard about somewhere. Look, the reality is that it's free, natural and grows like wildfire. So it's a yes for those times in winter and spring when there isn't much going on in the greens department. Nettle tastes similar to spinach and makes a killer pesto (which is in my first book. Go buy it. Now). The idea of the pesto is to blanch the leaves to remove the toxic sting, squeeze the water out, then, just as for basil pesto, simply blend with some olive oil, salt,

garlic, grated parmesan and nuts of some kind, and voilà! Pesto. It can then be used on pasta, in salads, with roast vegetables or here on a pizza. Any why put it on a pizza? Well, I reckon you can put almost anything on a pizza and kids will eat it. And really, that's where a lot of my efforts go – towards getting my kids to eat real food.

Years ago I was in a northern Italian town called Bergamo and ate a pizza topped with basil pesto and thinly sliced potato. It was cheesy and full-flavoured, and has remained in my memory ever since. I love making this style of pizza. It's never as good as my memory implies, but for now it will just have to do. Nothing beats a great food memory.

Nettle Pizza

SERVES 2

What you need

2–3 large whole potatoes, peeled

1 Pizza base (page 295)

plain (all-purpose) flour, for dusting

90–125 g (3–4½ oz/⅓–½ cup) nettle pesto

250 g (9 oz/ 1⅓ cups) grated mozzarella

olive oil, for drizzling

semolina, for dusting

100–200 g (3½–7 oz) crumbly full-flavoured vintage cheddar, grated

salt and freshly cracked black pepper, to taste

Nettle pesto

6–8 cups nettle leaves

50–100 g (1¾–3½ oz/½–1 cup) walnuts, plus extra to taste

2 garlic cloves

90 g (3 oz/1 cup) grated pecorino, plus extra to taste

125 ml (4 fl oz/½ cup) olive oil, plus extra as required

salt, to taste

How to make it

To make the pesto, blanch the nettle leaves for a minute in boiling water to deactivate the toxins that make the nettle sting (wear gloves to touch the nettles until you've completed this step). Drain, set aside until cool enough to handle, then squeeze out the excess water with your hands.

Meanwhile, whizz the walnuts in a food processor until they resemble breadcrumbs. Add the blanched leaves and garlic, and whizz to make a paste.

With the machine still whizzing, add the pecorino then slowly pour in the olive oil until the mixture has your preferred consistency. If you like it cheesy or nutty, add more of these ingredients too. Making pesto is more about testing it and making it suit your taste. I like mine with plenty of olive oil, not too many nuts. Season to taste with salt.

Preheat the oven to its highest temperature (around 250°C/480°F).

Boil the potatoes until they're soft enough to pierce easily with a blunt fork. Drain and allow to cool, then slice thinly lengthways (if there is a lengthways).

Roll out the pizza base on a floured bench. Spoon over the pesto (I like it generous). Add a layer of the thinly sliced potatoes. Scatter over the mozzarella and drizzle with olive oil.

Dust a pizza stone or baking tray with semolina and heat in the hot oven. Add your pizza and cook for 10–15 minutes.

Crumble over the vintage cheddar, season with salt and pepper, and serve.

For a moment, drift back to beautiful Bergamo, where you can't understand what anyone's saying and you eat too much gelato.

Very little effort required

I have this inbuilt calendar that tells me it's time to check for a specific food that should be in season. Foraging is such a buzz phrase. You see it on menus at hip restaurants and I hear it's even entered the foodie TV world. Funny, because the whole point of foraging (where it has its roots, so to speak) is based around the necessity of feeding one's family. Nature's supermarket. It's also been a staple food source for many poverty-stricken communities over the ages, and somehow from that it's become embedded in numerous cultures across the globe. One of the most recent cultures to embrace foraging is that of the middle-class restaurant-goer. Which is ace, because they're eating food that's wild, food that's much better than over-processed rubbish. So let's take the good with the bad.

For me, foraging is a little more real than a sampled dish at a three-hatted restaurant. It makes up a good section of my food supply, and I particularly love it because I don't have to work hard for its production. I till no soil. I water no garden. I graft no branches. All I do is take. Nature does the rest. Now to me that makes very real sense. Nature does all the hard work? You're kidding me, right? That's too easy!

Nearing the end of winter, I keep my eyes closely fixed on the bare branches of the elder trees that grow on roadsides and in the bush near home. By early spring the buds have arrived and the leaves pop out a rich green. Soon after, the flowers develop and the white petals eventually come out on display. This is when I get excited. It's those aromatic flowers that are the key ingredient to the most refreshing cordial I've ever drunk – elderflower cordial.

Years ago, 'Hatto', a good-looking furniture-making friend of mine, got me addicted to elderflower cordial for life. He gave me a bottle of his freshly made cordial and that bottle made many beautiful summer drinks (mostly with added vodka). Unfortunately, it soon ran out and I begged for another, which with some clever trading (on his side) garnered me one further

bottle. But then it was gone. The elder trees had long finished flowering that spring, so I had to wait until the following year to make my own. Hatto was reluctant to give me the exact recipe for his cordial, so I researched my own. It all seemed so basic. All that's required is to steep the flower heads in a broth of water, sugar, citric acid and fresh lemons. Simple, right? All the recipes had slight variations, so I figured it would be easy enough to make up my own. No harm trying. It's not like I'm going to walk into a supermarket and buy elderflower cordial. Now I just had to wait that damn year until they flowered again.

Fast-forward to now! The trees on the country roadside were finally in flower. We'd also scoped out some elder trees in friends' backyards – often they had no idea what we were on about with this flower cordial, so we promised them a few bottles in return for our haul of their flowers. For one day we picked like mad. It was a beautiful crisp spring morning, the blue sky dotted with soft pretty clouds. We spent the day up ladders, clambering on fences and hanging from branches. By the end of the day we had bags of flower heads. The smell was from the old world. It's an aroma that reminds me of tea-cosies and grandmas.

I set up the large pot on the flame of a gas burner. This is the same large pot I use to boil the tomatoes for making passata (puréed tomatoes) – trust me, I washed it. The pot is massive, so large we could fit the entire haul of flower heads and the remaining ingredients inside for steeping (see page 75 for the recipe). Once the water was almost boiling, we turned off the heat, covered it and left it for two days to steep. Into clean bottles it went, which was probably the stickiest task I've ever undertaken! But the sweet smell kept us happy. We filled more than forty bottles, which was well and truly enough. Now we were set for those hot days of the oncoming summer, when our daily chores were finished and it was time to relax. Now I just need to learn how to make my own vodka.

Years ago a friend gave me a bottle of his elderflower cordial. I didn't think much of it, until about a week later I decided to try it and had one of those excited moments when food memories are made. I remember I kept asking Kate over and over again, 'Did you taste that? It's amazing!' What was even more amazing was discovering that it went particularly well with vodka. Well, let's face it, what doesn't go well with vodka?

I will say, though, that this has to be the most refreshing cordial I've ever drunk. You make it in spring but drink it in summer. When you've been slaving out in the patch and you need a break, nothing beats a big old pitcher of ice and elderflower. Just perfect.

I tend to make massive batches, as I find a bottle of home-made elderflower cordial becomes an excellent form of currency. And look, you can pick a hundred flower heads in no time.

Elderflower Cordial

MAKES ABOUT 8 × 700 ML (23½ FL OZ) BOTTLES

What you need

50–60 elderflower heads

3 kg (6 lb 10 oz) white sugar

3 tablespoons citric acid

5 lemons

How to make it

Put the flower heads, sugar and citric acid in a really large stockpot with 6–8 litres (203–270 fl oz/24–32 cups) water. Roughly remove strips of lemon zest from the lemons using a vegetable peeler. Cut the lemons in half, squeeze the juice into the mix, then add the peeled zest and the lemons as well.

Bring to the boil over medium heat and stir until the sugar has dissolved. Reduce the heat and gently simmer for 1 hour.

Remove from the heat, then set aside to steep, covered, overnight.

In the morning, strain the cordial into sterilised bottles and seal tightly.

Store in the larder for up to 6 months; refrigerate after opening. It's best after the first 2 weeks.

Making babies

When I started growing my own vegetables I used to buy all my veg as advanced seedlings from the nursery. It cost me a lot of money, which at that time I had because I worked a nine-to-five. But since taking the leap into the great unknown (becoming professionally unemployed), I've had to accept that it's too expensive to continue with this approach. So as the seasons came and went I learned how to raise my own seedlings. This approach has a few rad benefits other than just a cost reduction.

I guess if I were an extremist I'd say that buying seedlings from a nursery is contrary to my approach of reducing food miles. Think about it. The seedlings are raised on a farm somewhere in non-recyclable plastic pots and then transported to the nursery. I don't know how far they've travelled and I don't know what, if anything, has been added to the plants in the way of growth stimulants or fertilisers. I'm not an extremist, I'm a realist, but I also think that giving it a go ourselves is more rewarding than simply making a purchase at the nursery. Sometimes, though, when seeds don't germinate at home, we have no choice but to buy pre-raised seedlings.

To raise seedlings from scratch you need the seeds, right? I've found that there's more variety when buying just seeds than there is in seedlings. My nursery would only have advanced seedlings of two or three types of a particular sort of veg. I want a bit more variety than this, spice of life and all that. So back in the early days, when I turned my backyard into a food bowl, I found one of those online seed banks. No, not Monsanto ;-).

I found a seed company that served as a seed reservoir with the goal of preserving and supplying a heap of old-world (heirloom) varieties of vegetables and fruit. As I sifted through the varieties online I was gobsmacked! So many types I'd never seen before. So many old and rare beauties (just like me). After the excitement subsided I clicked on this variety then that one. Before long my digital shopping basket was overflowing and my credit card was getting a workout. A week or so later a package arrived in the post. Hundreds of my old-world seeds had arrived and now I had to take action to plant them. But before I mixed soil and seed I went through all the seeds, admiring all the rad names – like Zebra, Aunt Ruby's Green, Purple Sprouting, Christmas Lima, Flageolet, Painted Mountain, Slim Jim, Rosa Bianca, Futsu and Scorzonera.

It was then that I suddenly realised I'd been ripped off. Ripped off, but not by the seed company. They'd done the right thing and sent me the seeds I'd ordered. It was more the realisation that I'd been ripped off by supermarkets (again). This variety of seeds meant I'd soon be enjoying an array of new and interesting flavours, textures and even aromatics, something that had never been on offer at a supermarket, sensory pleasures I'd been missing out on all my life. Realising I'd been ripped off just fuelled my resolve, and before long the empty toilet rolls I'd saved were standing in trays, filled with seed-raising mix to house my seedlings. And thus my future of delicious food was written.

Years down the track, here I am picking the seeds from my own patch, the same variety of seeds that were collected for me by that online seed bank. I love seeing the process of providing the right conditions for a seed to germinate, the magic of plant birth and then the teenage years, the fruiting and then the retirement years where I come back to collect the seeds to ensure the process happens again the following year. And yes, sometimes if life gets too busy, the realist in me goes back to the nursery and buys advanced seedlings. It's a better alternative than out-of-season non-organic veg!

Smoky Bacon & Pea Broth

What you need

1–2 tablespoons olive oil
3 onions, chopped
3 carrots, chopped
3 celery stalks, chopped, leaves reserved and chopped
250 g (9 oz) smoky bacon (page 189), finely chopped
1 litre (34 fl oz/4 cups) Home-made veg stock (page 294)
3 tablespoons Old Bay Seasoning (or extra Home-made veg stock)
310 g (11 oz/2 cups) green peas (podded, you idiot)
handful of parsley, finely chopped
salt and pepper, to taste (optional)
sesame seeds, to garnish

It's such a treat when the green peas arrive in spring. It offers a much-needed break from the leafy winter greens and dried beans! I used to hate peas; I'd never eat them. When I started growing them it was a revelation of sorts. And now every year in they go, making slow progress over winter then when springtime really hits, boom! Green bombs of pea-ness.

If you're intimidated by any cooking process but want to learn to cook, this recipe is a no-brainer. It's so easy to make, but it's ugly as sin. Best to eat it with a blindfold. There's a reason why this meal will never be on 'master chuff' – it's as pretty as a dropped pie. But the upside is that it's loaded with stuff from the backyard and just happens to be relatively healthy. Yes, bacon is healthy. It's written in the practiculture law.

How to make it

Heat a generous glug of olive oil in a large stockpot over low heat and sweat the onion, carrot and celery stalks for at least 20 minutes. If it gets dry, stir through a splash of water. Gently cooking the veg this way will add to the flavour of the stock.

Stir through the bacon and cook for a few minutes. Now add the stock, Old Bay Seasoning, peas, reserved celery leaves and 1 litre (34 fl oz/4 cups) water, and gently simmer for 1–2 hours.

A few minutes before serving, stir through the parsley (reserving a little to garnish), and season to taste if desired.

Serve garnished with the reserved parsley and a sprinkle of sesame seeds.

I love pigeon, especially feral pigeon, which is an introduced pest. Sometimes I'll get asked to shoot some pigeons on a farm when their numbers get out of hand, or maybe I'll accidentally run one over on the road. Either way, meat is meat – I'll either shoot it, run over it or rip its head off. That sounds a bit harsh, but you can't cook a live pigeon. They just don't cooperate.

The idea of a pie for pigeon was a pure alliteration. It just sounded good, so I figured it must be right. The first time I made this pie was when I was asked to catch four feral pigeons in a chicken house. I'd arrived to pick up an unwanted rooster and noticed the four birds happily living in the pen with the chickens, getting plump from eating all the chicken feed. The property manager was glad to rid the pen of the pigeons. The only problem was that I didn't really arrive knowing I'd have to catch pigeons in a pen. All I had was my cap and some ninja swiftness. After a bit of agile hilarity, I caught all four birds and took them home.

The drive back was full of wild thoughts about how to cook them. I was going to skewer them on a stick and roast them over an open fire but in the end I decided to make a more civilised meal. I also caused a bit of a storm by involving my daughters in the killing process. I wrote a story about the day on my blog and boy, did it cause a stink! Which

is good, because it got people talking about the meat paradox. Should we be more in touch with how our meat is produced? Should we be aware and experience the killing of a sentient being in order to have the right to eat it? These are serious questions that need to be considered by many of us.

What I learned from the experience is first, that many people are confronted by the reality that an animal must be killed to 'transform' it into a meat product, and secondly, that teaching young kids this reality is apparently a no-no. Well, obviously I disagree on the latter point. It's only a Western cultural approach to hide certain realities from ourselves. In other cultures it's very much understood. In Morocco, for example, you go to a food market, pick your live chicken and then it's killed and processed before your very eyes. Imagine that at a supermarket! My kids have a total understanding of where meat comes from; they're not scared or grossed out. They understand the reality of meat and I hope, as they grow into adults, these experiences will help them make informed decisions as consumers.

The best thing I learned about this process is that pigeon pie is delicious. I now jump at the opportunity to get my hands on these tasty little birds.

Roadkill Pigeon Pie

SERVES 2

What you need

60 ml (2 fl oz/¼ cup) olive oil	1 tablespoon hot pimentón (Spanish paprika)
2 onions, finely chopped	salt, to taste
4 garlic cloves, finely chopped	½ teaspoon freshly cracked black pepper
1 wild pigeon, spatchcocked (see tip)	60 g (2 oz) chorizo (page 49), chopped
splash of Pedro Ximénez (Spanish sweet sherry)	250 g (9 oz) Shortcrust pastry (page 105)
525 g (1 lb 3 oz/2 cups) tomato passata (puréed tomatoes)	1 egg, lightly beaten
250 ml (8½ fl oz/1 cup) red wine	sesame or poppy seeds, for sprinkling (optional)
8–10 whole cloves	chips (fries) or wedges, to serve
handful of parsley, chopped	

How to make it

Preheat the oven to 180°C (360°F).

Heat half the olive oil (a generous glug) in a frying pan over low heat and gently sweat the onion and garlic for 10–15 minutes. The longer you cook them, the sweeter they get. Transfer to a flameproof casserole dish and set aside.

Using the same frying pan, add the remaining olive oil (another glug) and brown the pigeon for about 1 minute each side. The idea is to seal the meat, not cook it.

Splash over the sherry then transfer with the pigeon to the casserole dish with the onions and garlic. Add the passata, red wine, cloves, parsley, pimentón, salt, pepper and chorizo.

Add the lid, pop in the oven and cook for 30 minutes, then reduce the temp to 150°C (300°F) and cook for 1 hour. The meat should now be tender and soft. Remove the dish from the oven and increase the temp to 220°C (430°F).

Remove the bird from the casserole dish and the meat from the bones. Be sure not to leave any tiny bones in the mix! While you're pulling the meat from the bird, set the dish on the stove top over high heat to reduce the gravy. Return the meat to the dish and continue to reduce the gravy until it's thick, not runny.

Transfer the mixture to a pie dish and cover with a round of shortcrust pastry or cut strips of pastry and weave them over the filling. Brush with the beaten egg and sprinkle with some sesame or poppy seeds, if desired.

Bake for 30 minutes, or until the pastry is crunchy.

Serve with chips or wedges.

Tip: To spatchcock the birds I use a pair of scissors. I place the under blade through the bottom hole (where I pulled the guts out) and poke it out at the neck. I then cut through the breastplate (sternum) cleanly and open the birds out wide to cook evenly on both sides.

Ryan the gosling

My mate Jack is always working on some new project at his place. Years ago he had a few head of sheep that he'd fatten up for the freezer. I was totally jealous, as I didn't have the land for that, but these days he's moved on to a more dynamic approach to food acquisition. He grows a fair bit of his tucker and he's always looking for ways to improve his yield and his approach to DIY food. Now he's into geese. One male and a handful of willing females, and his goose population exploded. There were so many little goslings getting around that he gave us one. We couldn't help but call him Ryan. Unlike the megastar lady-loving Ryan Gosling, ours met an untimely death. I got up to check the nursery of ducklings and chickens and there he lay, quiet, still and very much dead. It's not easy killing an animal, and I've had to work on that for a few years now, but when one dies by itself and when it's so damn little, it just plain sucks. To lift my spirits I hired *The Notebook*, bought a tub of strawberry ice cream and stayed in bed all day. Not really. But I was sad.

With Ryan the Gosling gone, there were still a lot of geese in the neighbourhood. Jack had so many that eventually the amount of goose poo deposited at his place began to cause a problem. With sixteen goslings now mature, Jack decided they were all destined for the freezer. That's a great deal of labour for just one fella, so he wrangled me in to help. Payment? Yep. Five birds! Made my day! The thought of five of those large birds for my freezer – wow! What a brilliant source of good meat.

The day came and we did what needed to be done. We were well organised – well, mostly Jack was. I just grabbed the birds, dispatched them and gutted them. Jack was operating his home-made feather-plucker, which worked a treat and saved us a good deal of time. I had the dirty work, with my hands up cavities bringing out the reality – all blood and guts. Literally.

By the afternoon, we were both exhausted. We had all the birds in the freezer, including the livers and hearts, and we'd swept up and hosed out the feathers and inner workings of the birds. It was time to crack a coldie. I went home that night with five large birds and a heap of offal. Even though I was excited about cooking geese (which was a new experience for me), I was even more excited at the thought of all those hearts. I know it sounds a bit wrong, but I've learned to love these little hearts as a treat. They're rich in flavour and firm of texture, and eating the heart seems like another way to use as much as possible of the life that's just been taken. It's not really a way of showing the bird some respect – it's dead – but instead I see it as a way of respecting what's been provided by Mother Nature. It's important to give thanks, and this is a way of doing so. In fact, it's become a little bit of a ritual, mostly just with poultry, like ducks, chicken (see page 185) and geese. I eat all the hearts of these birds. There are cultures around the world whose traditions may seem odd to us, but now I have a better understanding of how these weird food traditions and rituals possibly developed and why they exist. In any case, if I blindfolded you and served you a forkful of goose heart with sherry glaze, I'm sure you'd be converted to my weird heart-eating religion.

Geese are magic animals. They keep the grass around the house block short during summer, they provide us with enormous eggs in spring and they also feed us with their delicious meat. They really are a backyard farmer's dream bird. I'm thankful that my mate decided to experiment in keeping a small flock at his place, because it was the introduction to geese that I needed. To be honest, I hate the concept of lawns and being a slave to mowing them, so geese really are just my edible lawn mowers. Keeping lawns green requires a heap of water,

which is a bit of a waste just to keep up appearances. And I'm yet to find a mower that doesn't use some natural resources to operate, electric mowers included. But a living lawn mower that fattens up on the grass – well, that just ticks many practical-living boxes.

I'd never cooked a goose before this year, so as for all new forms of meat cooking I looked to the masters for answers. For goose I headed straight to Hank Shaw, the author of the book Duck, Duck, Goose.

Herby Roast Goose with Crispy Skin

SERVES 4 (WITH ROAST VEG)

What you need

1 whole goose	60 ml (2 fl oz/¼ cup) olive oil
4 garlic cloves, peeled	1 teaspoon dried thyme
1 teaspoon black peppercorns	pinch of salt
grated zest and juice of 1 lemon	roast vegetables, to serve

How to make it

Preheat the oven to 180°C (360°F). Take the goose out of the fridge and keep at room temperature while the oven is warming up.

Using a mortar and pestle, crush the garlic cloves to make a paste. Add the peppercorns and crush well. Add the lemon zest and juice, half the olive oil, the thyme, and a generous pinch of salt, maybe two. Mix well to make a marinade.

Rub the marinade over the entire bird, then transfer the goose to a roasting tin and roast, uncovered, for 45 minutes.

Remove the goose from the oven and, using a boning knife, cut out the breast. Wrap the breast in aluminium foil and set aside to rest on the bench.

Cover the rest of the goose in foil, then return to the oven and roast for a further 45 minutes. Remove the bird from the oven and allow to rest.

Meanwhile, heat the remaining olive oil until quite hot in a frying pan over high heat. Sear the goose breast skin side down for 1 minute, then flip over once to finish the other side.

Slice the breast up, remove the wings and legs from the roasted goose, and serve with any other remaining bits of meat and roast veggies.

Enjoy!

I think the title of his book gives away his goose-cooking prowess. He has a technique I now use for cooking home-raised geese and it works magnificently. It's simply a matter of removing the breast halfway through roasting, so as not to dry it out, and then crisping the skin with a quick pan-fry before serving, making the most of that delicious crispy skin. You can season the bird however you like; here I use a simple classic that works well.

Collecting the blueprint

There doesn't seem to be any one time of the year when I collect seeds. A plant just gets to the point where it's finished providing the food, and then it becomes a priority for me to preserve the seed so the entire process can be repeated the following year. Seeds come in so many sizes and forms. Some we eat – such as beans – some come later, after the plant has flowered, after we've taken from her what we wanted. They're all different.

There are a few issues, however, when it comes to the world of seeds. First, the information the seeds possess is becoming more and more the property of corporations. This is a concern, is it not? It's surely something we should be questioning. Should one entity have control over a food source for the masses? Well, I reckon if that entity invented the seed then sure, it's their intellectual property. I don't really have any interest in any form of highly manipulated seed anyway. I think we all have the power to resist. Sure, it's good to question the power of corporations, I'm all for that, but I also prefer the approach of doing more than just complaining. Seed saving and planting are a way we can take back ownership of the problem. Little seed co-ops are popping up all over the Western world. Most of them seem to have similar ideals – to save seeds for the good of the people. The varieties are interesting, and they're often not generic, so they can cater for variable climates, soil types and other growing conditions. You can save these seeds yourself, so you're then in control. Isn't that a good thing? Hell, yes!

As a high-school student I was awarded dux in biology in my final year. I'd fallen in love with genetics. The study of life, of biology, had me fascinated. The idea that critical information about an organism could be trapped, harnessed and passed on to the next generation was mind-boggling. The concept that little changes (mutations) in that information (DNA) could be beneficial to a species was so intriguing. This knowledge transfers to growing veg at home. If you were to try growing a range of varieties of the one species, say different types of tomato, eventually you'd find one that grows the most successfully in your yard. One or two varieties will stand out as clear success stories. You want to save the seed from those plants. Each season, tiny changes may occur with that variety. It might mingle with another, cross-pollinate and produce a new variety even better than the last. It might grow and improve over the seasons to work more productively with the conditions available. This is how we got these varieties in the first place. Corn, for example, was a pretty lame wild grass until it was improved season after season by growers until at last it was nothing like its original form but a food source that spawned centuries of prosperity in South America. So you see, it's important for us to continue that process. We have that ownership, that responsibility – we needn't rely on a money-hungry corporation to do that for us.

Spring marks a great resurgence in fresh food from the patch. It's the renaissance of the annual seasonal progression. It's when eating veg is cool and in fashion again. The winter has been hard – sure, there's been plenty of kale, chard, etc. – but now some variety comes into play. Not only is it a time to delve in to freshly podded peas, fluffy-housed broad (fava) beans or stunning-tasting broccoli, it's also a time to be mindful of preserving the seed for planting these beauties the following year. There's a catch for those of us with limited space for our patch, and let's face it, that's most of us. If I were to leave rows and rows of vegetables to go to seed, I'd likely miss out on the right time to plant the vegetables for the oncoming season. This year I was caught out by leaving broad beans in too long.

First I buggered up by planting the beans a little late, and secondly I was greedy and waited until the beans were plumper to gain a freezer full of beans for the following winter's dry spell. But I also allowed the broad beans extra time, to ensure as many flowers as possible formed bean pods, allowing me not only to collect buckets of food, but also a bucket or two of beans I could keep for seed, readying me for early winter when it's time to replant them.

So how can we get around this dilemma of managing our valuable backyard real estate? Well, I figured out one approach when a mate of mine offered me a haul of broccoli seeds. He'd feasted on the florets, and he'd allowed one or two successful plants to go fully to seed. He then plucked the plant from its earthly grasp and hung it in a shed with a cloth underneath to collect any falling seeds. Now this might not seem like a solution at first, but consider this. He didn't collect and cure any broad bean seeds. But I did. See where I'm going here? A seed swap ensued. We didn't moan and whinge about corporations owning seeds, we just swapped seeds for plants we'd both grown, for plants we both enjoy eating. Now that's taking back control.

This is the seed I collected in spring–summer. I don't grow every imaginable vegetable, so the list is modest. The ideal conditions for drying seeds is somewhere cool and dry – avoid high moisture or dampness.

Things that grow in pods, dry in pods

- Peas

- Broad beans

Note how much 'stock' you have remaining on the plants. Don't eat it all because those beans and peas you munch on are next year's seeds! If you're battling for space and you need to make way for your next crop, I suggest pulling the plants out, pulling off the remaining bean and pea pods (don't shell them!) and storing them somewhere undercover. Dry, warm or cool is fine, just not too much humidity or they may rot. The next element to be mindful of is pests. Just like us, the mice, rats, possums and tigers all want to eat your produce. So keep it up high and free of pests. In a month or so, depending on the weather, the seeds (peas and beans) will rattle loosely in their pods. They're ready when this happens. I normally test a few by crushing a bean pod. If the pod cracks and crumbles dryly in my hand, it's ready for the next stage in the process. I then remove all the peas and beans and store them in a large glass jar with the lid off for another month. Keeping the lid off allows any final moisture to evaporate and ensures a clean dry.

Things that need to be hung up

- Silverbeet (Swiss chard)
- Rainbow chard
- Rocket (arugula)
- Parsley
- Broccoli
- Celery
- Mustard
- Cress
- Kale

For these veggies I tend to pull out the entire plant after I've allowed it to form seed. I hang them upside down in the shed and tie around them a bag of a breathable fabric such as fine hessian or calico. The seeds will eventually dry and fall into the bag for easy collection.

Some of these, such as rocket and chard, will self-seed if you allow them to. Rocket is one of my most successful garden weeds!

Spring has truly arrived when the peas are in season. Being a grower of food for the family, I've turned into one of those people who lives more by a seasonal calendar than a regular one. It may be spring by the diary's account, but I refuse to accept that fact until the peas arrive. Philosophically speaking, I reckon the calendar of nature is more real to live by than the old human calendar, but that's just me. Either way, the peas are here, and they're fresh and delicious!

I get excited when the first flowers arrive, then when I see bees fussing around them, and finally I tend to lose my shit when I pick the first pea off the vine. That explosion of pea flavour is – well, it's fabulous! There, I said it. These guys are the epitome of home-grown perfection. The kids and I gorge ourselves on the fresh green peas as we try to pick some for dinner. I reckon that's a bit of a winner veg, when the kids love eating them off the plant, but I do like to cook with them, and this little ditty is a snack that goes well with a cold ale on a warm spring day. Tapas, if you will.

Pea Bombs

SERVES 4

What you need

310 g (11 oz/2 cups) podded green peas

1 tablespoon sumac

25 g (1 oz/¼ cup) grated pecorino

1 tablespoon finely chopped mint

plain (all-purpose) flour, for dusting

1–2 eggs, lightly beaten

Toasted sourdough breadcrumbs (page 293), for coating

oil, for deep-frying

Chilli and smoked pimentón aioli (page 292), to serve

red chilli, chopped, to garnish

sea salt, to serve

How to make it

Parboil the peas for a few minutes just to soften them slightly. In a mixing bowl, mash the peas with the sumac, cheese and mint.

Line up three bowls on the bench: one with the flour, one with the eggs and one with the breadcrumbs.

Form a small ball of the pea mixture, coat it in the flour, then the egg, then give it a coat of breadcrumbs. Repeat with the remaining pea mixture, then pop them in the fridge for a few hours to harden.

Heat the oil in a heavy-based saucepan and deep-fry the pea bombs until golden brown.

Serve with chilli aioli, fresh chilli and sea salt.

Serving suggestion: *Cold beer.*

Summer

Summer

ummer is a funny old beast. By the calendar it starts on 1 December, but in reality it's a slow train. Up here in the hills, nothing seems to wake up until at least January. I'll often check with local friends (who grow veg) to see what stage they're at. I'm looking for some reassurance that I'm not doing something wrong: 'Have you got your beans in yet?', 'Have your tomatoes flowered yet?' Whatever news I get doesn't seem to make a difference. My garden is still dragging its summer feet.

I'm well aware of my impatient nature, so I remind myself that things will eventually happen and I distract myself with chores until the weeks pass, the warm weather arrives and the garden takes hold. There's a very short window of opportunity here, as we're exposed somewhat, being positioned on a large hill in an already elevated highlands region. Wind is a killer for the garden. In winter it's a fiercely cold wind, strong enough that last winter it blew every leaf off my young lemon tree. (Poor lemon tree. If it were a man, he'd be suffering from debilitating shrinkage.) In spring, the wind swirls and twirls, not really sure of what it's doing. And by summer the wind is hot. Damn hot. Hot enough that it can draw every last inch of moisture from the leaves of my vegetables, like they've just walked on the surface of the sun. Not that plants can walk. I'm aware of that. I haven't spent *that* much time living in the hills.

Just before Christmas, however, we get a little taste of summer. A mate has an extensive orchard with walls of climbing and bushing berries of all varieties. They seem to mark the real beginning of the warm-season food glut. Raspberries, gooseberries, blackcurrants and boysenberries are enjoyed as a welcome to summer. One year we were offered as many blackcurrants as we could

pick. Kate made a killer cordial, one that seemed to be best enjoyed with vodka. Always with the vodka.

In a short time, the berries disappear and the real food comes to the fore. Flowers mature to fruit, meals suddenly shy away from having any association with meat, and we become faux vegetarians for a few months. Why eat meat when you've got access to veg this pure, this fresh? That's what my whole approach to living is – to go wild over summer growing enough storable food for the winter lull.

This system seems logical, but it's fraught with challenges. Timing is paramount. I've realised this over many a summer now. It's okay for some varieties, but for those sensitive summer-lovin' varieties it's critical to get the timing right. If you get it wrong, the outcome is simple – less food. It's as brutal as that. I must admit, that fact has taken a bit of getting used to since I stopped buying fresh produce from a supermarket. I guess that's because I'd had the convenience my entire adult life. I'd grown accustomed to it. But now, out here and deciding to live this way, there is no convenience. I've made a commitment to live like this, with nature, with the seasons. It's the most deliberate of choices.

Transition

By early summer I had rows of broad (fava) beans and peas still occupying the precious real estate I needed for summer crops. The damn things just kept on providing us with heaps of food! How annoying is that? Fresh, organic food. OMG, so annoying. I was reluctant to pull them out, but eventually I had to make a call. I spent an afternoon pulling every pea and bean from the plants, then I pulled those very plants from the ground.

The chooks had a mega-feed, as they tend to when I do a spell in the patch. But this time, they weren't to be fed second-class weeds. No, this time, the chooks were to dine on fresh pea and broad bean leaves! I look after the girls and they look after me. There was, however, too much in the way of vegetative matter, so half of it went into a big pile destined to be compost for the following year. Not much gets wasted around here. First, I don't have much cash, and secondly I just don't like waste. There's no point to it.

That evening we sat in the family room podding the little green goodies. Around 12 kilograms (26½ pounds) of broad beans went into the freezer. The first store of veg for winter (that is, if we could just hold off eating them during summer). I do want to share something with you, though, because I made a mistake and we can avoid that happening if I tell you this now. I didn't blanch the beans before freezing them, and when I cook them now, they're harder and taste slightly different. They're still palatable, but they need to be cooked longer to soften them up. I guess I should have done to them what I do with corn pre-freezing, and blanched them then cooled them in iced water. Next year I'll be all over that. And now I've saved you the pain of finding out by making the same mistake I did.

With my cache of peas and beans stored away, it was time to start some real planting for summer. With a long-handled shovel I dug a shovel's depth into the soil and turned it over. This seems to help with drainage and mixes up all the detritus and detritivores, resulting in a nice friable medium for the soon-to-be-sown seeds to start their growing career. It's at this point that I drag in some kid labour. Not because the job is easier with their 'help' but because I want them to feel some ownership over the veg garden.

I try to match up the right kid with the vegetable they most enjoy eating, with the idea that when the veg is mature, said kid can harvest it and will appreciate the experience. Well, that's the intention anyway. It doesn't always work, but no harm trying, right? In went a few rows of corn, a few varieties of summer beans, rocket (arugula) and more peas. You can never get enough fresh green peas.

With our fingers black from the rich volcanic soil, we stood back and admired our laborious effort. Nothing but a few rows of dirt – so unfulfilling for the kids! I go to great lengths to remind them that the germination process is just a few weeks and they'll soon be able to see baby veg plants, but who am I kidding really? Off they go, under the cypress pine to the swings from whence I'd just dragged them to 'play' in the garden. One day, though, these kids will remember. I know this for a fact, because this is exactly what my mum did for me, and I remember it and I cherish it, and those childhood experiences have made me the man I am today.

I have a habit of looking over my handiwork in the patch, and at this time of the year, early summer, the garden doesn't give back a great deal of visual stimulation. It's transition time and you see more soil than you do plant matter. It is, however, a garden full of promise. And were it not for the fact I've been growing summer vegetables for a few years now, I'd probably crack the sads and hang out on the swings with the kids. But I know that only a few months away the family will be enjoying as much summer veg as they can consume. I can rest easy in the knowledge that it's still early summer and I have all my beans and corn in the ground. Now to wait with fingers crossed.

Summer babies

Back in spring I propagated a heap of seedlings for summer planting. I give lots of vegetables the direct-planting treatment but some respond very well to being nurtured in small pots until they're of size and can be released from the baby plant nursery. It's mostly zucchini (courgettes), pumpkins (squash), eggplants (aubergines), tomatoes, basil and coriander (cilantro) that get this special treatment; almost everything else for summer I plant directly into the garden beds. I still use the toilet-roll method. I also have a bunch of old seedling pots I use year after year. It seems to work well, especially if you've made yourself a little hot house to give the new seedlings a head start. Unfortunately for me, I failed to get the plastic over my new poly tunnel early enough so I just sat

my seed trays in the boot room at the rear of the house. It's full of windows and it faces north, so it's blessed with plenty of light. For most of the plants I propagate, I'll add two seeds per tube, allowing for the chance of one not germinating and me having a wasted empty tube with no seedling in it. As the seeds germinate I pluck out the smaller of the two and allow the faster, more robust seedling to continue growing.

All my summer veg has popped up, the magic leaves have broken out of the seed casing and with two tiny leaves opened up, they look like they want to be hugged. Now I might love my veg, but I know a big ol' bear hug from this bloke will end badly for the seedlings, so I reserve my hug for later. Each day I give the little babies a gentle spray of water as I'm heading out

to my chores. It's not really a demanding job raising these babies. At least there are no shitty nappies or late-night screaming. And unlike human babies, it's totally legal to eat these.

As the plants grew I made sure their little patch of soil was ready for them. All weeds got removed, and the soil turned and lifted with a little compost. It feels like summer is starting. The baby plants are lovingly deposited in the soil, and I use cut-open plastic bottles to give them some initial protection. I breathe a sigh of relief, comforted that the summer growing season has really started and this time, unlike a few seeds buried in the soil, I can see results. All I have to do now is hope we get a long summer, with plenty of hot days and oodles of warm sunlight.

Escape

It'd been a while since we'd had a holiday, and we can't really afford a proper holiday so we bought an old caravan instead. We figured we'd get years of use out of it and it could also serve as a spare room for visitors. It was a bit of a steal actually – a 1971 Viscount six-berth for a few grand. The catch was a twelve-hour drive to pick it up, but once we had it back home and cleaned up, it was ready for us to drag to the closest beach, down on the Great Ocean Road. Off we headed with dreams of warm sand between our toes and endless afternoons fishing for dinner. Leaving the veg garden behind was worrisome, but I had some good folk stay over to keep an eye on the place for me. I didn't care what they did at the house, as long as the garden got plenty of water on those forecast hot days.

The annual summer trip to the beach means fishing for me. I don't surf, I don't sunbake, but I do love eating freshly caught seafood. And luckily for me, a week down on the beach means plenty of time for fishing and foraging for the coastal bounty. Where we camp is right on the beach – well, not literally, but it's just over the sand dune. From our caravan window we can see the waves rolling in, bikini-clad sunbakers, surfers having the times of their lives, and Henry the dog taking a dump on the beach. *Henry*!!!

As midday lazily turned to afternoon I'd grab my surf rod and head to the now much quieter beach. My dad had passed on his beautiful bamboo surf rod he made the year I was born. It hauls a mean cast, out past the breaker with ease. And with a bit of luck, I caught myself a nice Australian salmon and a few mullet. Not enough to feed an army but something to put a smile on my face and some food in our bellies. For days after that the fishing was harder work with little result, so I headed out on a local charter boat to access some deepwater fishing. Out we went into the blue, then finally the anchor was dropped and our lines went in. I had a pretty successful day with my guide, and as a result I brought home fish for us to enjoy for the next few days – mackerel, flathead, snapper and even dog shark.

When the fish is this fresh, I don't like to muck around with it. What's the point? You'll disguise the natural flavour of the fish, which is not cool because that's what should be celebrated, that fresh natural flavour – the richness of mackerel, the sweetness of flathead and the freshness of snapper, all beautiful fish in their own right. So I kept things simple. A bit of butter, salt and pepper, served with a wedge of lemon. Sometimes if I catch a good haul of Australian salmon, it's then that I'll play with different flavours. The meat of the Aussie salmon is all right on its own, but unlike these other fish it does tend to work well with a bit of introduced flavour magic.

After feasting on fish for a few days, we were ready to return home. We'd had a bit of a heatwave and the van was somehow becoming smaller and hotter, especially with four little girls on board, and Henry. Thankfully, the veg garden back home had been watered and, even with the extreme hot weather, I'd only lost some carrots, a few beans and the leaves of a patch of zucchini. The hot summer wind had been so dry that all the moisture had been drawn from some of the plants and they'd died, but the losses weren't big. I was still on track to have plenty of veg to come, and plenty of veg to add to my provisions for winter.

There are lots of species of fish that people turn their noses up at, many for reasons unknown. Australian 'cocky' salmon is one of those fish species that often gets returned to the water, as it's not a target species. I've loved it since the first time I caught it off a pier in Apollo Bay, Victoria. There was a good-sized school of them and my mate and I were pulling them in for a spell, filling our Eskys with fresh delicious fish. Australian salmon (Arripis trutta) isn't actually a salmonoid species, it just looks like a salmon and so we call it that. It tastes nothing like a true salmon; it has a taste of its own – which really isn't much to write home about. It's definitely not a strong flavour, like bream or flathead, and that's what I love about it. Its flavour is pretty light, which allows you to add a whole bunch of different culinary elements.

On the mainland in summer, we catch these beauties off the beach with a large surf rod, but when we visit the island state (Tassie) we use a tinnie in a bay and trawl off the back, with outstanding results. It's a real fighting fish, and when you hook a decent specimen you're in for a battle. The key to a good-tasting Aussie salmon is to bleed it once you've landed it. Cut the throat and let it bleed, and you'll have a good meal that evening.

We'll fire up the barbecue, open some chilled beers, tell fishing tales and cook fish for a few hours. It's one of my most comfortable moments of the summer – ice-cold beer, good company and fresh fish. In the van at the beach there's a herb garden with ingredients on hand we like to use: coriander, lemon thyme, chilli and dill. We just pick herbs, add spice, cook and sip beer. Really, is there anything more enjoyable on a hot summer's evening?

If you want to try this recipe and Australian salmon aren't in your local waters, give it a go with mackerel, bonito or tuna.

Australian Salmon Two Ways

SERVES 4

1. Ginger and chilli

What you need

3 tablespoons freshly grated ginger

75 g (2¾ oz/½ cup) plain (all-purpose) flour

4 Australian salmon fillets

1–2 tablespoons olive oil

30 g (1 oz) butter

1 lime, sliced, to serve

coriander (cilantro) leaves, to serve

chilli, sliced, to serve

salt and pepper, to taste

How to make it

Mix the ginger with the flour and coat the fillets in this mixture.

Heat a glug of olive oil with a knob of butter in a frying pan over medium heat, and cook each fillet for 2–4 minutes on each side, or until cooked.

Serve with a slice of lime, coriander and chilli, and season to taste.

Feast.

2. Pimentón and chilli aioli

What you need

1–2 tablespoons olive oil

3–4 garlic cloves, thinly sliced

3 tablespoons smoked pimentón (Spanish paprika)

75 g (2¾ oz/½ cup) plain (all-purpose) flour

4 Australian salmon fillets

Chilli and smoked pimentón aioli (page 292), to serve

1 lemon, sliced, to serve

How to make it

Heat a generous glug of olive oil in a frying pan over medium heat and fry the garlic for a minute or two.

Mix the pimentón with the flour and coat the fillets in this mixture.

Cook the coated fillets in the garlic olive oil for a few minutes each side.

Serve with a drizzle of chilli aioli and a slice of lemon.

Sumac-crusted Flathead with Lemon

SERVES 2

What you need

3 tablespoons sumac

sea salt and freshly cracked black pepper, to taste

150 g (5½ oz/1 cup) plain (all-purpose) flour

8 flathead tail fillets

30 g (1 oz) butter

1–2 tablespoons olive oil (or more)

1 lemon, cut into wedges, to serve

chips (fries), to serve

Chilli and smoked pimentón aioli, to serve (page 292)

Flathead, the tasty bottom feeder. Sounds like a tagline in a marketing campaign! Such a tasty fish, but a bit of a bugger. Their spikes are deadly sharp and have some sort of toxin that makes you bleed like hell, but if you use a towel or metal gloves to handle them you should be fine. In the crystal-clear waters off Bruny Island we dangle our baited lines down into the water and peek over the side of the boat, watching as the flathead race for the bait. It's such clear water you can sometimes dangle the baited hook to the closest fish. And as gross as this may sound, the best bait for flathead is flathead.

Each summer we target flathead for cooking in the caravan kitchen with the kids. Once we weren't lucky, so we headed to a fish shop that had a sign saying flathead tails were on special. I was so excited. I asked if the fish came from the fish co-op near the boat ramp. Nope, these fish came from the Melbourne fish market supplier. My jaw dropped to the ground. The absolute madness of our food system right there – a six-hour round trip for fish to be delivered to a coastal town with a fish co-op. Made no sense to me. Better go bait my lines.

There isn't much you really need to do to these fillets; they taste amazing cooked as simply as possible and served with some crispy hot spuds. But a little sneaky spice never hurt anyone. And sumac is always in the summer caravan pantry; I think it was invented to go with fish.

If you don't have access to fresh flathead, you could try this recipe with gurnard or cod.

How to make it

Mix the sumac and a little salt and pepper with the flour and coat the fillets in this mixture.

Heat a knob of butter with a glug of olive oil (I'd be generous with my glug!) in a frying pan over medium heat. Fry the fillets on each side until cooked through, which takes only a few minutes. Test one fillet in your mouth for 'doneness'. Oh, that was good, wasn't it? Better test another.

Serve with lemon, crispy fries and chilli aioli.

Like Christmas, but not the evil consumer Christmas

I've been asked so many times, 'Do you eat the zucchini flowers?' Look, I probably have at some fancy restaurant and they probably tasted good, but to be honest I like to grow zucchini so I have zucchini to eat. And I'm just not very fancy. Well, not flower-eating fancy anyway. Zucchini is a pretty loved veg in this house. It goes in everything from soups to pasta and cakes. It's loved for many reasons, notably its ease of growth, and it being the most prolific food producer in the garden. One zucchini plant can produce kilos of produce. Often there's more zucchini than we need, but over the years I seem to be growing more. Why? Well, I've been using it in dishes my kids are more inclined to eat; Kate bakes with it; and after a million meals of pasta, soups and grilled-veg salads, I use the rest to make a relish or chutney. So it all gets used up. Even the odd zucchini that has a bit of rot in it goes to the chooks for a treat. Every zucchini gets used. Just not the flowers. Maybe I *should* eat the flowers.

So it's really summer now. All my seeds have germinated. The garden is full of neat rows of beans and corn, and the poly tunnel is a hive of activity. All my darling zucchini plants are proudly boasting large leaves and happy bright-yellow flowers. So far this summer we've not really had much in the way of variety other than green peas, broad (fava) beans and the odd broccoli. Nothing else is really happening. I mean, sure, the poly tunnel is full of plants, but there's just no food dripping off said plants. The rows of beans and corn are months away from providing food, and in any case both are destined to be stored for winter consumption. The zucchini will be the first of the summer veg we can actually eat *in* summer. It's ironic, really, that during the peak growing season I don't have much to eat! Well, that's mostly my fault for not getting the plastic over the poly tunnel sooner in spring, but that's another story. For a few weeks this summer, we'll most likely have to rely on the humble zucchini more than anything else.

I wonder how I'll feel about this approach by autumn. Will I be over zucchini?

I have to tell you that I did try another one of my little experiments in the garden. As well as raising zucchini seedlings in toilet rolls, I've also tried the direct-sowing approach to see if it would make a difference to speed of growth and productivity. I tried this experiment once with peas, and the direct-seeded peas absolutely killed the seedling version, I guess because they didn't lose those few weeks seedlings do when they get transplanted. That root disturbance is a killer! So I tried the same experiment with zucchini and found no significant difference between the two. Kind of boring result, eh? I bet you were wishing I'd tell you something rad like the direct-seeded plants grow twice as fast and twice as large. Nope. Just boring old nothing. But both still gave me more zucchini than I needed.

'Don't try to feed me that hippie shit.' That's what I used to say in my head years ago when I'd go to someone's place and there'd be anything 'weird' on offer. I was such a douchebag foodist. My food ignorance is what held me back for so many years. I had to work really hard on my tolerance and acceptance of different foods, but that was way back when and these days I'm a sponge for food diversity. 'Pass the burghul salad', 'More quinoa, please', 'Is that hummus?' have all come from my mouth at one point or another. If my old Macca's-loving self could see me now, he'd probably throw the unwanted cheeseburger pickles in my face.

Zucchini are one of those vegetables I recommend people grow when they're starting out raising food in their backyard. It's a fast-growing crop that's as giving as Mother Teresa. Almonds, on the other hand, take a bit more patience and work to get a decent crop, but with a little perseverance you can get a few good baskets of these delicious nuts from your own backyard, or someone else's backyard in my case. See, years ago I got far too excited with converting my city backyard into a food bowl and planted too many fruit and nut trees. After one season of mega-growth, I had to accept that I had in fact gone overboard. A workmate with a country pad offered some space

Hippies' Zucchini, Nuts & Burghul

SERVES 4 AS A SIDE

What you need

2–3 garden-fresh zucchini (courgettes)	hearty handful of parsley
60 ml (2 fl oz/¼ cup) olive oil	small handful of mint
80 g (2¾ oz/½ cup) almonds	grated zest and juice of 1 lemon
2 garlic cloves, crushed	sumac, to taste
175 g (6 oz/1 cup) burghul (bulgur wheat), cooked according to the packet instructions	goat's feta, to serve

How to make it

Preheat the barbecue grill to high. Cut the zucchini into lengthways strips. Drizzle with half the olive oil and toss to coat. Cook the zucchini on the barbecue until soft.

Either roughly smash or chop the almonds and toast them in a hot dry frying pan over medium heat until they start to colour.

In a mortar and pestle, crush the garlic with the remaining olive oil (a glug).

When the zucchini are cooked, transfer them to a mixing bowl with the burghul. Chop the parsley and mint (reserving a few leaves of each as a garnish), then add to the zucchini and burghul with the almonds, lemon zest and juice, and garlic olive oil.

Sprinkle with sumac, garnish with the reserved mint and parsley, and serve with a generous helping of crumbled feta while burning sandalwood incense.

in his large orchard for me to relocate some of my trees. He even promised not to eat any of the produce. What a guy!

I no longer work that office job, but every year I return to my friend's orchard, catch up over a cuppa and pick some produce from my trees. Right next to my almond tree at this orchard sits an olive tree I bought for my friend when his father died. For some reason I get very emotional when I see how much the olive tree has grown. I never met his father, but I'm glad there's a tree living and well to mark his existence on this earth. See, I am a damn hippie. This salad is perfect for me. I might buy a kombi and start wearing tie-dye.

When I was in my twenties I was an ignorant fool. I guess it's all part of growing up. Just because legally you're an adult, it doesn't mean you're grown up, which can be a good thing, but also not so good. The topic of quiche is a good way to explain my under-developed mentality. I used to think quiche was somehow a very unmanly meal. If I was on a road trip and I'd stopped at a roadside café, and there was an option of meat pie or a quiche, I would have puffed up my dumb-arse manly chest and opted for the meat pie. My manly bravado is somewhat diminished these days – might have something to do with living in a house with five females – and I like quiche now. What I like most about quiche is that I can make it from backyard produce, and that's something that's very dear to me. The meals I love the most are those where most of the ingredients come from my direct practical efforts. I have egg-laying chooks, I have home-cured smoked bacon and there's more zucchini than I know what to do with. And if you stretch it out some more, you may even find some home-made goat's cheese in my fridge. What a way to celebrate all the effort you've made from producing all that tucker in your backyard – with a very manly quiche.

Backyarders' Zucchini & Smoked-bacon Quiche

SERVES 4–6

What you need

Shortcrust pastry

100 g (3½ oz) chilled butter, diced

200 g (7 oz/1⅓ cups) plain (all-purpose) flour, sifted, plus extra for dusting

1 small egg, lightly beaten

Filling

1–2 tablespoons olive oil

1 onion, chopped

2 garlic cloves, chopped

100 g (3½ oz) smoky bacon (page 189), chopped

3 zucchini (courgettes)

handful of parsley, chopped

90 g (3 oz/1 cup) grated pecorino

4 eggs, lightly beaten

pinch of salt

100 g (3½ oz/⅔ cup) crumbled goat's feta

2 jalapeño chillies, sliced

How to make it

To make the shortcrust pastry, whizz the butter and flour in a food processor until the mixture resembles breadcrumbs. With the processor still running, slowly pour in the egg and let the processor do all the work for you. The mixture should bind together to form a lump of dough. If it doesn't quite pull together, add small amounts of chilled water until it does. Wrap the dough in plastic wrap and refrigerate for at least 1 hour.

Preheat the oven to 220°C (430°F) and grease a 23 cm (9 inch) pie dish.

To prepare the filling, heat a glug of olive oil in a frying pan over medium heat, then gently cook the onion and garlic until softened. Add the bacon and cook for a few minutes. Using a potato peeler, shave the zucchini into long strips. Add to the frying pan and cook until they soften and colour. Turn out into a large mixing bowl to cool.

Roll out the shortcrust pastry on a lightly floured bench and use it to line the prepared pie dish. Trim the edges and poke the bottom of the pastry with a fork. Line the pastry with baking paper, half-fill with oven beans and blind bake for 10 minutes. Remove the beans and baking paper, and bake for a further 10 minutes, or until golden.

Turn the oven down to 180°C (360°F).

Mix the parsley, pecorino and eggs into the fried zucchini and bacon, season with salt, then pour into the pastry shell. Crumble over the feta and sprinkle over the chilli.

Bake for 30 minutes, or until set, then allow to rest for 10 minutes before serving.

Zucchini Fritters

What you need

3–4 zucchini (courgettes) (not tiny ones, not massive yacht size either, just perfect zucchini size)

pinch of salt, plus extra to taste

135 g (5 oz/1½ cups) grated pecorino

handful of parsley, chopped

3 garlic cloves, crushed

75 g (2¾ oz/½ cup) plain (all-purpose) flour

2 eggs, lightly beaten

pepper, to taste

olive oil, for shallow-frying

1 teaspoon smoked pimentón (Spanish paprika)

200 g (7 oz) sour cream

garden-fresh jalapeño chillies, sliced, to serve

Summer is a beautiful time here in the garden. My daily walk through the patch is a real pleasure. Sometimes I find myself sitting on one of the timber walls of a garden bed just staring at the plants and the insects, and listening to the very nature around me. The sun is warm, the aromatics are strong and I'll just sit there looking at the vegetables and herbs, thinking about all the meals I'd like to cook. When I first started gardening I always had more zucchini than I knew what to do with, which hasn't really changed much but now I have more dishes I like to cook for the family with this versatile ingredient. Fritters are super-easy and make great finger food for messy ratbag kids. They're one of those meals I suggest for people who tell me they're too time poor to cook real food. An easy prep, a few minutes in the frying pan and you have yourself a delicious meal that can be eaten hot or cold, for breakfast, lunch or dinner. Cooking isn't hard really, is it? Especially when you're talking about something as simple and easy as a zucchini fritter!

How to make it

Chop the ends off the zucchini and then grate the rest into a colander. Sprinkle over the salt then set aside to drain for a few hours.

Squeeze the zucchini well, then transfer to a large mixing bowl. Add the cheese, parsley (reserving a little as a garnish), garlic, flour and eggs. Season with salt and pepper, and mix well.

Heat a generous glug of olive oil in a frying pan over medium–high heat. Working in batches, cook generous spoonfuls of the mixture on both sides until golden brown.

Lay on paper towel to drain off any excess oil while cooking the next batch.

Mix the pimentón and sour cream in a bowl.

Serve the fritters with a dollop of the smoky sour cream, a garnish of the reserved parsley and some sliced chilli on the side.

Hello, summer!

Harissa the kisser

My poly tunnel is at DEFCON 1. I've got the biggest eggplant leaves I've ever seen, the highest tomato plants of all time and an entire side of the tunnel dedicated to chilli. Yes, it may seem like overkill, but I have a theory that's served me well these past few years, and that is to grow bucketloads of the stuff you really love. And I love chilli. I love it raw, I love it in cooking and most of all I love it turned into a sauce like a Salsa picante (page 113). I drizzle those chilli sauces on everything. Heat and flavour! You can beat an egg, but you just can't beat that combo of heat and flavour!

In the tunnel I have three varieties: jalapeño, habanero and fire chilli, which looks a lot like cayenne pepper. I'm guessing it is a cayenne, but the boys in the marketing department at the plant nursery must have thought 'fire chilli' sounded a bit more rad. That aside, my chilli have now flowered, most of them have been successfully pollinated and I now have fruit, mega amounts of chilli fruit. And my veg-growing mate Jack has heaps of chilli. So much chilli that he keeps bringing it over to my place to trade. I have so much chilli I could literally sell it at the Sunday market. But this chilli is too valuable as chilli to exchange for money.

In the depths of winter this chilli will warm me in two ways: first with its natural heat, and secondly it will warm my spirit. When days are short and dark clouds abound, that chilli sauce will lift my spirits. It will remind me of birds chirping in summer sun, plentiful flowers and the aromatics of a summer garden – all the things I'm taking care to enjoy right now while summer is in full swing. Each hot day of late will see me at the end of the hose, providing these productive plants with the gift of water. It's my way of nurturing them. Each few weeks the progress is phenomenal. First the flowers come out, then tiny green fruits and now hundreds if not thousands of chillies of various shapes and sizes dangle on these pretty green bushes.

I'm fortunate to have planted so many chillies that I can afford the luxury of eating them in summer. My precious beans don't get consumed at all over summer or autumn – I force myself to wait until winter, as they store indefinitely when dried – but chilli I can eat as much as I like. As for other fruits, there are so many applications that offer a multitude of culinary outcomes. When I first started growing chilli, it was one meagre pot plant that produced a few handfuls of chillies at best. Back then I didn't eat so much chilli, nor did I make a range of sauces, chutneys and relishes. But now my appreciation for these fiery gems has grown. Of late I've been enjoying a breakfast with some chorizo and egg and a whole jalapeño – beautiful crunchy capsicum (bell pepper) flavour with a little 'hello' heat! Lunchtime, chilli. Dinner, chilli. Chilli, chilli, chilli! Is good, yes?

With all this stock of chilli, I need to start preserving some for the larder. I have plenty of spare zucchini, so I've made a large batch of really hot relish. Kate's done her bit and made her killer harissa, which, incidentally, we love on everything. The first time she made it was one of those beautiful food memories for me. Harissa is a wonderful hot chilli paste that originates from North Africa. It's a heart-starter, for sure! Finding the balance between garlic and cumin seems to make it. Seriously, once you've made your own, you'll never go back to store-bought (see page 111 for my recipe). Just like every other food I've made over the years, nothing beats home-made. You get uniqueness in flavour and often the freshness of the ingredients is what takes it up a notch.

Jalapeño is my preferred chilli to grow. It's pretty hot but it's not as mad as habanero. Most of the crop is destined to be smoked into chipotle or made into my salsa picante. Man, I love this hot sauce! Over the years I've tried a heap of different brands, and the thing I've enjoyed about most of them was that balance of heat and flavour, tart and sweet. But most of all I love the smokiness of some brands. To get the smoked flavour in my sauce I add smoked pimentón and chipotle in adobo sauce. The beauty of this salsa is that I can capture summer's main prize. During the winter, I'll pour it over many meals when there isn't a fresh chilli to be seen.

The salsa stores well in the larder, and all I have to remember is to keep the bottle in the refrigerator after opening. To be honest, an open bottle doesn't last very long – it goes on everything! The beauty of making your own salsa picante is that you get to control the heat. If you like nuclear-powered heat then keep the seeds in. If you like your salsa a tad calmer, then remove the seeds. It's totally up to you. Now, isn't that how food production should be?

Each summer I go overboard with my chilli-planting. Most of the harvest ends up as salsa picante, which I'll use all winter to rid me of the winter blues. But there's so much fresh chilli at the end of summer that I can't help finding new uses for it. Harissa is amazingly tasty, and at times it's a bit dangerous – it just ends up being spread on bread and devoured. It has a bit of a punch to it, but it's the spice party that gets my motor running. Garlic, cumin, coriander and, can you believe, not a hint of smoked pimentón (Spanish paprika)! Making your own harissa doesn't take much time, and you can freeze the excess or

store it for a week in the fridge. But it doesn't last that long before it's used to smother something. During the time there's harissa in the house, everything starts tasting like harissa.

I'm not sure which chilli variety is traditionally used to make harissa, but I grow jalapeño because it's prolific and has the perfect heat for my palate. But use whatever type of ripe red chilli you want. And you can also grill them before you begin. I'm sure there's no such thing as harissa police. Or is there? Don't tell anyone I use jalapeño!

Jalapeño Harissa

MAKES 250 G (9 OZ/1 CUP)

What you need

1 tablespoon cumin seeds

1 teaspoon coriander seeds

1 large garlic bulb, cloves separated and peeled

2–3 tablespoons olive oil

10 red jalapeño chillies, ends removed, seeds in

juice of 1 lemon

large pinch of salt

How to make it

Toast the cumin and coriander seeds in a dry frying pan over medium heat until you start smelling spice town. Crush the seeds in a large mortar and pestle until they form a powder. Add the garlic cloves and crush them into a paste. Add enough of the olive oil to make a spice paste.

Whizz the paste, chillies and lemon juice in a food processor until they form a smooth paste. Season with salt.

Smother on everything!

My interest in Spanish food came about as an adult interested in my mixed heritage; I wasn't brought up with it. That hasn't stopped me, though, and it has been and continues to be a great journey, learning about Mediterranean flavours and applying them to the food I grow, hunt or, dare I say, forage. When I travel off the highlands and down to the city, I often visit a Spanish grocery store in Fitzroy called Casa Iberica. It's chock-full of spices, food and flavours from Spain and the Americas. I get a little giddy when I'm there. It's almost like I'm in a daze, a kid in a candy store. But it's not candy I'm interested in, it's pimentón, chorizo, salamanca and salsa picante, or hot sauce. There are so many versions of this sauce to choose from, and I think I've tried most of them at one point or another. But the reality is that they travel a great distance to get to me, so I only buy them as a treat now. I'm not going without hot sauce, though, so I figured out how to make my own.

I do tend to overuse this type of sauce. It goes on my eggs and chorizo in the mornings, and then in a sandwich or salad for lunch, then most likely a little bit might find its way onto my dinner when appropriate. So in order to maintain my habit, I need to grow a lot of chilli. An entire side of my poly tunnel is dedicated solely to jalapeño. At the tail end of summer and into autumn I make my sauce, and lots of it. The salsa picante keeps well in the larder for months – in fact, it will last me until the jalapeños have returned to my garden. But be careful, sometimes the bottle can get a bit fermenty and will open like a bottle of champagne. We have salsa on our ceiling. You get the drift. Or spray.

My favourite types of salsa picante have a slightly smoky flavour and a good kick of heat. I get this from smoking some dried chilli and, of course, from the ever-faithful smoked pimentón.

Salsa Picante

What you need

2 kg (4 lb 6 oz) jalapeño chillies, chopped, seeds in	⅓ cup smoked pimentón (Spanish paprika)
5 dried mulato chillies, soaked in 500 ml (17 fl oz/2 cups) water overnight	125 ml (4 fl oz/½ cup) malt vinegar, plus extra to taste
5 dried chipotle chillies, soaked in 500 ml (17 fl oz/2 cups) water overnight	100 g (3½ oz/½ cup) brown sugar, plus extra to taste
	1 garlic bulb, cloves separated, peeled and roughly chopped
4 onions, chopped	
4 tomatoes, seeded and chopped	

How to make it

Pour all the chillies, including any soaking water, into a large saucepan. Add all the remaining ingredients and bring to the boil over medium heat, then reduce the heat and simmer for a few hours.

Remove from the stove top, allow to cool a little, then process with a hand-held blender until the sauce is uniform and runny.

Taste the salsa when it's cool, then add more sugar or vinegar if necessary.

Strain through a fine-mesh sieve into sterilised bottles, seal them, then boil them in a large pot of water for 20 minutes before storing. (Transfer the seeds and pulp from the sieve into a sterilised screw-top jar and top with olive oil. It's great in cooking to add heat to a dish.)

This is just the beginning. Now experiment with different spices and flavours to make your own version.

Oh, bugger

I'm not much of a gambler. I do, however, love the movies *Casino*, *Maverick* and *Let It Ride*. Go figure. A few months ago I made a bet, and it's only now that I realise I bet on the wrong horse. In fact, I bet on the wrong crop. I'd managed to set up the vegetable garden last winter, which was ace, but it meant that I planted the broad (fava) bean crop a little later than usual. It's just one of the realities of setting up a new garden at a new house. You have to allow a season or two to really get into the swing of things. The beans took a lot longer to finish off, which meant we were still harvesting late into spring and even into summer. So when the bean crop had finally come to an end it was definitely midsummer. It's easy to get a bit cocky about the seasons when the sun is belting down and the hot wind blows in from the north. Feeling like I was in an endless summer, I decided to use the empty beds for growing corn. It was a gamble. I had two options: to plant a crop or to let the bed rest over summer. A bed resting over summer is out of the question. For this system of living off what you grow to work, you have to grow most of your food over summer. To leave a bed vacant for the remaining summer seems such a waste. So I wrangled a daughter or two and we set about planting a little corn crop.

At first there was promise. The germination rate was seemingly 100 per cent, and the tiny green corn shoots popped up in record time. The plants grew next to rows of white beans, summer broccoli and more beans. Did I mention I like beans? I looked after that corn crop with love and care. When the fierce winds came I roped the narrow crop together to give it strength. I kept the water up and the weeds down. But the season wouldn't last forever. And it started to run out. Sure, I managed to harvest some corncobs, but we pulled more corn out of the ground at the end of the season that didn't give us food. So I put all that energy and all those resources into something that didn't give such a great return. These things happen. It's not the end of the world. It just means that during winter I'll have to eat more beans and kale than frozen corn.

Black beauties

Eggplant (aubergine) is a warm-loving plant and so it's a no-brainer for summer, or so I thought. I've not had much luck over the last decade growing it up here in the Central Highlands. Our summer growing season just isn't long enough. It seems that just as the plant has flowered, autumn arrives and chills the flowers into submission, and the result is one eggplant per plant, and even that eggplant is a bit miserable-looking. This summer, though, I'm trying a new approach, for I have a poly tunnel. When it's hot outside, it's molten hot inside the tunnel! How much hotter does the eggplant want it, eh?

The results so far have been very rewarding. The leaves alone are massive, which is encouraging in itself. They're the biggest, healthiest eggplant leaves I've ever seen in my garden. As exciting as mega-sized eggplant leaves are, I can't eat them. It's the flowers I'm interested in. No, not for stuffing with foie gras and dipping in batter, finished with a foam of foraged treats. The flowers, when pollinated, turn into the much-coveted eggplant themselves. And now my plants have flowered prolifically and I have fruit! Autumn can come, it can bring its cold weather. We're no longer in fear, for this year I have my plants warm in my tunnel of love. Here's hoping I get so many eggplants I'll become sick of them.

Eggplant as a summer veg tends to be enjoyed in summer, not winter. I can grill it and store it in olive oil, but it doesn't store as long as I'd like it to. It's great barbecued or grilled, and often ends up on the chargrill pan with a sprinkle of salt and a glug of olive oil. I've even used it in making a hot tomato and eggplant kasundi. That kasundi will end up with bacon, rocket (arugula) and cheese in many a winter's toasted sandwich … mmm, manwich! But for now, I'll keep grilling these black beauties while the days are hot and long, and the barbecue weather reigns supreme.

One small piece of advice with growing the eggplants in the super-hot controlled environment of the poly tunnel. If you're going to go to all this effort and try this method, I suggest you stake your plants. Mine grew so large and had so much fruit on them that some fell over with the excess weight. That might not sound like such a big deal, but if the main stem snaps and the fruit isn't fully developed, you potentially miss out on eight to twelve eggplants, and in my world that's a significant loss. So get out those old nylon stockings and secure the plants as they mature. Just don't get busted trying on the old lady's tights in the poly tunnel. Not that it's happened to me.

Baba Ghanoush

SERVES 4

What you need

4 large eggplants (aubergines)
4 garlic cloves, crushed
handful of parsley
juice of 1 lemon
1 teaspoon cayenne pepper
90 g (3 oz/⅓ cup) tahini
2 pinches of salt
good-quality extra virgin olive oil, for drizzling
sumac, to serve

Eggplants have always been a bit of a veg favourite, but in this cold climate they're a real pain to grow. Our summer just isn't long enough. The plants are just flowering when they should already have been in fruit, so by the time autumn comes there are one or two sad-looking eggplants for us to eat. It's not smart to have large eggplant bushes taking up space when I could be growing something better suited to our climate. Sucks, right? But then I built a poly tunnel and brought the summer up a peg or two. Now I have a month extra at the end of summer and my eggplants thrive. They just love the heat, warm soil and steamy hot air. I plant out in spring and harvest in summer. It's made such a difference. Being able to eat fresh, full-bodied eggplants from my own garden is a real treat, and every summer now my poly tunnel is full of these delicious fruits.

I love to grill eggplants on the summer barbecue, but someone told me about this technique of cooking them straight on the gas stove top. I was sceptical at first, but then I ate the baba ghanoush they made and it had a slightly smoky flavour, just like the real deal. Another DIY home-version tick! Obviously you can add different spices and herbs, even use cheeses and different oils. This is simply a basis from which to start.

How to make it

Wrap the eggplant in aluminium foil and cook directly on the gas stove top. If you don't have gas, cook them under a hot grill (broiler). Turn over with tongs every 5 minutes or so – the idea is for them to cook evenly. You'll start to feel them get very soft, and at some point they'll become difficult to pick up with the tongs – that's usually when they're ready.

Take the foil off and slide a fork under the skin to start to separate the 'meat' from the skin. Discard the skin. (Take note of how good it smells. Reminds me of campfire-cooked potato. Weird?)

Transfer the cooked eggplant to a mixing bowl. Add the garlic, parsley (reserving a little for a garnish), lemon juice, cayenne and tahini. Whizz into a paste using a hand-held blender, and season with salt.

Serve with a drizzle of olive oil, a sprinkle of sumac and a garnish of the reserved parsley.

Now I know these aren't really 'kitty cakes' – the classic Japanese okonomiyaki – but me being the hillbilly country bloke I am, I'd never heard of them. It's one of the pitfalls of living in a bubble in the bush! A friend of mine (enter Kitty) told me what I could do with all the cabbage I had lying around and, thankfully, it was something nicer than what she normally tells me to do (Kitty has a potty mouth). Intrigued by the idea of making cabbage palatable for the ratbags, I accepted her idea on the proviso that she show me how to cook them. The process seemed easy enough, but it was the eating that hooked me like a stupid fish. How could this be made of cabbage? It felt like something a bit naughty! I ate a bunch of them, loved them, then a few days later asked her to make them again. That was when she really told me where I could put the cabbage.

Kitty Cakes

SERVES 6

What you need

The brown sauce (no jokes, please)	The mayo	The cakes
250 ml (8½ fl oz/1 cup) Catsup (page 164)	250 g (9 oz/1 cup) Mayo (page 292)	150–300 g (5½–10½ oz/ 1–2 cups) plain (all-purpose) flour
125 ml (4 fl oz/½ cup) mirin	1 tablespoon ready-made wasabi	2 whole cabbages, hearts removed, finely shredded
80 ml (2½ fl oz/⅓ cup) tamari		100 g (3½ oz) dried slippery Jack or shiitake mushrooms, finely chopped
90 g (3 oz/⅓ cup) dijon mustard		10 spring onions (scallions), finely chopped
		170 ml (5½ fl oz/⅔ cup) mirin
		8–10 eggs
		sunflower oil, for shallow-frying
		handful of dried nori (seaweed), cut into strips, to serve
		sesame seeds, toasted, to serve

How to make it

To make the brown sauce, simply pop all the ingredients in a small saucepan and simmer over medium heat until the sauce reduces and thickens.

For the mayo, simply mix in the wasabi.

To make the kitty cakes, in a large bowl, mix 250 ml (8½ fl oz/1 cup) water with enough of the flour to make a soggy paste. Add the cabbage, mushrooms, spring onions, mirin and eggs, and mix well. The idea is to make a battered mush of well-stirred ingredients.

Heat the sunflower oil in a large heavy-based frying pan, then use a large mixing spoon to dish a few patties into the hot oil. Cook until golden brown on both sides. I tend to flip them over a few times to get them evenly cooked through – nothing worse than raw cabbage in a thick kitty cake! Lay on paper towel to drain off any excess oil while you cook the next batch.

Serve with a squirt of both sauces, a healthy topping of seaweed and a generous sprinkle of sesame seeds.

Gold in the bottle

In early summer we enjoyed the odd feed of berries we'd traded with friends, as well as a few apricots, plums and now peaches. Soon there'll be apples and pears to boot! So much fruit gets wasted as second-grade fruit that never ends up being sold commercially, and that's where you can make a good store for your larder. It's pretty cheap compared with A-grade fruit and if you think about it, most of it will be peeled before canning anyway, so any blemishes can be cut out.

Having a fully operational fruit and berry orchard will take time. And being a renter makes longing for such a thing even more frustrating. To overcome the possibility of having to move (yet again), I've planted my mini orchard in large wooden crates with the idea that when I do have to move, I can lift the crates onto a lorry with a tractor, then plant them at our 'forever house'. At least I'll get some fruit from the trees over the next few years while we save for land. In the meantime, I get my fruit from organic commercial growers, friends' trees or the bush.

If you have a good greengrocer you might chat to them and see if they have access to commercially grown second-grade fruit for preserving. It's a much cheaper alternative than buying the pretty stuff, and honestly you can't tell the difference once you've processed and bottled them. We use the old Fowlers Vacola vacuum-sealed jars. They last forever and only the lids and rubber rings need to be replaced (although we tend to use the lids over and over again). These kits are everywhere to be found, a remnant of the old days when more people preserved their own, a time before we had large factory canneries. I reckon at some point in the 1950s these preserving kits were a mandatory wedding gift. You can pick up the boiling pots for a few bucks and if you buy in bulk the glasses are reasonably priced, especially when you consider you can use them year after year. The OG recycler. There are other brands out there that do the same thing, so use what's most abundant and within your price range.

One of the best purchases I made from an old-wares shop years ago was a tiny handbook written sometime in the 1950s by the Fowlers Vacola company. It contains instructions on how to preserve almost every fruit, vegetable and sauce imaginable. It's worth more to me than gold itself! Each year from spring to summer I refer to the handbook for instructions. It tells me how to prepare the fruit, what temperature to boil it to and for how long. It works every time. And the best thing is, I know we have fruit we can eat in winter that's organic and stored in a light sugar syrup with no additives or preservatives. That's worth the effort just for peace of mind. Now if I can only figure out how to avoid the wrinkled hands from preparing buckets of ripe fruit!

Bottling Fruit

I lack any form of sweet tooth, but my kids sure love the sweet stuff. They love fruit. One kid in the family loves eating fruit so much that it's a rarity not to see her holding some form of fruit in her hand. All the kids love picking it from the trees and bushes when it's in season, but they also want to eat it in the middle of winter – which means I need to preserve like crazy from summer to autumn. In winter and spring the kids are fed with bottled fruits from the warm season, and this keeps them happy. And that's important to my happiness. Let's face it, as a parent you'd rather feed your kids some preserved fruit than mass-produced sweets. Am I right?

When summer comes, I start hunting around all my spots for fruit. I check in with friends who have established trees and bushes, I check the fruit-set in my wild fruit locations, and I start chatting up the local commercial growers for deals on second-grade fruit. By the end of autumn we've got the larder well stocked – that is, if we've had a season of luck and high productivity. It's not really a hard task to preserve fruit, it's simply laborious. It's a chore best done with someone to keep you company. We work as a team, which speeds up the process somewhat, and we can both laugh about our wrinkly fruit-processing hands.

We preserve the fruit that grows in our area, so we're limited to mostly stone fruits, berries, apples and pears. After that spiritual moment of tasting a peach off a friend's tree (see page 196), I discovered the variety was 'Anzac' and later bought one as bare-rooted stock. It's still a few years away from providing us with buckets of peaches, so for now I'll make do with our current system of labour for fruit. But there are other fruits I now enjoy that I never did before. I guess it may sound strange to many people that I didn't really ever eat fruit, but I completely blame the large-scale commercial and supermarket system. It offered little variety, and because the fruit wasn't always in season, it wasn't at its peak, and no doubt put me off fruit altogether. To experience fruit from the trees when it's ripe and in season, amazing. Funny, isn't it? I now pick pears from a few secret wild trees. I allow them to get nice and ripe, almost overripe, then I devour them. Never had I tasted a pear like this – soft, sweet and juicy.

When preserving, we add a little bit of sugar to the syrup it's stored in but try not to do too much else to it. That way we get to eat them as they were intended. We do make a nice spiced plum, though, which is great for adding to muffins in winter.

To make our light sugar syrup, we boil 5 litres (169 fl oz/20 cups) water at a time then add 110 g (4 oz/½ cup) sugar and stir until it's dissolved. We process the fruit, stuff it firmly and tightly into sterilised jars and pour over the sugar syrup, allowing time for it to fill all the gaps and cracks between the cut fruit.

We seal the jars then stand them in a preserving unit and fill with enough cold water to almost fill the thermometer well (the water reservoir attached to the outside of the preserver). With the lid on the preserver, we bring the temperature slowly up to 92°C (198°F), which takes 45–60 minutes. Depending on the bottle size, we hold the temp at 92°C for a further 45–60 minutes. This works for all fruit.

Here's what we preserve each summer and autumn

Fruit	Preparation	Preserving liquid
Apples	Peeled, cored and halved or quartered depending on size or variety	Light sugar syrup
Pears	Peeled, cored and halved or quartered depending on size or variety	Light sugar syrup
Nectarines	Halved and stoned	Light sugar syrup
Plums	Halved and stoned	Light sugar syrup
Spiced blood plums	Halved, stoned and stewed to soften	Light sugar syrup with spices such as cinnamon, star anise and cloves (please experiment!)
Peaches	Halved and stoned	Light sugar syrup
Apricots	Halved and stoned	Light sugar syrup

A mate of mine needed a hand laying a concrete slab for a garden shed. He's Polish and he loves a deal – heck, I reckon it's in my Mediterranean blood to be a deal-maker too. Everything comes down to sharing skills, labour, knowledge or produce. No money need be exchanged. It's a great community asset, although I'm sure the taxman would disagree. The deal was labour for fruit, which seemed pretty fair to me. So on went the gumboots for a morning spent laying concrete and an afternoon picking fruit – a day well spent with a mate. My Polish

brother has an extensive fruit orchard he's been adding to for years. He's got more than a hundred trees, shrubs and berries that provide his young family with a fruity cuisine. From spring to autumn he has food in his backyard to be harvested, including a proper functional vegetable patch. This guy has it made in the shade.

He took me over to a patch of blackcurrants, which were dripping off the branches in clumps of black. He told me to pick as many as

Blackcurrant Cordial

MAKES 1–1.5 LITRES (34–51 FL OZ/4–6 CUPS)

What you need

1 kg (2 lb 3 oz) blackcurrants, stems removed

440 g (15½ oz/2 cups) white sugar

2–3 lemons

How to make it

Put the blackcurrants, sugar and 500 ml (17 fl oz/2 cups) water in a large saucepan. Cut the lemons in half and squeeze the juice into the mix, then add the lemons as well. Bring to the boil over medium heat and stir until the sugar has dissolved. Reduce the heat and gently simmer for 20 minutes. The currants will soften, but to get the most flavour from the fruit, squish them down with something like a potato masher or even a hand-held blender (cool a little first) to release all that flavour. You can steep the mixture overnight to concentrate the cordial.

Strain through muslin (cheesecloth) and store in sterilised bottles.

Goes great guns with soda water (club soda) and vodka. Just sayin' …

I wanted, as he'd had his fill for the season. I guess when you have so much fruit to choose from you can get over different crops easily! Even though they're fiddly to pick, I'm glad we filled a few buckets, because it makes a refreshing cordial for summer. It's a very basic process, which furnishes some high-value produce. And of course, if you make a few too many bottles, you have more things to make deals with.

Little nippers

Each summer I try to get a good feed of yabbies (small freshwater crayfish). I just love the taste of them. It's another food source that brings annual variety to the mix of food types. I mean, who wants to eat kale all year round? Yabbies are at their peak in summer, when they're done with breeding and birthing, and simply concentrate on eating and fattening up. Good time to go harvest nature's bounty, eh? They're not overly hard to catch, either. You simply use an opera house net, pop some rotting stinky meat in the bait pouch, throw the net in the dam water and wait. Sometimes you get a magnificent haul, enough to feed the family, and sometimes you get a more modest catch, which just goes to the parents. Come on, don't judge me!

What I find hilarious about 'harvesting' yabbies is the contradiction it presents to the anti-hunting idea in this country, notably anti-duck-hunting. Yabbies are native, they're part of a natural wetland ecosystem and they're obviously living beings – one may even suggest they're sentient beings – so why is there no outcry when a haul of yabbies is eaten? Why is some meat deemed acceptable and other types unacceptable? An interesting conundrum. I ask the same question about fish. Why is it okay to kill a slimy wet trout but murderous to cut the throat of a live chicken? From what I can gather, it has something to do with feathers and fur. The more feathers and fur an animal has, the more valued it is, or the higher its potential for the snuggly, schmoopy-poopy, cutie-pie cuddle factor. See, you can't cuddle a wet trout or a crab. It's just gross. I've tried it. You can, however, cuddle a fluffy little duckling or a cute Ryan Gosling … mmm, so dreamy.

It's a phenomenon born of a society that's too distant from the reality of food. If you've eaten, say, chicken meat all your life but never seen the conditions that chicken lived in, how can you have an informed view about said meat? If you've never caught a yabby for dinner or shot a wild duck for food, how can you have an informed opinion about it? You just can't.

With this in mind, each year in summer I catch yabbies to eat. Why? Because it's real food that nature provided. Sure, I have to kill a living being, but I've been doing that all my life. I've been a meat eater all my life. I've been killing animals all my life. It's just that I used to outsource the killing part. Catching yabbies is yet another reminder that an animal will be killed so I can utilise its meat to continue my survival. That sickens some people. And that's okay. It means more yabbies for me.

With my summer bucket of yabbies as full as it's going to be, I head home for a feed. I've been boiling yabbies and freshwater crayfish since I was a wee boy. As a kid, I'd get out on the river on a Sunday, all my chores done the previous day, and catch some freshwater crayfish – beautiful large spiny crustaceans with a big tail and sweet meat. If I caught a few big ones, I was well fed, as they're much larger than a yabby. I'd simply light a campfire, fill the billy with river water and pop the crays in when the water was boiling. I'd suck every bit of meat from the shell – it sure was a prized feed, more loved even than trout. As the years progressed, I'd make a garlic, butter and white wine sauce for the yabbies, a sure winner. This summer I wanted to try something different. I didn't get as many yabbies as I would have liked, so I came up with a meal (page 129) that would harness that sweet yabby flavour but could be stretched out and fill the stomach like a good po'boy needs.

Yabbies (small freshwater crayfish) are a real delicacy – they're not something I can get my hands on in quantities large enough to be frivolous with in the kitchen. The yabbies in my dam are a real challenge to trap. I know they're there, but they simply refuse to cooperate by walking into the traps for me. Maybe they know I like eating them – word gets around fast out here. Thankfully, I have friends with better behaved crustaceans. And when a bucket of snapping yabbies gets dumped in my kitchen I go for this recipe. It's a bit of a mash-up of ideas, really, and it may not look the most beautiful, but it tastes great!

There are two parts to this dish: the chowder and the fried dumplings. I'll admit that there's a bit of work to it, but the results are worth it, especially if you love freshwater crustaceans. If you can get your hands on about 30–40 yabbies, you'll be able to feed a few adults. If you're not so lucky out on the ponds, then make a smaller batch and serve it as an entrée.

Yab-chow

SERVES 4

What you need

30–40 yabbies (small freshwater crayfish) (300–400 g/ 10½–14 oz meat)	5 eggs
	200 g (7 oz/2 cups) Toasted sourdough breadcrumbs (page 293)
1–2 tablespoons olive oil	
2 onions, chopped	750 ml (25½ fl oz/3 cups) sunflower oil
2 carrots, chopped	
1 litre (34 fl oz/4 cups) yabby stock (see below)	45 g (1½ oz/½ cup) grated pecorino
handful of chives, snipped	150 ml (5 fl oz) pouring (single/ light) cream
8–10 potatoes, peeled	
150 g (5½ oz/1 cup) plain (all-purpose) flour, plus extra for dusting	salt and pepper, to taste
	1 jalapeño chilli, chopped

How to make it

Preheat the oven to 200°C (400°F).

Cook the yabbies in boiling water until they turn red. Drain, allow to cool a little, then remove the meat from the tail and claws, and set aside. Put the remaining shells (containing the head and body meat) on a large baking tray.

Bake the yabby shells for 40 minutes, then transfer to a large stockpot with 3 litres (101 fl oz/12 cups) water. Simmer over medium heat for 30 minutes, then strain the stock. Discard the shells, and reserve 1 litre (34 fl oz/4 cups) stock for the recipe; store any excess for future cooking.

Heat a generous glug of olive oil in a large stockpot over low heat and sweat the onion and carrot for 30 minutes, stirring regularly. To get the best results, the heat must be very low. This slow cooking of the veg will intensify the flavour.

Add the reserved yabby stock and the chives (reserving a little as a garnish) and simmer for another 10 minutes. Finally, cool a little, then whizz with a hand-held blender until you get a consistently smooth soup base. I leave the soup in the pot for now, off the heat, and start making the dumplings.

Boil the potatoes until you can easily pierce them with a fork. Allow to cool, then push through a potato ricer or mash them using a potato masher until silky smooth. Transfer to a large mixing bowl, add half the flour and 2 eggs, and mix well. What we need to create is something of a thick potato mash that's dry enough to form a ball.

Line up three bowls on the bench: one with the remaining flour, one with the remaining eggs (lightly beaten) and one with the breadcrumbs. Form small potato

dumplings (a tad smaller than a golf ball) and coat them first in the flour, then with egg and finally with the breadcrumbs. Leave them on a flour-dusted tray in the fridge for a few hours to set.

Heat the sunflower oil in a heavy-based saucepan and fry the dumplings in batches, laying them on paper towel to drain off any excess oil while you cook the next batch.

Now we're ready to put it all together! Pop the soup back on the heat. When it's hot like a soup, add the cheese and the reserved yabby meat, and stir through the cream. Season to taste.

Place some fried dumplings in each bowl, then pour in the soup base, making sure each bowl gets a serving of the cooked yabby meat. Garnish with the chilli and the reserved chives.

Hothouse

Jerry Reed had a classic song, 'When You're Hot, You're Hot', and when it's hot here it's really hot. Even though we have a shortish summer due to our high altitude, it doesn't mean we don't have hot days. And when it's super-hot, imagine how hot the hothouse poly tunnel is. It's got to be over 50–60 degrees Celsius (122–140 degrees Fahrenheit) some days. When I built the tunnel I added two vents at one end and a door at the other. The idea is that the hot air has some directional flow, helped some days by a light breeze, and then escapes out any available exit point.

On a sunny day you can walk past one of the open vents and feel the heat desperately trying to escape from the tunnel. It's amazing how much heat is generated simply from sunlight being trapped under plastic. I have to be careful to remember to open the vents during the daylight hours and close them in the evening. It's an attempt to maintain a consistent temperature – not just the ambient temperature, but also the soil temp. The warm soil keeps the sensitive crops happy, and I'm keen to keep these guys happy. Think about where they originated: chilli, tomato, eggplant, capsicum – they're all from the Americas. All of these summer vegetables I love to cook with are heat-loving plants. Wouldn't it be easier if I just liked cool-climate vegetables like radishes? But man cannot survive on cold radishes alone. He must have chilli! Well, I must have chilli anyway. And I really don't like radishes.

So far the poly tunnel has been an absolute hit with the crops. Everything's ticking away as it should. The eggplant has massive leaves, flowers and fruit. The chillies have flowered, and a good crop of jalapeños has formed. There are plenty of cherry tomatoes for the kids to steal, and the zucchini plant is giving us a handful of fruit every week without fail. This poly tunnel is the best investment I've made for this garden and it looks like it's really paid off. In late autumn I'll plant green peas and broccoli, which should grow well during the winter months.

Corn-fed

I'd never really grown much corn, other than a small patch for fun, but last summer I had a nice little crop and it's encouraged me to be a preserver this summer. With some help from one of the darling kids, we planted a long garden bed with handfuls of corn kernels. Within a week or so the bed was full of little emerging corn plants. Even though I think we've got the seeds in a little bit late in the season, I'm hoping that as summer rolls into autumn we might just get a mega crop. Here's hoping.

The beaut thing about growing corn is that it's easy to store frozen, which means it's now a high priority on my list of things to grow. And as a grass species it doesn't seem to be too thirsty, which works well for a dry summer. Last winter, with our little crop of corn stored in the freezer, we made corn fritters, which were magic for putting smiles on faces. Imagine being all sad with the winter blues, then biting into a fritter where corn kernels explode with each bite, popping out a burst of summer! It's a great distraction from eating winter bean stews and kale, kale, kale. Let's face it, corn is a happy food. Who doesn't have memories of butter-smothered corncobs and corn particles stuck unavoidably between their teeth? Well, I do! And every time I bite into a corncob, I'm immediately transported back to a childhood dinner, with Mum wanting to watch *Moonlighting* and me wanting to watch *Magnum P.I.* Good corn-filled times.

Even though my corn hasn't quite matured (still at the Justin Bieber stage), I've been getting my hands on corn from my veg-growing farmer friend Rod. And it's so good, I often eat it raw. Here we go again, Rohan advocating raw food. What a damn foodie hipster! I do prefer it cooked, it's just that sometimes I get too excited, kind of like sex. You know those moments when you just can't get your pants off fast enough? Well, not that corn enters the bedroom, but it's a damn exciting time in summer when the corn arrives. And this year from my garden it may be autumn corn. I'll keep you posted.

Watching the growth

Summer's been absolutely beautiful. I'm feeling good to be alive, surrounded by so much beauty. The bees are buzzing in the patch, the veg is growing, the weather is perfect … it's utopia. Well, a little bubble of utopia. The days are long, the sun warms the skin – and the heart. Food is plentiful and fresh. The kids play outside all day long. I've even had a few spare moments to slip off into a hammock and snooze while the gentle summer breeze lulls me away. I've only seen a few snakes, and none on the house block, which is a good sign. We haven't had any bushfires close by this year, and the water tanks are full, as is the spring-fed dam, allowing me to water the veg garden as much as I like. It's an oasis. If only I owned the place.

Rental dilemmas aside, it's just a beautiful time of year. Late summer is when everything seems to be a happy land. Most days, by late afternoon we'll stop whatever we've been doing and hang out in the garden. A cold beer races down into the tummy, followed by another. There's often good conversation in the garden, about one's day, or plant progress, politics and world events. Everything happens outside. Even the cooking moves outside. Often at this time of the year, I'll simply cut off some veg like zucchini, eggplant and capsicum, drizzle over a little olive juice and grill it on the barbecue. I'll serve it with fresh basil, jalapeño and feta, seasoned with sea salt. Or I'll set the rotisserie in a spin with a herb and pimentón–marinated rabbit or two. Some nights I'm sure I could just fall asleep on a blanket, staring up into the summer heavens. It's a time that must be cherished because in five months it's going to be as cold as a polar region. All this growing better get its act together or we'll starve. Not really. We'll always have plenty of kale. *Kale!* No more kale! (insert crazy-man eye twitching).

One thing that makes this time of year so gobsmackingly wonderful is the progress in the patch. Back in spring and early summer, it was in transition mode with more soil visible than foliage. But now it's a sight to behold. Beans are in flower and climbing their way to the heavens. Sometimes I think the scarlet runner beans would grow to the clouds if only I built a ladder tall enough for them. The zucchini patch is so dense with large green leaves that you have to fight past the jungle to get to ground level and find your feed! Tomatoes form in groups like loitering teenagers, hanging out on aromatic branches. Broccolis stand firm, upright and proud, with blue–green leaves and large healthy florets, just begging to be picked. Visually, it's a stark contrast to the beginning of summer. Often I'll be watering the garden and shake my head at how much growth has taken place. All I did was plant the damn seed and look what happened! All this food. It's real food, grown right here in my backyard.

This visual splendour makes me laugh at those sayings we have, like 'paddock to plate' or 'spade to fork'. It's just food! Do you think the families growing their food in rural Vietnam refer to the food they grow in their backyard as paddock to plate? No, they just call it food. Why, then, do we have to complicate things and confuse people with all these terms and phrases? I think it diminishes the message somewhat. Let's face it, it's just vegetables grown in your backyard or someone's paddock. And anyway, all whole food is 'paddock to plate'. Think about it.

I wish I could better describe this garden to you. I wish I had the literary capabilities to paint a stunning picture that would create a nice feeling for you to experience. I wish I could walk every one of you through the garden at this time of year, hand you fresh peas and beans, and send you on your way with a basket of produce.

It's an amazing feeling walking through the gate to my veg patch and looking over all the produce I've grown for the family. Sometimes I just peruse and grin. Some people tell me I'm lucky to have a vegetable garden flourishing with food, but luck has nothing to do with it. I worked for this. I made the deliberate choice to grow as much food as possible so as to remove myself from supermarket reliance. It's involved some digging, some propagating, some planting, some weeding and watering, and a great deal of learning. And it pays off every summer growing season. My garden in full flight is a sight to behold. Anyone's vegetable garden at the height of summer is amazing to look at. To be able to bend down and pick out something to eat that's been grown

the natural way will give you a phenomenal feeling. And then to cook and eat it – wow, that's another feeling altogether! It's not as good a feeling as an afternoon of love or a bottle of aged whisky, but it's still a pleasure worth incorporating into your life.

Cooking in the garden is practical. It's better than a hot summer kitchen, and even better with a crisp dry lager washing down the dust and grit of a hot summer breeze. The smell of olive oil and vegetables cooking on the grill is enough to drive me wild. A big bowl of this food sets me up really well for an afternoon siesta in the tree hammock.

Summer-veg Afternoon Delight

SERVES 4

What you need

2 eggplants (aubergines)	3 tablespoons chopped parsley, plus extra to garnish
2 red capsicums (bell peppers), seeds removed	200 g (7 oz/1⅓ cups) crumbled feta
2–3 zucchini (courgettes)	1 jalapeño chilli, chopped
60 ml (2 fl oz/¼ cup) olive oil	sumac, to serve
rock salt and freshly cracked black pepper, to taste	sesame seeds, to garnish
juice of ½ lemon	
3 tablespoons chopped mint, plus extra to garnish	

How to make it

Heat the barbecue grill to high, open a cold beer.

Slice all the veg lengthways and put it in a large mixing bowl. Drizzle over the olive oil and crack over some salt and pepper. Toss to ensure an even coating of olive oil.

Cook the veg on the hot barbecue grill, turning frequently until charred and softened. When the veg is cooked, take it off the heat and give it a rough chop into bite-sized pieces. Transfer to a bowl or platter.

Toss the veg with the lemon juice, herbs, feta and chilli, and mix well.

Sprinkle with sumac and sesame seeds, use extra herbs to garnish, then serve with another cold beer.

Note: *This isn't a groundbreaking new edgy recipe. It's simple, real, no-bullshit food. It's food that I grew in my backyard. And that's what makes it special.*

Nothing to do with food, everything to do with comfort

It seems odd to be doing the most physically strenuous activity at the height of summer, but it's something that just needs to be done. The house we're currently renting was built just after World War II. It's a standard old farmhouse, the same as most houses around here from that era. It's weatherboard and well insulated, but even so, in winter it's cold. It's just plain cold everywhere here in winter. We have two fireplaces, but only really use one of them, which is a doored heater and very efficient at heating one end of the house. For any fire you need wood, and in this house it's my responsibility to collect it. Just as it is for much of the food in the larder, it's during summer that I need to concentrate on building my cache of fuel. And in case you're wondering why we don't use natural gas, let me tell you, we're so very fortunate as to be remote enough not to be connected to the gas mains. Our only option for warmth is firewood. In any case, if you think about trees as a natural resource, they're totally renewable, unlike gas reserves.

Now cutting firewood is one of those things that amazingly gives me a great sense of satisfaction. And I share this with a lot of other people, men and women alike. A good friend of mine, Jen, lives some of her time in a little place she calls the Pirate Shack, where wood heating is the only option. We've had plenty of talk about how we enjoy the process of cleaning fallen limbs, sawing the wood, stacking it for a year to cure and then splitting it and stacking it somewhere dry for winter fuel. Why is this chore enjoyed so much by so many? I blame Lego.

Think about it. It's the whole stacking thing. Each cut log is a piece of Lego that makes the final construction, a damn big pile of wood. Like working with those plastic Lego pieces, the process becomes mind-numbingly methodical. Each piece is cut to the same length, then picked up, stacked neatly and so the process continues. Each time, the worker steps back and admires the construction taking place, just like a child building a knight's castle with Lego.

I can spend a whole day getting lost with wood. I love the work the chainsaw does – it's a real performer. And I love the log splitter coming down with force, smashing into the dried log, splitting it in half. The reward is in the pile of split logs building and building as the day progresses. It's instant gratification. Secretly, your muscles are getting a workout, your shoulders working overtime, at first holding the chainsaw, next swinging the splitter. Mentally, I remind myself of the deposits I'm making in the fuel bank, and how this day will make my life in the future more comfortable. It's an old way of thinking, especially with regard to heating for winter. I used to simply turn on the gas heater. Now I have to work for my heat.

Our lives are so much less physically intensive these days. Instead of cutting firewood, we simple press a button. Even before houses had fireplaces, people still had to roam the bush, bending and lifting, carting and hauling wood to their campfire. There are so many examples of how we used to be physical and now we just press buttons. I've lived both lives, and I have to say that even though this version involves more hard work that's more physically demanding, it's definitely more rewarding than just pressing a button and paying a gas bill. I know it's not for everyone, and I don't expect everyone to cut down trees and burn wood for heat, I'm just sharing how I feel about it.

I have a pile of wood I cut out from the domestic logging coupe last year, but it's all too long, as I cut it for use in the large open fire down at the old schoolhouse where we lived a year back. I have the daunting task of recutting all the wood into shorter lengths, and then I have to start the splitting process. Then stacking. Man, I'm a glutton for punishment! It's been an ongoing project for me over the summer. When we have a day of mild conditions, I fuel up the chainsaw and get to work. I'll get into a trance-like state, lifting the next log, setting it in place, unlocking the saw, cutting, then adding the two new logs to the pile for splitting. Sometimes I wish the saw would run out of puff as I do, but it keeps going. Soon my pile of new logs is high and I start thinking about how long it's going to take me to split, so I change jobs. I split for an hour or so then load the truck for the final task of stacking. My cache is getting larger. I feel like winter will be warm and secure. I love that feeling.

My childhood memories of beetroot (beets) are not rad. It's taken me a few years to work up the courage to even grow this bugger in my patch. Every bit of soil is valuable in a small garden, and the thought of beetroot taking up space where I could be growing tomatoes or beans has challenged me for years. But I eventually broke and allocated a small corner of the summer garden to these beautiful root vegetables. Yes, I like them now, but don't let's get carried away – they're not so much a favourite vegetable, but they do add to the mixture of summer flavours. Man cannot live on tomato and beans alone.

In love-making, I think experimentation is the key to keeping things interesting. Same approach for cooking. You can make a similar version of this with roasted beets, which will bring out a bit of a sweeter vibe. The sugars of the beetroot caramelise and you'll end up with a completely different dish. So feel free to play around. Keep it fresh, baby.

Beetroot & Walnut Salad

SERVES 4 AS A SIDE

What you need

4–6 garden-fresh beetroot (beets)

handful of cress (water or pepper)

1 tablespoon chopped mint

100 g (3½ oz/½ cup) marinated goat's cheese

100 g (3½ oz/1 cup) walnuts, roughly chopped

1–2 tablespoons balsamic vinegar

salt and pepper, to taste

olive oil, for drizzling

pea shoots, to garnish

How to make it

Wash the dirt off your beets. Dirty buggers. Poach them in boiling water until they're soft enough to pierce easily with a fork. Drain and allow to cool. Peel off the skin (it will slip off easily), cut the beets into small cubes and transfer them to a mixing bowl.

Throw in the cress, mint, goat's cheese, walnuts and balsamic vinegar, and toss well.

Season to taste, drizzle over some olive oil and garnish with pea shoots.

Tight lines

I've been dreaming about getting back on the water all summer: the cool water rushing between my legs, the sweet taste of snow-melted stream water, and the thought of the fly line whizzing and holding tight with a spectacular trout on the end of it. Instead, I've been cutting wood for the oncoming winter, tending the garden and delivering vegetables to the city. It's easy to get caught up in what we think is important, and as much as growing the food and cutting firewood is important for keeping the house running, I still need to get out on the water. It's imperative for my spiritual wellbeing. Jeff my fly-fishing mate has been on my back for months now, so it didn't take much of a nudge to pack up the truck and head for the high country.

I do fish the local lakes and the odd creek and stream near home, but nothing beats time spent up in the high country fishing for trout. The drive is an absolute pain in the arse, but the destination is mind-blowing and spectacular. We drive for hours on flat, dry and barren land until we start the climb up. At first we cover the low hills, where the road meanders and winds its way around the landscape with rhythmic sway. Through plantation pine forests and aromatic eucalyptus we drive. The bush eventually changes from majestic towering mountain ash to stubby, gnarly snow gums. The air is pure up here – it's crisp and your body feels excited with a sense of freedom. There are sparse human settlements here; it's mostly just bush.

We have a few spots we've returned to, and every time we traverse the rocky track to our preferred campsite we both cross our fingers it's vacant. We've actually never seen anyone there, just the remnants of dickhead campers who leave their rubbish for us to collect. The secret track is 4WD-access-only and my old truck manages it with ease. The rocks and loose stones make the truck slip with the descent, but taking it easy and slow is a sure bet. As we pull away from the last of the snow gums, the track opens out to a large valley clearing. The view here is amazing. The crystal-clear river snakes its way through the valley, with grass and native flowers covering the slopes back up to the bush line. It doesn't take long until we can see the camp. No one there. What a relief!

The last bit of track is the most dangerous. It's fallen away with heavy rain over the years and it's a tight steep corner before the land flattens out. This is where it's easy to tip a truck, so I take it nice and slow. The last point is so steep and unbalanced you can't actually see the track over the bonnet – you kind of hope for the best. I land safely and, full of fisherman's excitement, we both lunge from the truck straight to the water for a stickybeak.

It's the height of summer now and blowflies buzz around our faces. The heat from the sun breaks out a summer sweat. The water is pure here; it's mostly snow melt, and there's no cattle for miles. It's my favourite water to drink in the world – untouched by human interference. We set up camp and wait for the evening rise. Sure enough, the river delivers. Rise after rise and cast after cast, and then bang! The first trout of the trip. It's a little one, so I let him go back to his home to get fat over the next year.

We fish every day without fail. Mornings are hot in the tents, so we get up at an early hour, cook a hearty meal, slide into our waders and head off to fish. Some days are just perfection and some not so much. Jeff has a stellar day catching more than twenty trout. I come in at a handful each day, and even though I never catch as many, I'm overjoyed nonetheless. The extreme heat in the middle of the day and afternoon keeps us hidden under shade back at our camp, for a siesta and a patient wait for the coolness and an evening rise. We eat well on these trips. I prepare before leaving home with a bit of emergency food just in case the trout aren't on. It all comes from the backyard so we eat like kings, but most nights we smoke a trout or two, fry up some potatoes, and drink whisky and wine well into the evening. We tell tales of past fishing trips, pass around a doobie, and wax lyrical about how the world is a bit fucked. Each night I climb up into my rooftop tent with the biggest smile on my face. Here I am, totally happy. There's no internet connection, no sign of mankind's infrastructure, just us and the best damn river I've ever fished. Oh, and at night you drift asleep to the howl of the alpine dingoes singing their soulful tune. Could it get any better than this? I doubt it.

Beware the wankers

In any 'sport' there are wankers. They're unavoidable. They love having all the best gear. They love telling you how expensive everything they have is. And they always get the newest equipment, just to ensure they're above everyone else. Fly fishing is full of these wankers.

The reason people pay thousands of dollars for specialty fly rods and gear is that the trout are so intuitive they only strike at rods valued over $1000. No shit! This is what the wanker fisherman will tell you anyway. Now I'm not the world's best fly fisherman. I'm well aware that I'll be a student of the craft all my life. But I do know one thing: I've caught more fish on a cheaper, more affordable rod than I have on a more expensive rod. It's that bloody consumerism disease – bigger is better and all that rubbish! I once found a secondhand fly rod for less than $40. It sat in a bargain bin of secondhand goods, out the front of a hunting and fishing store, and guess what? It catches fish! So beware of these wankers, and don't become one yourself.

Summer is the best time for fly fishing, with the water flowing clear and fresh, and a multitude of insects on the water – a plethora of food for the fish to fatten up on, and for us to replicate with our flies. I don't have much in the way of flowing water near home, just one sole river that's a dangerous river to fish at the best of times. Most of my fly fishing is on the still water.

We're very fortunate to have a spring-fed dam on the property we rent. Late last winter I dropped in around forty-five yearling rainbow trout I purchased from the hatchery. It was more of an experiment, really – I didn't expect it to work very well, but it was worth a try. So now in summer the trout are feeding on the surface, showing off their sleek silver flesh, taunting me. I've been out of a morning, waving my fly rod backwards and forwards, presenting the fly and hoping for a strike. These fish are totally onto me – they must read my blog. No matter what type of fly I present, no matter how close to their noses it is, they simply refuse to strike. Frustrated by these smart trout, I've resorted to using a spinner. In the lure goes with a long cast. Plop! Into the water it drops. I reel in slowly, and the lure jiggles and wobbles like the sexy hip swagger of a lady. Nothing. But just to add salt to the wound, the trout follow the lure in to the bank, wink at me, then swim off. Bastards!

So, frustrated as I am, I have nowhere to turn but to my teenage approach – worm on a hook. By this time in summer, the water is low and the water plants are thick from the excess sunlight, so I use a float. I cast a few lines to double my score. I wait patiently as the trout gracefully rise to feed right in front of my very eyes. But again, I'm dodged. Not a trout on a hook. They're laughing their fishy laugh at me. They're talking to each other, they're planning, talking tactics and proposing sinister ways to frustrate me. But I will get them one day. Even if it involves a shotgun and TNT. I *will* eat that trout.

In the meantime, while I'm mad with those nasty trout, I plan the annual cure for the fly fisherman's itchy feet – the high-country fishing trip. A good mate of mine, Raynor, suggested we head for the Mitta Mitta, where his folks have a small cabin. Who in their right mind would say no to that? The Mitta is a beautiful river. It's now controlled mostly by man-made dams and weirs, but as far as wild trout is concerned, it's a fine river. As is the nearby Snowy Creek, which I've also never fished. What an adventure we had planned.

With another friend, Sam, we jumped in my truck and headed north-east to the mountains, with rods in the tub and hope in our hearts. We spent the weekend fishing beautiful water, but much of it in the Mitta was flowing fast, as it's high summer and the irrigators downstream are crying out for water. This made successful fishing nigh on impossible. And the Snowy wasn't much better. The hot summer weather had the trout sitting tight on the banks, keeping cool. My summer hasn't been the raddest with regard to trout fishing. You could say it's been a waste of time, given I didn't bring back any food. But I think the time on the water has a different value than just acquiring food. What that value is, is for the individual to discover. For me though, it's being there. Simply being on a river – so serene, so pretty – my dog walking alongside me on the banks, a friend to converse with, the sounds and smells of the bush. And even though I didn't catch anything on this trip, the exciting thought that I *might* catch something is good enough.

A few weeks after the trip, my mate Jack did a food deal with me. He caught a few trout from his big dam and exchanged it for some of my food. A compromise, I guess, but you can't get everything you want – especially when you're dealing with fickle nature.

One thing I love about a lifestyle of eating what you have in season is that you invariably come across some combinations that just seem to work brilliantly. Often recipes come from nothing more than having to make a meal with what you have on hand – this is probably the basis for most of my cooking. I had a bunch of slow-cooked venison meat in the fridge, a bag of fresh broad (fava) beans from Mum's garden and a good cache of onions. And thus this meal was born. It was such a winner it's now on the menu for the kids. When the kids remember a recipe I take it as one I should memorise, write down or photo-document.

Hah! I got my kids to eat broad beans. Sucked in, dudes.

Broad Bean & Venison Warm Salad

SERVES 4

What you need

The venison	The salad
small venison shoulder	1–2 tablespoons olive oil
100 g (3½ oz) lard	4 onions, chopped
100 g (3½ oz) butter	350 g (12½ oz/2 cups) podded broad (fava) beans, boiled and peeled
handful of sage	
handful of thyme	handful of mint, chopped, plus extra to garnish
cracked black pepper, to taste	
250 ml (8½ fl oz/1 cup) red wine	handful of tarragon, chopped
	2 preserved lemons, skins only, finely chopped
	200 g (7 oz/1⅓ cups) crumbled goat's feta
	sumac, to taste
	salt and pepper, to taste
	chives, snipped, to garnish

How to make it

Preheat a hooded barbecue to low or the oven to 125°C (260°F).

To prepare the venison, sit the shoulder on large-sized aluminium foil, making sure the bottom is as watertight as possible and bending up the sides to make a rough bowl shape. Break up the lard and butter and spread it out around the meat. Add the herbs and pepper, and pour over the wine. Tightly wrap the shoulder in the foil – the idea is that the foil will prevent the meat drying out. Wild venison can be quite dry if not cooked with some form of moisture, so the lard, butter and wine all help. They also add mega-flavour.

Transfer to a baking tray and cook for 2–5 hours in the barbecue or oven. It's ready when it's falling off the bone and is obviously easy to chew ;-). When the venison is done, remove from the heat and set aside to rest for 30 minutes.

While the deer is resting, start preparing the salad. Heat a generous glug of olive oil in a frying pan over low–medium heat, then cook the onions for 30 minutes. The slow-cooked onions will add a sweet element to the mix. Stir constantly but not OCD-style. No offence.

Remove the venison from the bone, pulling it apart into smaller pieces, and transfer to a mixing bowl. Add the broad beans, herbs, sweet slow-fried onions and preserved lemon, and stir through.

Top with the feta and a sprinkle of sumac, season to taste, garnish with the extra mint and the chives, and serve.

Lamb Neck & Summer Broad Beans

SERVES 4

What you need

60 ml (2 fl oz/¼ cup) olive oil

1 onion, finely chopped

5 garlic cloves, finely chopped

4 lamb neck cuts

1–2 tablespoons fino sherry

1 dried chilli, finely chopped

6 whole allspice berries

725 g (1 lb 10 oz/2¾ cups) tomato passata (puréed tomatoes)

350 g (12½ fl oz/2 cups) podded broad (fava) beans

The couple we rent our property from are sheep farmers. My landlord kindly offered to buy us a lamb and we very excitedly accepted. So one fresh morning I found myself up at the shed seeing our lamb being broken down by the mobile butcher in a matter of minutes. I was asked if I wanted the neck for slow-cooking, and I was a bit intrigued as to what to do with it. Surely a slow braise would do the job! Now, this is by no means a fancy meal, but it's very tasty. The slow-cooked lamb melts in your mouth, and the freshness of early summer broad beans in the broth is a yum buddy.

How to make it

Heat half the olive oil (a glug) in a heavy-based stockpot over low–medium heat. Simmer the onion and garlic for at least 10 minutes, or until browned.

Heat the remaining oil in a frying pan over high heat and seal the lamb for a minute each side. Transfer the sealed lamb to the stockpot with the onions and garlic.

Deglaze the frying pan with a splash of fino sherry (there will be flames) then pour it into the stockpot.

Add the chilli, allspice and passata, bring to the boil, then reduce the heat and simmer, very gently, for at least 2 hours, or until the meat is tender.

When the meat is cooked, it's time to blanch the broad beans in boiling water (they only take a few minutes if they're fresh). Drain the cooked beans, allow to cool a little (so you don't burn your hands, silly) then peel off the skins.

Lay a serve of the beans on each plate, then ladle over the sauce from the slow-cooked lamb. Pop the lamb neck on top. Enjoy.

I'm no gardening expert. I do grow vegetables, herbs, fruit and some nuts. It's just a matter of giving it a go and harvesting whatever results you get. A few years ago I started planting pea seeds directly into the soil of my garden and you'll never believe it, but pea plants started to grow in the same spot I left the seeds. Amazing. The tiny little plants grew larger and larger, eventually flowering. Those pretty flowers turned into peas and I ate them. Fresh off the vine, bursting with that pea-ness flavour in my mouth. Yes, you just said that in your head. Ha, ha, ha, got you!

Jokes aside, fresh garden-grown peas – amazing food, right? And in the garden bed right next to them sits a crop of potatoes. I probably shouldn't harvest the potatoes yet – it's a bit early – but, bugger it, I'm going to make a meal of tucker straight from the patch and it's going to taste like amazing. And just because fresh garden peas are so damn healthy, I'll add bacon to even out the nutritional balance. And, well, smoky bacon just makes everything all right.

Pea & Whole New-season Potato Creamy Salad

SERVES 4

What you need

10–12 baby potatoes, washed

60 ml (2 fl oz/¼ cup) olive oil

155 g (5½ oz/1 cup) podded garden-fresh peas

2 rashers (slices) smoky loin bacon (page 189), cut crossways into strips

100 g (3½ oz) mascarpone

25 g (1 oz/¼ cup) grated sharp pecorino

handful of parsley, finely chopped

handful of mint, finely chopped, plus extra to garnish

juice of 1 lemon

salt and pepper, to taste

How to make it

Preheat the oven to 200°C (390°F).

Parboil the potatoes, then drain and place in a roasting tin. Drizzle over a bit more than half the olive oil (a generous glug), then toss the potatoes well to coat evenly in the oil. Roast for 30 minutes, then check for 'doneness'. The best roast potatoes are crispy on the outside and soft in the middle.

Cook the peas for 5 minutes in boiling water, then drain and transfer to a mixing bowl.

While the peas are cooking, pan-fry the bacon in the remaining olive juice (it'll be a light glug).

When the potatoes are cooked, add them to the bowl with the peas, along with the bacon, mascarpone, pecorino, herbs and lemon juice.

Season to taste, garnish with extra mint, and eat straight from the bowl. Whoops, I mean serve to your family.

I plant a lot of root vegetables by direct seeding. I don't always get a mega-rad strike rate, but when I do, there's often an impending root-veg extravaganza.

For some reason, I've had great success with parsnips this year. I have no idea how I did it. There aren't any tricks, it just worked really well. Now I have more parsnips than I originally expected, and I've come up with a better way to use this stunning root veg than playing parsnip swords with the kids in the backyard. To be honest, I'd only really been cutting the parsnips into chips, roasting them, and dipping the heck

out of them in some sort of dirty home-made mayo or aioli (page 292). But like an episode of Friends, it gets boring pretty quickly.

It's the roasting that brings out the best in a parsnip, so I stuck with that technique and made a dip. The thing is, though, it can end up a bit like peanut butter, in that if you put a big spoonful in your gob, your greedy tongue will stick to the roof of your mouth and you can't talk for a while – which I've found really useful when Kate gets a bit chatty. 'Here, hon, try a spoonful of this delicious dip.' Gets her every time.

Roast Parsnip Spread or Dip

MAKES 250–500 ML (8½–17 FL OZ/1–2 CUPS)

What you need

10–12 young parsnips	¼ teaspoon chilli powder
olive oil, for drizzling	handful of parsley, chopped
50–100 g (1¾–3½ oz) chèvre	salt and pepper, to taste
45 g (1½ oz/½ cup) grated pecorino	
3 teaspoons lemon juice	

How to make it

Preheat the oven to 200°C (390°F).

Cut the parsnips into chunks to help them cook a little faster. Lay them in a roasting tin and drizzle over some olive juice. Bake for 20 minutes, then flip each chunk over. Bake for a further 15–20 minutes, until mega-soft. If I can pierce them with a fork I reckon they're done.

Blitz the roasted parsnip in a food processor, then add the two cheeses, lemon juice, chilli powder and parsley.

Season to taste. Offer to chatty member of the house.

Tip: With parsnips, pick 'em small, like carrot-sized – I reckon they're sweeter and less woody that way. Oh, and be careful with the amount of lemon you put in. I've made it with too much lemon and it's like a punch in the face for your tastebuds. Start with a quarter of a lemon (about 3 teaspoons of juice) and go from there.

Little red

Looking at a ripe tomato is looking into the very heart of summer. They've been the symbol of summer for me for so many years now. I have fond memories of biting into ripe tomatoes when I was a kid on the farm. Warmed by the sun, those tomatoes had fleshy insides that would burst with sweetness. Darling miniature cherry tomatoes, eaten straight off the truss, enjoyed like a fruit from a tree. Most summers in my adult life I've grown tomatoes. Any house I've lived in that's had a little patch of soil, I've planted a tomato or two in November. My whole life I've appreciated that aromatic signature, that smell you enjoy when you rub past the plant or water it.

I've loved every new set of flowers, and the potential of the ripe fruit they promise. Each meal with tomato in it is akin to eating a slice of summer. It's sweet and fresh. To anyone who asks me to suggest which veg they should start their own patch with, I'll often recommend tomatoes. They've had a strong influence on my life. I hope they can do the same for others.

I know. It sounds odd that I'm going on about bloody tomatoes! But they're pretty amazing when grown by your own hands, on your patch of earth. The taste is unreal, and miles more enjoyable than a tomato grown in a solution on a hydroponic farm.

Growing tomatoes is purely a summer thing. The plant represents everything about summer – healthy green foliage, sunny yellow flowers and bountiful fruit. And that smell, there's no mistaking it, it's the aromatics of summer. Eating them any other time of the year is just odd.

I'm glad it only comes to visit for a few months of the year. Its absence gives me some time to long for it, and it's not just the tomato itself that I long for, but warmth, the sun's rays of life that make the plant grow. In the depths of winter, when my toes ache from the cold, the thought of walking through the garden picking ripe tomatoes is enough to improve my dull winter mood. We'll reminisce about the previous summer, the crop we enjoyed, and the time it took to raise it to maturity in order to fruit. It's quite an achievement not to let a plant die. It's not necessarily hard labour, it's simply remembering your role as a nurturer.

Each spring I'll select a range of tomato varieties to propagate. It doesn't matter which varieties I select, what matters is the practical outcome I wish to achieve, which is quite simply tomatoes to eat. I do like to try a few new types each year, for the sole purpose of keeping life interesting. Sometimes in winter I'll flick through some tommie seed packets in a shop and just pick out a few. It's buying into the idea of hope. Holding the seeds in my hand is the first step in a project aimed at eating them. It's holding the promise of summer.

My tomatoes have been a challenge this year, just as the situation was last year. The yard I planted in last year just didn't get enough full sun and, as a result, I had more unripe green tomatoes than ripe. This year, in a new backyard, I was a month or so behind in planting due to my delayed poly-tunnel construction, and I've missed out on a mega crop again. That's just the reality of being a home grower. Sometimes you have a win, sometimes not. I'm not too disappointed, though. I've still been able to harvest enough tomatoes to keep the kitchen happy, just not enough to make big batches of passata (puréed tomatoes) or sauces.

We're not far from autumn. The wind has returned with its bite. The house fire has even been lit, and the cobwebs dusted from my jackets. For now my tomatoes remain in the poly tunnel. Some are still flowering and some carry ripe fruit. I can't bear to pull them all out – each year the thought of it gives me anxiety. I can't help but compare the inevitability of pulling the plants out to my own mortality. These plants were born of a seed carrying genetic information, they grew

and served their natural purpose, and eventually they will be removed from this earth – just as I will some day. But if one is to live with nature then one must accept what cannot be changed. And the reality is, we all live with nature. We all face the same shitty reality. We'll all be pulled from the poly tunnel. Unlike the tomatoes, though, we'll be able to ask ourselves if we served our purpose.

The best looking tomatoes, those that succeed above all others, are the ones whose seed I'll keep for next season. The seeds are scooped out, cleaned of flesh and laid out on paper towel to dry. I write the name of each variety, and often, as for all vegetables, I'll rename them. I like creating more memorable names, like 'Yellow Gems', 'Tia's Favourite' or 'Jack's Revenge'. There are no rules with gardening. You can do whatever you like. It's your garden. You rule. I have a sign on one of the gates to my garden – 'Rohan's Garden' – which was a gift from the kids. When you enter, you walk onto sovereign soil where practical thinking triumphs over rules and regulations; where food is produced without chemical enhancement; where the approach to growing food relies on soil, water, plants and sunlight. It's where everything makes sense.

It's time for me to make way for autumn. The plants must go. There were some really late bloomers that I didn't even get fruit from. They're the first to be pulled out. My heart aches pulling these bastards out. There's no escaping the reality that it's the end of summer. It seemed so damn short. I have so much unfinished business, so many things I never got around to finishing. But what can I do? I'm only one man. I can only be in one place at a time, performing one task at a time. I can't expect anything more from myself other than to try my best, to persevere when it's easier to give up, to make peace when there's still a fight. I know my enemy. It's time.

I love shanks. If they come off a wallaby, kangaroo, deer or lamb, it doesn't matter. The thing that makes them all good is the muscle and its gelatinous nature, which gets me excited. Normally, I'd cook shanks in the cooler months, but the last few years I've enjoyed them in summer. Summer is a veg fest for us backyard growers, so the very thought of a meat fest in the middle of summer gets me wobbly at the knees. And even though I could serve these shanks with a side of fresh summer veg, I blatantly refuse to. It's a bowl of tender melt-in-your-mouth meat. Why add anything to it? Well, it sure makes a change for me, anyway.

Patience is super-important when cooking shanks. I recommend you set the dish cooking then bugger off out to the garden to potter for a few hours. For your effort in the garden you shall be rewarded with a summer meat fest. Hot and spicy, too, so you're required to knock the top off a coldie to wash down all that spice.

Spanish Shanks

SERVES 2

What you need

1 tablespoon cumin seeds	1 tablespoon chilli powder
1–2 tablespoons olive oil	725 g (1 lb 10 oz/ 2¾ cups) tomato passata (puréed tomatoes)
2 onions, sliced	
5 large garlic cloves, sliced	
2 large lamb shanks	salt, to taste
250 ml (8½ fl oz/1 cup) red wine	parsley, to garnish
1 tablespoon smoked pimentón (Spanish paprika)	

How to make it

Toast the cumin seeds in a dry frying pan over medium heat. After a few minutes they'll start to heat up and release the beautiful aromatics. Remove from the heat and crush to a powder in a mortar and pestle.

Heat the olive oil in a flameproof casserole dish over low–medium heat on the stove top, then toss in the onion and garlic, and fry them gently for at least 10 minutes.

Add the shanks and brown them evenly, then pour in the wine. Add the cumin, pimentón, chilli powder and passata. Pop the lid on, reduce the heat to very low, and simmer for 2–3 hours.

Season with salt and serve with a garnish of parsley.

Autumn

Autumn

Don't pat the dog

There are many things I like to grumble about in this modern world. The fact that most of us have zero contact with other living beasts (other than cats and dogs) is one of my gripes. Being around animals is something that's been taken away from us over a few generations. It's one of those by-products of living in a modern world so sophisticated that we consumers are no longer required to meet the food we eat, especially when it's alive. In days past, people had animals in the backyard or knew someone living on the land. That's not really the case for everyone now.

It's not like it's a human right or anything, and it's not like we all have to get cuddly with a lamb or snuggly with a duck, but having contact with animals or at least an understanding of how they live is kind of important. Living with animals that end up on the plate has been part of human culture since the get-go – well, a few thousand years, give or take.

Why exactly is it important for us to have contact with animals? Consider this hypothetical. I give you a handful of cute ducklings, all fluffy and beautiful. They smell sweet. They make little ducky noises. You're convinced they're just the cutest things on the globe. You immediately fall in love. You spend hours just watching them. Cuddling them. You raise them, you care for them. Time goes by. They get plump. You battle internally whether or not to eat them. OMG, how can I kill Gary? Fred? Fluffy? And yes, Daffy? But man, you just love a duck risotto. But you can't! You couldn't!

You're now faced with a meat paradox. With duck meat on the brain, you head to the supermarket, buy duck meat and cook that damn risotto while looking out the back window at your happy little ducks. The point is that the contact you had with a 'meat' bird has changed your perspective: you can't kill and eat a pet. But going to the supermarket to buy meat, there's no connection. No emotion. It's robotic. It's thoughtless. Hard pill to swallow, eh? I know, it sucks, right! I've been there. I cursed myself for all the years I'd been doing it. And that's why I'm a grumpy man. Because this reality sucks.

I often wonder, if we were all to reintroduce contact with the various species of farmed animals we consume, how it would impact on our food choices. I wonder how many of us would decide we don't want to eat something that was a living animal because we gave it a pat when it was breathing and its heart was pumping. I wonder, if we all had a better understanding of the reality of the killing process involved, whether we'd choose

to buy less meat. It's definitely something worth thinking about when we bite into that low-fat chicken sub.

Over the years I've put myself in situations that have been confronting. I've taught myself how to kill an animal, how to butcher it, and how to cook it. It's far removed from my previous way of getting meat to the table, which simply involved making a selection from an open supermarket fridge. Instead of just considering hypotheticals, I went that extra step and made myself experience the harsh reality. What has it done? Has the process served any purpose? I definitely now value the meat I eat much more than I previously did. And with that in mind I tend to eat less of it. I'm also now slightly ruined, culinarily speaking. I now prefer the flavours of home-raised animals or wild meat to most farmed species. There's just so much more excitement in the flavour, and when you've worked hard for that meal you've plucked, gutted, skinned or scaled, there's a whole other level of appreciation that has nothing to do with flavour.

The first nut

When I was a wee laddie, my parents took me to visit some family friends who lived a block away from my grandparents. In their backyard was a thriving walnut tree. So many nuts had fallen to the ground that they couldn't eat them all themselves, so they offered us the chance to eat some. I remember the feeling of holding a whole nut in my hand and thinking, 'Gee, this is just like the nuts at the supermarket.' Weird, huh? Of course they're the same ones, you douchebag younger version of me! It was a realisation that food that comes from a tree is the same food as at the shops.

Years later, when I was married, my wife and I stayed the night in a little Victorian town called Dargo. Where we camped grew a huge old walnut tree – sure would have been more than a hundred years old. It was Easter time and the nuts were dropping to the ground, ready to harvest. I was gobsmacked. How could all these free walnuts just be lying on the ground?

I couldn't believe this great bounty was sitting there, not being used by anyone.

After that road trip, I returned to my lame-arse office job, remained caught up in trying to beat the guy beside me for the next promotion and forgot all about those walnuts. A decade later, a friend came to work and told me about his weekend. His family had been foraging for walnuts. What the? What's foraging? He explained that it was a good way to spend time with the kids, collect some natural food, yada, yada. But something intrigued me about those walnuts. I loved the experience all those years ago of picking them off the ground near my grandparents' place. Maybe I should take the kids out the following weekend for this activity they call foraging. It was around the same time I was starting to think a good deal more about food, its origins and how it was produced, so collecting something that simply fell from a tree worked well with my developing food philosophy.

The kids and I had a ball that day filling bags with fallen walnuts. Well, actually, I was the kid excited about the walnuts; the actual kids' attention span lasted about ten minutes before they noticed nearby distractions and left me to my own devices. I didn't care – it was like I was let into the bank vault to take as much as I liked, and with no consequences. These nuts would have simply rotted back into the ground or been eaten by the clever possums, so I wasn't doing anyone any great harm by collecting them.

Each year since then, I've taken the girls to the same tree. We forage for ten minutes or so, then they go off and get distracted, returning sporadically to help. When the baskets are full, we lie down in the grass, happy with our haul, and discuss future meals involving walnuts.

Nuts are an important part of our annual food supplies, and I like to get a cache of a few other species for the larder. Right now, in early autumn, the almonds are almost ready to harvest. They're the first nut. The second is hazelnuts, then walnuts and finally chestnuts, but they're all a little way off. The best thing about all of them is they store well. So when I'm working hard to fill up the food stores for winter, nuts get a big tick.

Bee

The first frosts have arrived. My climbing and bush beans are starting to look a little the worse for wear, but they still have a way to go to finish filling out the bean pods. It's not been the best bean season. I think the combination of two extreme heatwaves and a lack of pollinating bees might have something to do with it. I can't change the weather, but I can buy some bees.

Which I've now finally done after all these years of putting it off. I don't really hate bees, I just don't get all the fuss about them. People have been asking why I don't have a beehive, and in some situations they've plainly criticised me for not having them. I just haven't needed them in the past. At our other houses there have always been bees that just came to my garden of their own accord. But this place, being in the middle of monoculture agriculture, is somehow different. It's been exciting to see a rare bee in the garden, but I want to change that. I want them to be a common sight. This current bean crop is my first in this garden, and it's been the first time I've ever noticed such poor pollination. It's pushed me to make the phone call to my bee-loving mate and order a hive.

He's an amateur expert, I suppose, and man, he really does love his bees. In fact, he generally loves the crap out of nature. His Instagram feed always has great bird and bee photos, and not much else. I think that's an indication of what's important to him in his life. I wonder how his family feels about being trumped by birds and bees. I might talk to him about that. A new hive frame was constructed for me and some bees put inside it. I imagine there's more precise apiarist terminology for that process, but you get the general idea.

I picked up the hive in my truck and drove home gingerly. With a beehive sitting in my rear-view mirror, I took all the well-made roads home. Thanking my lucky stars there were no disasters on the way, I pulled into the drive and headed out the back, just near the veg garden. I lifted the heavy hive off the truck and sat it, as I was told to, facing north with a slight incline so rainwater could run off. I unclamped the frame and waited a good while for the bees to settle before I gently pulled off the tape covering their entrance.

From a safe distance of a few metres, I watched as the first bee popped its head out to investigate its new home. This first bee was shortly followed by another, then another, until there was a busy coming and going of bees. They're such busy little dudes, with a complex team system that's very admirable. All those bees working together for a common cause, looking out for each other, helping feed and nurture the young. It's a beautiful thing to observe, such community-driven goals. Nature is a phenomenal beast at times. We could learn a lot from bees. Stop being so interesting and get to work pollinating my patch!

I don't know if I'll get much honey. I have to wait until next summer anyway, as they need all the honey they have to survive the winter. I do like honey. I have it in my coffee and tea every day. And more and more, I'm using it as a natural sweetener in cooking. I hope I get the results I'm after, both better pollination and honey for the kitchen. It's uncharted territory for me, and like most things I guess it's just going to take some time to get used to. If it all fails, I guess I'll just have to get another hive and start again. Let's see how we go.

There's not much of a gamble when it comes to raising chickens. When fertilised eggs are activated (i.e. incubated), the odds of getting male or female chicks are about 50–50. That's why I've shied away from commercially grown chickens. The realisation that 50 per cent of the baby chickens born get dumped simply because they're male and aren't viable commercially speaking, is shocking. And look, it's just plain insulting! We males really do have to put up with a lot of rubbish from the ladies, and this treatment is just biased and unfair. Just because the females have the nice breasts and rump, while the males are all muscles and leanness …

Jokes aside, I think you'd agree that the fact that all the baby males get discarded in a dumpster – well, it's just plain shit. So as soon as I found myself living in a place suitable for keeping a few chickens, I set up shop. And yes, when springtime comes and a broody hen sits on the fertilised eggs and activates them, we get 50–50 results. The difference is we allow the roosters a bit more life than just a few weeks. When the guys are 6 months to a year old (teens to mid-twenties in chicken years) I give them the chop.

This year, however, the roosters had other plans. It seems most of them had a death wish! They harassed my egg-collecting girls, and friends and neighbours who came to visit. If only they attacked the unwanted visitors to the house, I'd have kept them a bit longer, but alas they became too much of a problem. I say that in the past tense, because, well, they're no longer with us. They're in our bellies! There was one beautiful-looking white cockerel I called Whitey – I know, witty, aren't I? He looked so strong and beautiful as he grew. With a fine set of tail feathers and a healthy comb, this guy was hot stuff for the ladies.

That is until I started hearing stories from the kids that he'd been chasing them and pecking madly while they stole his girlfriends' eggs. I thought there may have been some 'eggsaggeration' going on, so I let it lie for a while. Until, that is, I saw with my very own eyes the evil-spirited bastard attack the smallest kid. She screamed in fear as his feathers puffed up and he got in the air to attack her. In a second I ran out from the kitchen, grabbed him by the neck, and snap! Twist and wriggle. It all happened so fast. I held the shaking dead bird in one hand and tried to console the screaming child with the other. In any case, that was the straw that broke the camel's back. The boys had to go. All of them. Too much cock in the hen house is bad news for the hens, good news for our bellies!

Cheeky Chicken Calzone

SERVES 2

What you need

1 cheeky cock	a few wild mushrooms, finely chopped (optional)
3 eggplants (aubergines)	salt and pepper, to taste
1–2 tablespoons olive oil	1 Pizza base (page 295)
1 capsicum (bell pepper), roasted	plain (all-purpose) flour, for dusting
handful of thyme	1 egg, lightly beaten
handful of oregano	dried oregano, for sprinkling
200 g (7 oz) ricotta	
50 g (1¾ oz) mozzarella, cubed	
handful of olives, pitted and chopped	

How to make it

Preheat the oven to 200–220°C (390–430°F).

Gently poach the rooster in water for 3–4 hours, until the meat slips from the bones. Allow to cool, then separate all the meat from the bones, chop it into small pieces and transfer it to a large mixing bowl.

Heat a chargrill pan on the stove top over high heat. Slice the eggplants lengthways, drizzle them with a little olive oil, then grill them on the chargrill pan, slice them into small pieces and add to the mixing bowl.

Grill the capsicum on the chargrill pan until soft, then slice it and then add it to the mixing bowl.

Pick all the thyme and oregano leaves from the stems, then chop them and add to the mixing bowl with the cheeses, olives and wild mushroom, if using. Season with salt and pepper, and give it all a thorough mix.

Roll out the pizza base on a lightly floured bench to 1 cm thick, spoon a wad of the mixture onto one half of the base, then fold the other half over and seal it by pressing the edges with a fork. Brush with beaten egg and sprinkle over some dried oregano to be a bit old-school.

Bake for 25–30 minutes, or until golden.

Big star sky

In the witching hour, I wake. Most nights. It's a bit annoying, but it's part of my nightly routine. When I was a stressed-out dude living in the city, I could never get back to sleep. These days I'm a little more fortunate. I think my lifestyle choices are paying off. But I digress.

Often around 3 am I hear the pitter-patter of Henry's paws down the hallway, which signals that he needs a trip outside. I swing out of bed and take him out. Some nights there's a howling wind coming up the valley, and the big old oak and cedar trees bend to and fro with the mighty gusts. Sometimes it's still, scary still. I say scary, because more often than not it's windy here, so a still night feels out of place. When it's calm here I feel like something's about to happen, even when it's not. My first reflex when I get outside is to look up. The Milky Way can be clear and bright, stars and planets shine brightly, and the moon – wow, when it's in full swing it's ethereal. When these nights come, I drift out barefoot onto the grass for a better vantage. You have to take these opportunities as a gift. I'm sure we're meant to treasure this view. It's what can remind us of our reality, our place in the universe.

It gets me thinking, under those night skies. Are we the only animal that looks up and says wow? I'm not sure, but I do know we're the only animal on the planet with the ability to understand our true place. We have a sense of existence, a sense of consciousness. It gives us the ability to know right from wrong, or at least gives us the illusion that we know right from wrong. In any case, we can stare at the stars and ask questions. That alone is a precious gift.

So if that's the case, then why don't we (that is, most Westerners) ask questions about how we're treating this beautiful world? I mean, if we can look at the stars and at the same time have our feet firmly planted on the earth's surface, which we acknowledge is part of a larger system we're gazing at, you'd think that this understanding, this powerful observation, would make us care more about the earth we're living on. Am I thinking this way because it's 3 am and my mind's a bit wonky?

I often lament at the thought of future humans looking back at us. I'm sure we won't be known as a spiritually enlightened bunch of people. I think, unfortunately, we'll be remembered simply as consumers. More than ever we're dazzled by wealth and the bits and pieces we can purchase and collect. A few cultures, however, are thankfully carrying the torch. Some of the poorest people in the world, with maybe a bowl of rice for their daily meal, are some of the happiest. They have very little yet feel so very content, while we Westerners have so much, yet are burdened with such discontent. We're popping antidepressants like popcorn at the movies. We're living lives that take a heavy physical and mental toll on our bodies, and to cope with that we're medicated with tablets to keep us together. I know this because I was that person. I had dangerously high blood pressure from a combination of stress, smoking, drinking, eating salt-rich processed foods and living a sedentary existence. When my GP discovered this, he prescribed me medication immediately, as he did for my anxiety and depression. That's his job. He's a good GP. And it's not his fault that I'd dug myself into a shitty way of living. All he could do was make some suggestions for me to improve my lifestyle, and prescribe me some drugs to keep me alive and improve my state of mind. You may find this an over-share, but as embarrassing as I may find it to reveal this past of mine, it also comforts me now to look back at that version of myself, because it's my greatest personal discovery.

For so many years I felt like the lifestyle options in my middle-class existence were shit. I never really liked my jobs, never really liked the stress and disjointed community. I never liked the drive for a shallow wealth. I consider it a blessing that my poor health made me realise that the lifestyle I was living had the very real potential to shorten my life. So I made changes. I didn't know if they were the right changes but I knew something had to change. I wanted to stay alive. Selfishly. I wanted my kids to have a happier dad, one who'd be around longer than just his mid-forties. I'm not saying that my approach is perfect for everyone, but it's sure made my life and my little family's life a million times better.

At the witching hour, standing outside in my backyard, I can look at those stars now, with my dog pissing next to me, and feel unashamed to be happy and alive. I'm happy to be poorer in wealth but richer in living a more natural and healthy lifestyle. I'm no guru or shaman, but I've experienced a life worth living. The stars told me so.

I reckon one of autumn's great treats is the stubble quail. I find most hunters have their favourite seasonal food to hunt, and for me it's quail. To hunt them is tricky due to their size and speed. You could almost say it's like trying to pin Speedy Gonzales! I use my pointer to find the birds that lie hidden in thick pasture or freshly cut stubble of crops like maize, then the two of us flush them out and off they fly with a flutter of wings. If I lay my shot carefully and with good control, the bird will drop to the ground – another one for the pot, or in this case the campfire grill.

If you haven't tried wild quail before, I suggest you play around, cooking it with minimal flavours, to get a real feel for the taste of the meat. Well, that's what I did anyway. These days, though, I like to mess around a bit, by experimenting with some companion flavours to make life more interesting. Not that quail really needs it, but hey, I'm just having fun.

I'm not sure exactly what it is that's so alluring about cooking over a campfire, but it sure has me hooked. Maybe it's simply that I have so many childhood memories of it that I get all nostalgic, or maybe it's something innate in us humans, so raw and primitive. Either way, it's part of me, and it's probably part of you, too. Try this recipe with a few friends or your kids, all rugged up around an autumn campfire (check your council's fire regulations first) while the birds simmer away and taunt you with their aromatics.

Tip: To spatchcock the birds I use a pair of scissors. I place the under blade through the bottom hole (where I pulled the guts out) and poke it out at the neck. I then cut through the breastplate (sternum) cleanly and open the birds out wide to cook evenly on both sides.

Campfire Quail

SERVES 4

What you need

12 quail, spatchcocked (see tip opposite)

salt and pepper, to taste

1 lemon, quartered

thyme sprigs, to garnish

Marinade

2 jalapeño chillies

1 garlic bulb, cloves separated and peeled

1 teaspoon black peppercorns

3 tablespoons chopped thyme

3 tablespoons olive oil

1–2 tablespoons hot pimentón (Spanish paprika)

pinch of salt

How to make it

Start by making the marinade. Using a large mortar and pestle, crush the chillies, garlic, peppercorns and thyme until the mixture forms a bit of a rough paste, then stir in the olive oil, pimentón and salt.

Rub the marinade all over the birds. Refrigerate them overnight then remove from the fridge when starting the campfire, to allow the meat to get to 'room' temperature.

When the flames have calmed down a bit and a bed of coals has formed, pop the birds on a metal camp grill over the flames. (My grill isn't very technical – it's actually a steel wire shelf from an old oven that works brilliantly as a camp grill. Waste not!)

Turn the birds a few times. They'll take 15–20 minutes to cook, but bear in mind that every fire is different with regard to heat, so check your meat before you pull it off the flame. When you think they look ready, remove one and check it for well-done-ness by piercing one with a skewer or knife. If it drips red, keep cooking for a little longer, until it drips a bit clearer when pierced.

When they're all done, remove them from the fire and rest them on a metal tray for a few minutes. A bit of seasoning, a squeeze of lemon juice, a garnish of thyme, then on to the feasting.

Catsup

MAKES ABOUT 4 × 700 ML (23½ FL OZ) BOTTLES

What you need

2–3 kg (4 lb 6 oz–6 lb 10 oz) ugly tomatoes

60 ml (2 fl oz/¼ cup) olive oil, plus extra for storing

3 large onions, chopped

1 garlic bulb, cloves separated and peeled

125 ml (4 fl oz/½ cup) malt vinegar

100 g (3½ oz/½ cup) brown sugar

1 tablespoon whole cloves

1 tablespoon whole allspice berries

1 tablespoon cayenne pepper or chilli powder

2–3 tablespoons dried oregano

1 tablespoon freshly cracked black pepper

salt, to taste

When I found out how much sugar and other rubbish is in store-bought tomato ketchup, I had to add it to the list of food that I no longer wanted to buy. Over the years I haven't really missed it – I always seem to have some other home-made condiment to fill its shoes. With a box of left-over tomatoes and the year's supply of tomato passata taken care of, I figured why not make a batch. And I've been making it ever since. It's a recipe I reckon will evolve over time, but for now here's what I've been using. It's great out camping with camp-cooked sausages or on crisp roasted potatoes and fries. And the best thing is, you know the contents because you made it yourself.

How to make it

Preheat the oven to 200–220°C (390–430°F).

Halve the tomatoes, place in large roasting tins, drizzle over about half the olive oil and toss to coat. Roast for 30–40 minutes.

Meanwhile, heat the remaining olive oil in a large stockpot over low heat and gently sweat the onions and garlic for about 30 minutes.

Transfer the tomatoes to the stockpot with the onion and garlic. Add the vinegar, sugar, spices, oregano and seasoning, then simmer gently for 30 minutes, stirring occasionally.

Allow to cool a little, then blitz using a hand-held blender. Strain to remove any solids and skins, then transfer to sterilised bottles or jars, leaving enough

room at the top of each for a glug of olive oil for storage. They will keep for at least 6 months in the larder. Refrigerate the sauce after opening.

Sounds gross. Maybe I should have workshopped the name slightly more. So I raised some chicks that turned into roosters, which turned into little mongrel bastards that attacked the kids, so I ended up with a lot of rooster in my freezer – i.e. frozen cock. The roosters sat there while I waited for a bit of inspiration re the cooking approach. Then we had one of those frigid yet stunningly beautiful autumn days when I was out searching for fresh field mushrooms. So successful was my search that I returned home with a laden basket and a happy heart.

In the days that followed, I cooked some mushrooms, gave some to a friend and traded some for a home-made sauce. But I still had

a decent cache, and if I didn't cook with them soon, they'd be funky fungus. This is when the idea came to try cooking one of those classic meals I had vague memories of eating as a kid. Something along the lines of chicken and mushroom casserole? I kinda had the same ingredients. Field mushrooms are closely related to supermarket mushrooms, and a cock is just the male version of a chicken. Surely this could work.

This is actually how many of my meals originate. I look to my old life and try to recreate meals but with one main difference. I source, grow, raise or hunt the ingredients myself. And this one really takes the

cake. It makes use of the male bird, which in the commercial world is discarded as waste, but in my backyard gets to live for 6 months or a year. It's a bit fairer and for centuries it's been a practical way for humans to make the most of something that's, let's be honest here ... unwanted.

Almost everything for this meal comes from my backyard or the surrounding fields. Even the wine is from a local maker. I guess I've realised that I can still enjoy my favourite meals even when I use my own ingredients.

Cock, Leek & Fungus

SERVES 4

What you need

1 year-old cock	180–270 g (6½–9½ oz/2–3 cups) sliced field mushrooms
60 ml (2 fl oz/¼ cup) olive oil	
4 garden-fresh leeks, sliced	couscous, to serve
5 garlic cloves, sliced	salt and pepper, to taste
4 thick slices jamon (pancetta or bacon will work too)	butter, to serve
250 ml (8½ fl oz/1 cup) red wine	

How to make it

Preheat the oven to 170°C (340°F).

Cut the legs and wings off the bird. Heat half the olive oil (a glug) in a frying pan over medium heat and seal all sides of the body, legs and wings, then transfer to a large cast-iron casserole dish.

In the same pan, heat the remaining olive oil over low heat and gently sweat the leek and garlic until they soften. Add the jamon then transfer the lot to the casserole dish with the cock. Deglaze the frying pan with the red wine and add the wine to the casserole dish with enough water to just cover the chicken.

Into the oven with the casserole dish, then drop the temp to 150°C (300°F). After 1 hour, add the mushrooms and stir through, then reduce the temp to 130°C (270°F) and cook

for another hour, or until the meat starts to pull away from the bones.

Remove the casserole dish from the oven, take out the bird and pull all the meat from the bones, discarding the bones. Ladle out 500 ml (17 fl oz/2 cups) of the cooking water and use it to cook the couscous according to the packet instructions. Leave the remaining liquid in the dish.

Return the picked meat to the casserole dish, add seasoning, then set over medium heat on the stove top. Bring to a simmer and reduce the liquid to a sauce-like consistency while the couscous is cooking.

Serve the casserole on the couscous with a dirty big knob of butter on top, because mushrooms and butter are lovers.

Life's short, right? With that in mind, why don't you treat yourself to some fine-o dine-o? And this, my friends, is a pretty easy-to-make meal that gives some pretty rad results. When the hunting season starts again in autumn, the cauliflower is in abundance, and if you're lucky so are the wild mushrooms. I'm still a firm believer that some magic happens when you cook ingredients together that are all in season at the same time. Something just makes it work. Maybe there are food fairies out there who cast magic spells over our food to give the illusion that the seasonal approach to cooking is right. Maybe it's just all that acid I took when I was at uni. Fairies or no fairies, this meal is the business.

Sometimes the early autumn rain isn't so early. Sometimes we've had unseasonably dry autumns – something to do with climate change, apparently. So I'm using wild mushrooms I dried last autumn. If you're not a raving-mad bearded forager, you may go ahead and use dried porcini. It will produce equally good results.

Herby Hare & a Naughty* Gravy

* SERVED ON A HEALTHY ROASTED CAULIFLOWER MASH TO EASE YOUR HEALTH-CONSCIOUS MIND

SERVES 4

What you need

4 hare backstraps

1–2 tablespoons olive oil

Herb marinade

2 rosemary sprigs

4 garlic cloves

1 teaspoon juniper berries

1 teaspoon mountain pepper berries or black peppercorns

3 tablespoons olive oil

salt, to taste

Naughty gravy

handful of dried wild mushrooms, roughly chopped

2–3 tablespoons olive oil

2 onions, finely chopped

4 garlic cloves, finely chopped

125 ml (4 fl oz/½ cup) Pedro Ximénez (Spanish sweet sherry)

90 g (3 oz) fresh chorizo (page 49), diced

1 tablespoon cornflour (cornstarch)

50 g (1¾ oz) butter

salt, to taste

Roasted cauliflower mash

1–2 garden-fresh cauliflower heads

1–2 tablespoons olive oil

handful of parsley (I use curly), chopped

50–100 g (1¾–3½ oz/½–1 cup) grated cheese (I use cheddar, tasty, pecorino, Grana Padano)

juice of 1 lemon

salt, to taste

How to make it

To make the herb marinade, bash the rosemary, garlic, juniper berries and mountain pepper in a mortar and pestle until they form a paste. Add the olive juice, season with salt, and stir together. Rub this all over the hare and refrigerate overnight in an airtight container.

Before you start to make the gravy, soak the dried mushrooms in 500 ml (17 fl oz/2 cups) water for 1 hour. Reserving the liquid, drain the mushrooms and set aside in a bowl.

To make the gravy, heat the olive oil (a generous glug) in a frying pan over low–medium heat and gently cook the onion and garlic. It's important not to have the heat too high, as we want to really take our time cooking here. As the onions start

to cook, add a splash of the mushroom juice. It should smell amazing. Continue the process of cooking out the mushroom juice, letting the onions dry somewhat and then adding more juice until you have about 60 ml (2 fl oz/¼ cup) remaining in the pan. On the last splash of mushroom juice, add the sherry, mushrooms and chorizo.

Mix the cornflour with 250 ml (8½ fl oz/ 1 cup) cold water and whisk well using a fork. Add this to the gravy, then simmer and reduce until you have a fine sauce. Melt in the butter and season with salt.

Preheat the oven to 200°C (390°F).

Now make the cauliflower mash. Rip apart the cauliflower and place in a roasting tin

with the olive juice. Roast for 40 minutes, when the cauliflower should be getting a bit of burn action.

Blitz the roasted cauliflower in a bowl using a hand-held blender. Add the parsley, cheese and lemon juice, then blitz again until fluffy. Season with salt.

Now cook the hare. Heat the olive oil in a cast-iron frying pan over high heat. Sear the herbed backstraps, turning regularly to ensure they cook evenly. Remove from the heat and allow to rest for a few minutes.

Slice up the hare, sit it on a bed of cauliflower mash and smother it all with naughty gravy.

Eat this with a lover. And wine.

Deer

Imagine shooting something so large that it could fill your freezer in one go! I'm still not in a position to raise large farm animals for meat consumption at this stage, so my next best option is to hunt something large. My options are fairly limited – by law, that is. In reality, though, my options are great. Native kangaroo is plentiful and literally in my backyard. There are more kangaroos in the state of Victoria now than there were before European settlement! The landscape has been hugely altered for agricultural purposes, and the large spread of grass-filled paddocks is heaven for the kangaroo population. Seems logical to be able to hunt them, right? It's no secret out here that farmers, often frustrated with the number of kangaroos eating their crops, 'cull' them, often in fairly brutal hillbilly nights with boozy shooters mowing down the 'pests'. That may sound like a generalisation, but it's more common than you might think. Often the meat is left to rot in the bush somewhere, which is an obvious waste. It's also illegal. In fact, in Victoria it's illegal to hunt kangaroo unless you've been issued a 'destruction order' by the government, which they don't hand out too easily. So politics and hillbillies aside, I have to accept that I can't shoot the most sustainable source of red meat around, so I have to look for other alternatives.

The next best option is deer. Deer were introduced to Australia for game-hunting but in many parts they seem to have become a bit out of control, with populations getting big enough to warrant culls in some districts. There's a number of different species – sambar, red, fallow and hog deer. Fallow are the species in my turf. They're not as common as the roo – they're actually a bit of hard work to find. You can spend three days on a trail and get nothing, and I don't have that kind of time to waste. Coming home empty-handed is always a reality, but it's the lowdown cheap jibes from Kate that are the hardest to deal with.

I'd had deer-hunting on the cards for a while but never got around to it. First, there were the official licences, then finding a rifle that I could afford and justify. But there are only so many rabbits a man can eat, so this year I finally took the plunge. First up I applied for the licence – that was easy enough. The good news, too, was that the population of fallow deer is so high that it's now open season all year round. Next, I had to sort out a new rifle. My .22 Magnum just won't cut it for these big animals, and by law the minimum calibre for hunting fallow is .243 while for red deer and sambar it's a minimum of .270. So I figured, just in case I do get onto a larger species of deer, I might as well be prepared. Practical approach, right? So I settled on a .308. It makes my other rifle look like a toy gun, but it's the right tool for the task at hand. Heavy as all buggery, too!

The government provides guidelines for 'ethical' hunting, and this involves things like giving the animal a sporting chance and not spotlighting deer at night. I'm glad there are guidelines, because everyone's different. I'm not hunting for trophies, I'm trying to source a lot of meat from an animal that's, let's face it, introduced and feral. The only reason it's never described as feral in Australia is that it's considered 'game', and I'm definitely sure I'm not into that kind of thing. I'm probably going to cause a storm here by saying I hunt for meat. If I get a mega-sized deer that's all well and good, but really I'm trying my best to fill the freezer.

As for any new pursuit, I like to ask around and get different opinions and advice from people who know what they're talking about. Not the cowboys who give us hunters a bad name, but the real-deal blokes. I got the impression, after speaking to a few of these blokes, that there's still a bit of the trophy-hunter in most of them – which I don't really understand, but it's not my call. I got all the tips, like pack some good rope, don't wear red, walk at a snail's pace. I also got told that stag meat is pretty poor eating, so just take the head and cut out the back strap and leave the rest. I heard this tip from a few blokes, which kind of disappointed me. Not that the meat was poor eating, but the obvious fact that male deer were being hunted for trophy purposes only. Was this meat so bad that it had no culinary benefits? There was only one way to find out.

I had everything ready to go, my licence and my boom stick. I had yet to set aside a time to get away for a few days to hunt, but it seems fate had other plans for me. The whole deer thing came up in a casual roadside conversation with a friend, who told me they had deer in almost plague proportions where she lived. That settled it for me. Pest animals are high on my list of things to hunt, so the following weekend we headed out there.

Kate and I, accompanied by Henry my English pointer, loaded ourselves into the truck for the trip out bush. The country was drier than I expected – it'd been a harsh summer. The afternoon we arrived, we went out to the bush and spotted deer tracks and scats straight away. In fact, it wasn't long before we spotted a few inquisitive does staring back at us through the grey–blue foliage. There was hope I might get a deer for the freezer after all, even as a total novice.

cont.

We set up a small camp in a dry creek bed, and soon had a fire crackling away and wine in our bellies. That night we slept on the tray of my truck, looking into the abyss of stars. I had no idea what was in store for tomorrow. Would I shoot a deer? Would it die quickly? How would I skin it? 'Shit, I've never processed anything this big before! Will I stuff it up? Is that a spider crawling in my swag?' Eventually I stopped asking myself questions and drifted off to sleepy town.

Morning came with a fresh crispness that helps you spring out of your swag. There's nothing quite as raw as sleeping outside – it makes me feel a bit more real, in touch with the nature stuff. A brew of hot coffee washed down the eggs and chorizo, then off we went. It was still early dawn and the sun was asleep, hanging low in the east. We followed a trail for a few hours, looking for fresh scats and tracks. The deer tracks were amazing. We could see that a few had walked together over wet soil, their tracks as clear as the minute they were made. As it was the time of the rut, I kept my eyes open for rub trees – the males rub their antlers on their favourite tree to remove the velvet.

With all the signs pointing to deer, but no actual deer sightings, we started getting a little downhearted. It was then that I picked up not only the growl of a male but the clank of bashing antlers. Two males fighting! We crept closer as quietly as we could, but the two deer were so preoccupied with their man fight that they wouldn't have heard us anyway. We got to a point where we could just make out the bucks, working to and fro in the bush, growling and clanging with each blow. I felt like David Attenborough on location. What a thing to witness! There were moments when the deer would move further away from us and we'd wriggle behind them trying to get a better vantage point, but we just couldn't get close enough for a safe and clear shot. I could see the deer through my scope but they didn't stay still enough for me to shoot, so I made the call to return to the main track and leave the deer to themselves.

We returned to camp for a civilised break and then headed down another track. We found the same signs of deer, tracks

and scats. We continued on this track, hoping to spot something and making the most of the track being almost free of leaf litter and branches that would give away our location to a deer a mile away. Walking along the track side by side, I got a whack on the arm from Kate. I looked at her as she looked ahead, eyes fixed. She'd spotted a buck standing in the middle of the track, staring back at us. He spooked and headed off to the side to the dense bush, and we followed. My eyes scanned the bush looking for him, hoping for him to be still. And sure enough, out in the distance he stood. He must have been more curious than scared by us. He stood there long enough for me to raise my rifle, chamber a round and take aim. In an instant and a blast the deer dropped to the ground. My entire body was shaky. Kate stayed put as I walked towards the buck. Just like a fish, rabbit or duck it wriggled out its last bit of life before going limp.

I don't think it's an odd thing for a hunter to feel remorse. In fact, if you don't feel it there may be something wrong with you. I stood above the animal, watching blood pour from the wound I'd inflicted. I'd taken this life and it seemed so much more drastic than the small animals I'm used to hunting. This thing was massive. It was a beautiful creature of nature, wild and a bit grand. I felt so bad for having killed it.

Later that afternoon I shot a second deer, this time a doe. It was a productive day with regard to acquiring our meat. I gutted, skinned and butchered both animals, using the same basic principles I'd been using for rabbits and hares (just on a much larger scale). We bagged and labelled every cut of meat. We also labelled

it doe or stag, as I wanted to experiment with this notion that stag meat was near useless in the kitchen.

It turns out there is a slight flavour difference, but if you immediately bleed the stag by stabbing its chest and piercing its heart, the meat will taste normal. You can also soak the meat in water with a pinch of salt to remove the gaminess.

That night we sat around the campfire with our friends who'd invited us to the hunt. Our conversation centred around food and the day's events. I couldn't help but spend most of the night thinking about who I'd become, what I'd done. Years ago, I'd happily eaten beef, lamb, pork and chicken without a moment's thought as to how that meat was raised, what was done to it or how it got to my plate. But now things are different. Now I know the scenes in a meat factory, where the animals hang on conveyor belts getting zapped one after the other. Animals on conveyor belts? It's just insane! What have we become? Cheap meat means corners are cut. Once I realised this, I chose to be more aware and active regarding the meat I eat. So much so that today I had blood up my arms and the unmissable smell of deer on my shirt. The person I've become is well dedicated to a cause. I'm so damn set in my beliefs that I'm now an *active* killer. The old passive me used to outsource the dirty work to some other human in a factory. Although I struggled to comprehend the size of the animal I'd killed that day, I was in some odd way comforted that I'd just walked the talk.

Deconstructed Gnocchi with Venison Bolognese

SERVES AT LEAST 4

What you need

Bolognese

2–3 tablespoons olive oil

3 onions, chopped

4 garlic cloves, chopped

handful of parsley

500 g (1 lb 2 oz) minced (ground) venison

250 ml (9 fl oz/1 cup) red wine

725 g (1 lb 10 oz/2¾ cups) tomato passata (puréed tomatoes)

1 teaspoon smoked pimentón (Spanish paprika)

3 tablespoons chopped thyme

½ teaspoon chilli powder

1 teaspoon cumin

salt and pepper, to taste

Deconstructed gnocchi

1 kg (2 lb 3 oz) potatoes, peeled and halved

200 g (7 oz) butter

60 ml (2 fl oz/¼ cup) full-cream (whole) milk

salt, to taste

One night, a weeknight, I promised the kids gnocchi with a meaty venison bolognese. Most afternoons after the school pick-up, I get distracted with chores and then get to cooking time and have one of those 'Oh shit!' moments when I realise I've run out of time to make the meal for which I had grand plans. This is how this meal was created, from an 'Oh shit!' moment.

Now deconstructed gnocchi is normally something you'd find at a Michelin-starred restaurant. It takes a lot of effort to make and can be quite expensive to order. It's often only attempted by experienced chefs, but I'm happy to share my secrets, as I have a great shortcut.

So what is deconstructed gnocchi? Well, obviously it's derived from the gnocchi plant itself. The actual deconstruction process that chefs tend to use involves laying the gnocchi on a bed of dry ice for 16.5 hours, then using a blowtorch to heat the gnocchi to extreme temperatures until it begins to crumble. It's at this stage that it's transformed into a dust-like state. It's then placed in a rehydrating vacuum machine (very expensive), which turns it into a foamy substance. This foam is then layered on copper trays for refrigeration. When someone orders the deconstructed gnocchi, the chef simply spoons some of that substance from the tray and reheats it in a frying pan (with a glug of olive oil).

Even though it's a simple enough process, I've come up with a much faster method. Instead of making the actual gnocchi, deconstructing it then reanimating it, I simply boil potatoes and mash them. The kids have yet to notice the difference.

How to make it

To make the bolognese, heat a generous glug of olive oil in a frying pan over medium heat, brown the onions for 5 minutes, then add the garlic and cook for a further 5 minutes.

Cut the stems from the parsley (reserving the leaves), and chop them finely, then add to the pan. Add the meat and brown it for a few minutes. Splash in the wine

and cook for another minute or so while you chop the parsley leaves, saving a few as a garnish. Add the passata, pimentón, thyme, parsley leaves, chilli powder and cumin, then simmer for 30 minutes over low–medium heat. Season with salt and pepper.

To make the deconstructed gnocchi, boil the potatoes until they're soft enough to

pierce easily with a fork. Drain, transfer to a large mixing bowl and add the butter and milk. Using a potato masher (you can easily get these from kitchen supply stores …) mash to a soft creamy consistency. Season with salt.

Spoon out a portion of the deconstructed gnocchi, then ladle over that fine bolognese and garnish with the reserved parsley.

Around mid-autumn I tend to stop eating the fresh corn and start to snap-freeze it in bags for winter. In the following cool months, when food can be a bit dull at times, I reckon corn can be a sure heart-warmer. When you bite into a feed of corn in midwinter, it has a way of reminding you of warmer days. That sweet burst of corn is pretty powerful! While the corn is fresh in autumn, though, I love to cook this meal – and it has to be done right, over the hot coals of an outside fire (if your council will let you). Well, look, sure you can cook it inside, or even on a barbecue, but it just feels like more fun sitting around a crackling fire on a late afternoon. When the sun drops and the cool night air of autumn sneaks in, there's nothing like the hot corn and chilli

rub straight from a warm fire. It may be obvious by now that I'm partial to a bit of the hot stuff, so if you're shy of chilli heat, discard the seeds. I know it's hilarious that I'm using smoked pimentón – again! – but this buttery rub just has that Mexican vibe about it: smoky and hot. Hola!

Get the heat up on the fire for at least an hour before you want to cook. This makes a good base of hot coals and provides constant heat for cooking.

PS: I stole this recipe from Kate. Thanks, beautiful.

Mexicorn!

What you need

6–8 garden-fresh corncobs (still wrapped in nature's packaging, i.e. unpeeled)	**The butter rub**
	50–100 g (1¾–3½ oz) butter
grated pecorino, to serve	3 tablespoons olive oil
	1 tablespoon smoked pimentón (Spanish paprika)
	½ teaspoon ground cumin
	2 jalapeño chillies, finely chopped
	salt, to taste

How to make it

Soak the whole unpeeled corncobs in cold water for about 30 minutes. This gets some moisture into the outer leaves so that when the corncobs sit above the flames the kernels inside will steam and cook.

When the fire has been going for a while and has a good body of hot coals, place the corn on a grill over the flames. Cook for about 10 minutes, turning regularly to cook evenly on all sides.

While the corn cooks, mix all the ingredients for the butter rub in a bowl and leave just next to the fire, so that some of the heat starts gently melting the butter. Once the butter has melted, stir all the ingredients together well to make a sauce.

To finish off the corn, remove it from the fire and peel back all the leaves to expose the kernels. Put them back on the fire for about 5 minutes to get a bit of colour on those beautiful corncobs, then serve each one up with a spoonful of buttery rub smudged all over and topped with plenty of pecorino.

I've been making this meal for years but I've never really bothered to photograph it. There are two main reasons for this. First, I think it's just plain ugly – there, I said it. Most stroganoff just looks like a pile of blurp, or is that just me? It's definitely nothing special to look at, and pretty uninspiring to photograph! Secondly, every time I make it, I'm usually busy making love sounds while I shove it in my mouth. It's one of those meals you can cook for years and years and it never gets dull. Sure, it's a bit naughty, but hell, life's short and I want to enjoy myself. Don't you?

There are variations to this meal, and I can't help making them all the time. You can switch the cured meat from chorizo to salamanca, sopressa, pancetta, jamon – anything that's going to share its flavour with the taste sponges that are saffron milkcaps (pine mushrooms). You can also make this with other wild mushrooms, such as field or horse mushrooms. And you can switch your booze from red to white, and from fino to Pedro Ximénez. It all works equally well. It's like a Rubik's cube – so many combinations it can become mind-boggling. I even once tried adding a squeeze of lemon juice at the end, and

Mushstrog

SERVES 2

What you need

1–2 tablespoons olive oil

6–8 large sage leaves

5–10 mushrooms (I use saffron milkcaps/pine mushrooms)

2–3 garlic cloves, finely chopped

2 jalapeño chillies, finely chopped (optional, but go ahead, do it)

50 g (1¾ oz) fresh chorizo (page 49), sliced

a few thyme sprigs, leaves picked, plus extra sprigs to garnish

1 tablespoon fino sherry

1 heaped tablespoon mascarpone

salt and pepper, to taste

sourdough, toasted, to serve

How to make it

Heat a little olive oil in a cast-iron frying pan over medium–high heat with half the sage leaves. Slice the remaining sage leaves and set aside.

While that's warming up, discard the stems from the mushrooms then slice up the caps. Into the pan they go, then cook them for a few minutes until they start to release their moisture. Toss in the garlic, chilli (if using) and chorizo, followed by the thyme and the sliced sage leaves.

After few more minutes of sizzling, splash in a glug of sherry and toss it through – the mushrooms will soak up that flavour pretty quickly. Now add a naughty dollop of the mascarpone and a splash of water to make it all gravy-like.

Season lightly to taste, then serve on sourdough toast garnished with a thyme sprig.

it totally worked. I know there'll be some purist mushroom-lovers out there who'll think this is diabolical and I'm adding too many flavours, blah, blah, but that's the beauty of cooking at home – you can shut the door and keep the turkeys out of your house!

This is the combination I tend to make for those frosty mornings in autumn when I need the kind of spiritual-happiness injection that a good feed like this can provide.

Ownership of self

This morning, before starting any work, I sit in the veg garden, tea in hand. Just still. Everything still. Slowly my mind clears, I admire the superb fairy wren darting in and out of the bushes, through tall trees and around fine-looking rows of vegetables. I can hear the buzzing of busy insects fussing about with daily chores. The gentle breeze caresses my neck and rustles the oak leaves above the garden. It's a peaceful and natural place both physically and mentally.

It's in this space that I can think, my mind clear and free from distraction. My thoughts head to current research about a fella called Edward Bernays. He was the American godfather of propaganda or, as he coined the term, 'public relations'. Edward was the nephew of Sigmund Freud and used some of his uncle's philosophies to manipulate the masses.

The guy was a genius. Learned in the science of psychoanalysis, he believed the population could be kept under control if they were kept happy, content and distracted, that it would keep the mob-animal mentality at bay. So people were under the impression that their lives were happy and content because they were convinced (via the media) that certain stuff would make their lives better. It was the start of the twentieth century, and the beginning of the mad accumulation of stuff and consumerism.

Guys like Edward Bernays used psychoanalytical ideals to 'trick' people into wanting things they didn't need. Edward thought of people not necessarily as individuals, but as a mass to be persuaded. He saw that many people could be manipulated without them even knowing it was happening: 'If we understand the mechanism and motives of the group mind, is it not possible to control and regiment the masses according to our will without their knowing about it?'

Yes, that's a quote. Edward actually thought that way. Presidents, governments and big business employed him to turn twentieth-century America into the biggest consumerist society of all time. That way of managing the masses has spread throughout the Western world. It's no longer an American thing, it's Australian, English, South African, Singaporean. It's a worldwide problem. And it's a very effective way of keeping people in check. We, the people, are so busily distracted that most of us can no longer think past much more than what we desire or want, based on what's presented in front of us. This keeps us content. It might be big houses, flash cars, better job promotions, more money, new-season fashion, it doesn't matter. What matters is that it's distracting our minds from the reality of what life is about. It distracts us from

realising the impact we as individuals have on each other, and the impact this lifestyle of ours has on the natural world. That reality doesn't make money, does it?

It's so easy to be distracted by these things. I know because I was so distracted by them that I was in fact blind to the real reason for living. I worked so hard for more money, a job promotion, a better car, more appliances and new fashion. Not one of these things made me any happier. In fact, most of them just dragged me further into debt. In the back of my mind, I wanted people to think of me as successful because I had these things. I hoped people would think better of me because I ate at a particular fancy restaurant or drank a certain brand of beer or smoked a certain brand of cigarettes. Totally blind was I. Often I wonder what my obituary would have read if I'd died back then. 'Rohan got some good job promotions because he worked hard, he drove a nice car, he owned a lot of stuff, and, oh yeah, he spent $400 on his jeans … so … what a great guy.'

Isn't it amazing that we have this ability *not* to see past the crap? Why is our society driven by the ideals of consuming and public status and perception of wealth? Why can't we base our ideals and goals, personal achievement and success around things and acts that have more spiritual and community value? Like helping each other out, teaching each other, sharing with each other, living with less. What about the ideals of loving all humans and respecting that which supports us, that thing we used to know and respect: Mother Nature?

Are we chained to the mob mentality, just as Edward believed? Do we need to be controlled by the 'smart' people at the top, or can we think for ourselves? More people are asking these questions of corporations and government. How long do we let our society be driven by consumerism when we know it's destructive to the environment? Or do we just turn a blind eye and put trust in the puppeteers holding the strings?

Out here in this garden there are no puppeteers. Just reality. You could wipe all human civilisation into oblivion and here would still be those birds, those plants, those insects all working together. That's the reality. That's what we should respect, that's what we should value. Because without that reality, we won't survive. We need to break free from the cycle of our blindness for the crap. We all need to spend more time in the bush, out in fields and paddocks, on rivers and lakes. We need to feel that reality of nature, to smell it, touch it, hear it. We need to stick those natural experiences firmly in our minds and use them as a guiding force. It will help us make better choices

regarding our consumerism. We need to ask ourselves, 'Do I really need that plush teddy bear hugging a heart-shaped box of chocolates that says "I love you"?' Probably not.

It's not only our future that's threatened. It's the next batch of kids and their kids. Do you ever wonder if the planet will take it if we, the masses of the Western world, continue consuming as we are, hyped up on shopping steroids? All that sucking-dry of natural resources, all that pollution and climate-meddling? There's only so much of each finite natural resource for us to 'plunder'. Only so much the soil can take of intensive agriculture. Only so much pollution the atmosphere can take. I'm not saying never drive a car again, but maybe we should just drive it less. Savvy?

What's at stake is the continuation of humans living the comfortable lives we live. Who knows, maybe people actually want to live in a post-apocalyptic society and go all Mad Max aka Road Warrior. The evidence is here in front of us. We're surrounded by man-made unnatural things. I walk into a shopping mall, totally freaked out by shop after shop of things that won't make anyone's life better. These things we consume, they're slowly killing our natural world, our eyes closed, our greedy hands open to take it all. Perhaps it's time to wake up. Time to realign the goalposts. Time to reduce.

If we saw more of the natural world, if we had a better understanding of nature's importance for our own health as a species, wouldn't that knowledge carry us humans to a new level of consciousness? One where we make more deliberate and informed decisions about what we consume?

I know no one can tell anyone else the best way to live. It's something we need to search for and discover individually. But we need a collective way of thinking regarding the need to withdraw from consumerism's tractor beam. It's a powerful force. There are so many resource-hungry things that we don't think twice about consuming, we just buy frivolously.

I could give so many examples but here's one that immediately comes to mind. I was once given an electric popcorn-maker as a Christmas present. Don't think I'm ungrateful, but I didn't want or need the damn thing (so yes, I was totally ungrateful). First, the themed novelty-printed paper is a damn waste. Humbug! Every time I unwrap a Christmas gift I can't help but be a killjoy and think of all the other people in the world (who celebrate Christmas) ripping paper off some novelty throwaway gift. Imagine all that landfill paper. Imagine all the trees that had to be cut down for that moment of unwrapping.

cont.

Secondly, a popcorn-maker. Fuck. Really? A perfect example of a totally unnecessary electronic item, most of which will just end up in the trash along with the wrapping paper and the lame novelty card. All that plastic, metal and packaging, for what – the 'convenience' of making popcorn with just the touch of a button? Am I too busy to make popcorn using a perfectly good saucepan? How did the Native Americans survive so long without electric popcorn-makers?

That wonderful experience was about a decade ago, but it's firmly planted in my memory of stupid human behaviour. Now, when I walk into a department store to buy socks and undies, I can't help but look at all the unnecessary 'stuff' that fills the shelves. People buy this stuff; they fill their houses with this junk. It wouldn't be a problem if it weren't harming the natural world, but it is. Electric cupcake-makers, licensed merchandise, electric hotdog-makers, festive-season trinkets, Valentine's Day, Australia Day … all crap useless stuff that ends up as landfill but has used more natural resources. And let me tell you, I see it at the tip. As someone who spends a lot of time at tips looking over what people throw away, I see this mess of our society. We're such a wasteful people, blindly consuming without a thought. If we don't wake up, we'll consume until the planet is so unhealthy we'll have only one option: to consume each other's resources and eventually, inevitably each other. Maybe then the planet will be able to breathe again.

It's not like we can't have stuff. It's not that we need to live in tepees and throw spears, although any hipster reading this might like the idea of tepees, arrows and a feathered headdress. I know you may be thinking, 'Where does this guy get off telling me I need to consume less? Does he eat dust and walk around nude?' No, of course not. I'd scare the hell out of everyone. I'm just suggesting that we become mindful, maybe even sensible about what we consume. For example, I used to own thirty pairs of shoes, most of which just gathered dust. I'd look at a new pair in a shop and get sucked in by that consumer tractor beam and buy something I didn't need. I'd buy a new style in fashion shoe because

I wanted to look cool and 'up to date'. Eventually I saw through this. I gave all those shoes to charity, some of which I'd never worn before other than trying them on in the shop. Crazy, right? Now I have a handful of shoes that all serve a practical purpose. A pair of waterproof Bean boots for winter hunting. A pair of steel-cap slip-on workboots for daily use. Some lace-up leather Red Wings for hiking and hunting, and a pair of summer flip-flops. I'm well covered in the footwear department. I'm never without a pair of shoes, and I haven't made any frivolous purchases that require yet more resources to produce. So I hope I've explained my thoughts on reducing our consumerism bug. I know I do go on about it a lot, but don't you think, if we all second-guessed our consumer choices and acquired less stuff, it would make a difference to our environmental woes?

A sad reality is that before Edward Bernays, stuff used to be sold to people based on how long it lasted, how useful it was, how well it was made. Nowadays, much of the advertising is about what the product will do for you, how it will make you feel better, how it will improve your status, but definitely not how practical a service it will provide. And let's face it, cheap manufactured goods just don't last like the stuff from the old days. I know that sounds obvious, but so many things I use are already old and well used, yet they just keep on keeping on.

I value everything now based on its practicality. Will it till my garden for decades to come? Will it shoot harder, longer, faster? Will it last a lifetime, or at least will it give me many years of service as opposed to a year of service? Years ago, I used to buy those Teflon-coated frying pans. The little buggers would only last a year or two and then the seal would be compromised and I'd throw it out and be forced to buy another. I got sick of that so I looked for a better, longer lasting alternative that did the same job. My mum gave me a cast-iron frying pan that her dad had given her as a gift. It's heavy-duty and I guess it's going to last longer than a lifetime. I may need to replace the handle at some stage, though. Often, when applying the practical-thinking approach to stuff, I'll identify

some real benefits. Like the cast-iron frying pan, for example. It cooks better than a thin Teflon pan as its thick metal base retains heat longer and distributes it more evenly. I'm sure Teflon's not a natural health ingredient, either.

The challenge is, though, that we're constantly bombarded with advertising that's trying to convince us otherwise. Take, for example, an advertising spread in a food magazine. You'll be sure to see some famous celebrity chef telling you they *only* use this brand of frying pan because of its technological advancements, blah, blah, blah. But if you walk into that chef's famous restaurant, you'll see the staff using reliable cast-iron or aluminium pans because the reality is that they're harder wearing and a much cheaper alternative. Oh my. We're being lied to? Never!

My cup of tea is cold now and I have chores to do. I've done enough thinking for today. Out of the vegetable garden I go with mind a-buzzing and a heavy heart.

I keep chickens primarily for egg production and as a waste-disposal service. The chooks are happy and well fed. We're supplied with plenty of eggs and our kitchen and garden scraps are converted into chicken poo, which is seasoned and eventually returns to the garden as fertiliser.

Each spring new chicks hatch, and the inevitable result is that half of these are male. Boy chickens are really lame at laying eggs, so we let them get bigger for half a year (or so) and then we eat them, a system that's been in place on farms and in backyards for centuries. At our place, we can't afford to let a single animal go to waste, so we let them mature then we use the meat. Might sound rough, but I think it's a better deal than being able to live for just a few short days in a shed.

On the day I butcher the birds I cook this meal. I've been cooking it for a while now, and I guess it's a way to use more of the bird than just its meat, livers and bones for stock. A lovely American lady called Trish introduced me to the idea of cooking chicken hearts when I ran a workshop. She told me they were a delicacy, and proceeded to show me the basics of how to cook them. Trish poached the hearts then pan-fried them in butter with salt and pepper. They were amazing.

Chicken Hearts

SERVES 1

What you need

6–8 chicken hearts	pinch of chilli powder
50 g (1¾ oz) butter	salt and pepper, to taste
1–2 tablespoons olive oil	parsley, to garnish
Pedro Ximénez (Spanish sweet sherry)	mascarpone, to serve

How to make it

Poach the hearts in water for 20–30 minutes.

Once they're done, melt the butter with a glug of olive oil in a frying pan over medium heat. Pan-fry the hearts until they start to colour, then splash over some sherry, watching out for flames. Sprinkle in the chilli powder and season with salt and pepper.

Garnish with parsley and serve with a good dollop of mascarpone.

I still use the same process to soften the hearts in boiling water, but now I add some naughty stuff to the frying pan.

You need to boil them first to soften them, because the heart is a hardworking muscle. Then it's just a matter of frying them until you're hungry enough to eat them. Don't be squeamish. They taste nice, trust me. And if you've just taken the bird's life, try to use as much of it as possible.

So if you smoke fresh jalapeño it then turns into chipotle? Wow! This was an actual revelation to me. I even think, with regard to my cooking, it was life-changing. I've bought those massive cans of chipotle in adobo sauce and spooned the chilli on top of every second meal. It's addictive, but after a while everything just tastes like chipotle so you have to find some self-restraint. With a half-decent crop of jalapeños in the poly tunnel, I decided to try my hand at smoking these chillies and making my own chipotle. I fired up the cold-smoker and smoked those chillies for ages, 10 hours at least. In the morning I went out to check the smokehouse and the chillies sure smelt smoky, but they were still coloured and moist, whereas they were supposed to be totally dried out. Fail. So the next step was to try to hot-smoke them. I used my converted 44-gallon-drum smoke generator from my cold-smoker (see page 190). I simply took the lid off and placed a wire grill over the top with the chillies secured on top. I smoked them for about 5 hours, continually turning them and checking the coals for smoke. Success! They ended up dried and smoky like bought ones. Victory! I made this little sauce, which is a simple base from which to start. I think every jalapeño season the hot-smoker will get fired up and most of my crop will end up being smoked.

Smoked Jalapeño (Chipotle) Sauce

MAKES ABOUT 2 LITRES (68 FL OZ/8 CUPS)

What you need

2 kg (4 lb 6 oz) jalapeño chillies, seeds in

1–2 tablespoons olive oil

5 onions, chopped

1 garlic bulb, cloves separated, peeled and chopped

725 g (1 lb 10 oz/2¾ cups) tomato passata (puréed tomatoes)

¼ cup smoked pimentón (Spanish paprika) (to be sure of smokiness)

60 ml (2 fl oz/¼ cup) white vinegar, plus extra to taste

50 g (1¾ oz/¼ cup) brown sugar, plus extra to taste

large pinch of salt

How to make it

Hot-smoke the chillies (see opposite) and watch them magically turn into chipotle. Remove the stems.

Heat the olive oil in a large heavy-based saucepan over low heat, then gently sweat the onion and garlic for 30 minutes. Add the passata, pimentón and chipotle. Increase the heat to medium and simmer for 30 minutes.

Remove from the heat, allow to cool slightly, then blitz to a fine purée using a hand-held blender. Strain to remove the pulp and seeds, then return to the saucepan and to the stove top. Add the vinegar and sugar, then simmer to reduce and thicken. Season with salt.

You might like to add more vinegar or sugar to suit your taste.

Pour into sterilised bottles or jars. They will keep for a few months in the larder. Refrigerate after opening.

Years ago I visited a Polish deli and bought a slab of double-smoked pork belly, and I was done for. I sliced that smoked pork into little bits and added it to almost every meal until it ran out. I've been wanting to figure out how to make it ever since. One of the drivers for the construction of my cold-smoker was the idea of home-smoked bacon. But before I struck a match I had to learn how to make bacon.

Bacon-making was also a mystery to me, but it didn't take very long to figure out how to make it. The basic principle is to cure the meat using salt, which will draw out the moisture, then to add some flavour or sweetness in the form of spices, honey or sugar. I've experimented with spices and such, but as usual I've ended up favouring the basic flavours, especially now that I use pork from pigs that have been raised well. I have a friend who's a pig farmer and he raises a pig for me each year that I butcher myself. If you want good bacon, invest in an ethical pig farmer. There seems to be no shortage of those these days, which is a real victory for people who give a shit about the way their meat is raised.

A bit of effort goes into lighting the large smokehouse, so it's best to smoke a bunch of stuff at once. Before I fire up mine, I like to have ready some cured trout, jalapeño chillies, pork belly, sausages, pork loin and even some garlic. It is, after all, the practiculture approach.

Cold-smoked Bacon

MAKES 2–3 KG (4 LB 6 OZ–6 LB 10 OZ)

What you need

1 × 2–3 kg (4 lb 6 oz–6 lb 10 oz) side of pork loin	100 g (3½ oz/½ cup) brown sugar
250 g (9 oz/1 cup) salt	apple wood

How to make it

Trim any loose bits of meat from the loin, leaving the skin on. Coat the pork evenly with the salt and sugar, then seal in an airtight container and refrigerate. Once a day for 9 days, flip the pork over to allow the moisture to drain.

Rinse the loin thoroughly under cold water then pat dry with paper towel. Refrigerate the pork, uncovered, overnight to allow a pellicle (sticky film) to form.

Cold-smoke the bacon for 12 hours with apple wood.

The temperature of the smoke shouldn't be too hot or it will start to cook the meat.

When the smoking has finished, cut the skin off and slice for cooking.

I've not met many people who don't love cold-smoked trout or salmon. I know they're out there, but I've yet to meet them. Cold-smoked salmon was something I loved buying from the supermarket and using in salads, breakfasts or simply throwing in my gob whole. Cold-smoked trout is even better, but was always harder to find. I've been hot-smoking trout for many years now and I still love to do it, especially in summer after a successful fish. Cold-smoking had been a bit of a mystery to me, until I built myself a large smokehouse. I cut down a heap of weed pine trees and built a little log cabin that would serve a few purposes: smokehouse, kids' cubby and somewhere to camp out, albeit rather smoky at times. I designed it as a cold-smoking facility, with smoke piped in from a smoke generator (44 gallon drum) at a distance that would allow the smoke

to cool before touching the meat, cheese, chillies or vegetables. The difference compared to hot-smoking is that meat isn't actually cooked by the smoking process as it's already cured. Instead, the smoke acts as a flavour enhancement and extends the use-by date of the food. Smoke has curative powers of its own, and has been used by many cultures around the world for centuries.

I tried cold-smoking trout a few times in the new cold smokehouse with terrible results. I was so distracted by getting the amount of smoke right that I always forgot to cure the fish and the end product would just be dry and smoky-flavoured, but smoky-flavoured like tongue-kissing a trout with a pack-a-day smoking habit. I went back to the drawing board and took time to brine the fish and allow it to dry and finally for it to form this special gooey layer called the pellicle.

Cold-smoked Trout

MAKES 1 SMOKED TROUT

What you need

3 tablespoons salt

3 tablespoons brown sugar

1 whole trout, butterfly filleted

How to make it

Sprinkle the salt and sugar evenly over both sides of the trout. Seal in an airtight container and refrigerate for 2 hours.

Rinse the trout thoroughly under cold water, then pat dry with paper towel. Leave on a wire rack in the fridge (uncovered) to dry overnight. This is the crucial step, as it will form the pellicle, the sticky skin to which the smoke will adhere.

Fire up the smokehouse and hang the fish inside. Keep the fire stoked and smoking for a minimum of 10 hours. The temperature of a cold smoke should really be no higher than about 50°C (120°F) – the idea is to allow the smoke to cool before it reaches the meat, so it won't cook it but simply smoke it.

Note: *Also use this process for freshwater eel.*

This was the missing step that made all the difference. And once I incorporated that crucial step, my trout ended up magnificent!

Firing up the smoker returns in autumn. In summer it's out of the question, due to the risk of starting a grassfire in the field. In late spring I've been known to smoke a lot and bag and tag for the coming summer, when the smokehouse is banned.

These instructions are for one fish, but practically speaking I tend to wait until I have at least five or ten to fire up the large smokehouse. Oh, and like everything in this book, this is a guide only. You can add heaps of different spices if you like.

Thyme-crumbed Quail with Roast Beetroot Mash

SERVES 2

What you need

3–4 garden-fresh beetroot (beets)

60 ml (2 fl oz/¼ cup) olive oil, plus extra for drizzling

handful of dried thyme sprigs, leaves picked

100 g (3½ oz/1 cup) Toasted sourdough breadcrumbs (page 293)

salt and pepper, to taste

plain (all-purpose) flour, for dusting

2–3 eggs, lightly beaten

6–8 quail, quartered

oil, for shallow-frying

1 tablespoon balsamic vinegar

handful of basil, chopped

Quail isn't something I eat all the time – it's definitely an autumn treat. My pointer and I hunt for quail over the wet fields of stubble. My dog does most of the work; I just try to keep up with him as he leads me on point to a bird. A pointer is the perfect dog for this kind of bird-hunting, as the quail are so tiny we're hard-pressed to see them, but the dog will sniff them out and then stand on point with a bee-sting tail and a flattened posture. He'll stand like that, dead still, until I catch up from maybe a few hundred metres behind him. We then flush out the bird and I'll take aim with the shotgun. The pointer is also excellent for retrieving the fallen bird. By the end of a hunt, we're both exhausted and sleep heavily in the warmth of the campfire. I love to cook quail over the coals of a campfire, but I also love cooking with this delicious bird in the kitchen once I've returned home.

Quail-hunting season is in autumn, so I like to use the root veg that's growing in my garden at the time, and right now I have plenty of beetroot. I also have plenty of fresh herbs and a bag of quail. This is going to be a nice fresh meal for two.

How to make it

Preheat the oven to 200°C (390°F) and grease a roasting tin.

Wash the dirt off the beetroot, cut off the leaves (good for the chooks) and slice the beets in half. Toss them in half the olive oil and arrange cut side down in the prepared roasting tin. Bake for 45 minutes, or until soft enough to pierce with a fork.

Meanwhile, mix the thyme with the breadcrumbs and season with salt and pepper.

Line up three bowls on the bench: one with the flour, one with the eggs and one with the thyme breadcrumbs. Dust each quail piece with the flour, then dunk in the egg, then coat in the breadcrumbs.

Heat the oil in a heavy-based frying pan and cook the quail pieces on both sides until golden brown, working in batches if necessary and laying them on paper towel to drain off any excess oil.

When the beetroot is cooked through, mash it in a bowl and mix through a splash of balsamic vinegar, the remaining olive oil and the basil (reserving a little as a garnish). Season to taste.

Serve the quail on the mashed beetroot, drizzled with olive oil and garnished with the reserved basil.

I'm totally stealing this one from Kate, but it's too tasty not to share. I don't know the story behind it – I wasn't listening, I was eating and moaning. The nutty mushrooms are good, but it's the gently cooked sweet onions that make this recipe. Like any pie, it's really all about the filling. You can't really go wrong with puff pastry, and no I don't make my own, I buy it from the shop. If I had a gazillion hours spare I'd make it, but the reality is that we only have so many hours in the day. I think picking the mushrooms, growing the onions and sage, and foraging for the mountain pepper berries is enough effort. Oh, I didn't fashion my oven from scrap metal either – it too was purchased. Lame humour aside, please try this recipe in autumn. It's now become a family favourite, which tells me it's pretty good. And the best part is, because it's one of Kate's special recipes, I can sit back and let her cook it. I just eat it. Hurrah!

Kate's Magical Forest Mushroom & Onion Pie

SERVES 4

What you need

1–2 tablespoons olive oil	1 tablespoon balsamic vinegar
3 large onions, chopped	1 sheet ready-made puff pastry
4 garlic cloves, chopped	50 g (1¾ oz) blue cheese
180 g (6½ oz/2 cups) chopped wild mushrooms (typically Kate would use a mixture of saffron milkcaps/pine mushrooms, wood blewits and slippery Jacks)	freshly cracked mountain pepper berries
	1 egg, lightly beaten
	poppy seeds, for sprinkling
50 g (1¾ oz) butter	10–15 large sage leaves
pinch of brown sugar	

How to make it

Preheat the oven to 180°C (360°F).

Heat a glug of olive oil in a cast-iron frying pan over low heat, and gently cook the onion and garlic for at least 30 minutes. If the pan starts to dry out, turn down the heat if you can and keep adding a little splash of water and stirring through so the onion doesn't blacken and burn. Cooking the onions slowly like this will bring out a magnificent sweetness.

Add the mushrooms and the butter and cook until the mushrooms soften. Stir through the brown sugar and vinegar, then remove from the heat.

Line a baking tray with baking paper, then lay the sheet of pastry on top. Spoon the mushroom and onion mixture onto the middle of the pastry then fold in the sides of the pastry to make an open pie.

Crumble over half the blue cheese and crack over a generous amount of mountain pepper berry.

Brush the pastry with the egg and sprinkle over the poppy seeds.

Bake for 20–30 minutes, or until golden brown.

To serve, crumble over the remaining blue cheese and garnish with sage leaves. Nom nom.

Bottled summer, in autumn

I just got a message from a mate – some fruit is ready for picking in his orchard. The fruit season has started! It's the season for preparing fruit for preserving and for wrinkled hands. Most of the fruit I want is in season from early spring to autumn. I don't know of much fruit being in season in the middle of winter. I'm sure it exists somewhere, but I'm interested in the summer fruits. And just like the summer veggies that I grow in order to eat in winter, there's a selection of summer and autumn fruits we collect for winter tucker. Before I bang on about fruit and how rad it is, I should make it clear that this is something I do more for Kate and the kids. I don't really like fruit that much. In fact, I don't even have much of a sweet tooth – I prefer vegetables. But the kids love fruit, and I feel like it's my duty to provide them with the food they need (or want). Having said that, I'm pretty sure I once had some sort of epiphany with a warm peach pulled straight from a tree.

For years I'd only eat bananas and maybe the odd apple from the supermarket. I tried buying other fruits but it was a real shit fight to eat them. I never liked the taste, the smell or the texture. I really had to force myself to eat fruit. It sucked. The watermelons were too watery, apples were too floury and smelt funny, bananas could make me gag. I'd eat a few grapes (with cheese) and the odd plum. I sound like an anti-fruity. And you're right! I really hated fruit.

Things have changed, though, and I can tell you the one reason why I'm now eating real fruit, pulled from a tree, branch or vine with my own two hands. What's the difference, you ask? Well, there was that peach epiphany. A bunch of us were at a friend's little orchard and he was offering me different varieties of plums and such, when we came across this beautiful peach tree. Now I'd never been much of a peach eater before – maybe processed peaches from a tin, but never straight off the tree. This peach was soft and furry. It was still warm from the sun's heat. It smelt amazing, so good that I wanted to snuggle up with it. When I finally broke into the flesh, peach juice squirted everywhere! This warm juice dribbled through my beard then down my neck. The flavour was sweet and warm, unlike any fruit I'd eaten before. I groaned a little.

Where had this fruit been all my life?! Why had I been deprived of such an experience?! It was only a peach, for fuck's sake, but man, was it a joyous occasion! I immediately picked another and devoured that too. Then asked if I could pick more to take home. After his reluctant 'Yes, but don't pick too many, these are my favourite', I gathered a few in my basket to take home. I did have the intention of bottling a bunch of them for later, but they didn't last long enough.

So here started a bit of a change in the way I viewed fruit. Instead of saying no to trying it, I'd say yes if the fruit was either on the branch or on the ground. I discovered a few things I'd been missing all these years. Freshness is an obvious one, but variety is what makes the whole fruit experience so much more interesting. Take pears, for example. At the supermarket there was one variety, maybe two on offer, but in a home orchard there could be ten or more to choose from, each one different in taste, and texture too. I never used to eat pears, but now I love them at the peak of the season. And instead of those hard mega-crisp unripe pears, I let them get all juicy and ripe over a few weeks, and roasting them brings out a whole new level of sweetness. Sometimes the girls and I will delicately peel a few very ripe pears and slice them, each taking a sliver one at a time – they're juicy and sweet. Never had I experienced a pear like this before, but to some extent I'm now hooked, even though I still like to say I'm not a sweet tooth.

So the news that the fruit season has commenced has me excited. Last year we picked huge amounts of fruit, some from wild trees, some from country roadsides and some from friends' backyards. The season tends to start with the berries, nectarines, apricots and plums, then peaches and pears, then finishes with many apples. There are so many varieties, and each will be ripe at a different time of the year, so if you plan your orchard well you can have fruit to eat from mid-spring to late autumn. Much as the fruit supply is great during these seasons, however, it's in winter that the kids want the fruit the most. I guess it's the age-old situation of wanting the thing you can't have. There is, however, a way around this, and that is vacuum-sealed glass jars. For years the system of putting food in

jars and boiling them to create a vacuum seal has kept people's food stores balanced. There's something amazing about the simplicity of this approach, because it requires no preservatives. Just fruit, water and a hint of sugar, and the latter is optional.

This season hasn't been so favourable for fruit-growing. The summer has been exceptionally dry, and a few extreme heatwaves stressed the plants so much that they dropped a good number of their flowers. Fewer flowers means less fruit. We start off with a few buckets of berries, then we move on to the larger fruit. The plums get a bit of the spicy treatment and are stewed with cinnamon and star anise. The pears, apricots, nectarines and apples are all simply stoned or cored, peeled and popped in the jars. (See page 122 for more specific instructions). We use a very light sugar syrup, as this real fruit tends to have a bit of sugar in it and we don't want to overdo that sweetness – and yes, sugar isn't that good for you. Moderation is the key.

I keep an old canvas bag in the back of the truck just in case I spot a lost fruit tree in the bush, on the roadside or in a field where an old-time farm settlement once existed. Some years I've found more fruit than I know what to do with, but this season is not one of those years. I'm not complaining, though. We've squirrelled away some nice fruit for winter and had enough to enjoy some now, fresh off the tree.

The best fruit this season was the wild pears, which I've picked two seasons running now. I found a pear tree on a roadside in the middle of nowhere that had a few kilos of fruit hanging from it. The first year I picked the fruit and allowed it a few weeks to soften and ripen to the point that they were the juiciest pears I've ever eaten. This year I returned, eager to see if I'd be the first to pick this bounty. With luck on my side, I found the tree untouched, full of fruit. I wondered if this fruit has been waiting for years for someone to enjoy it. Maybe no one knows about it. Which is a bit sad, really, because it's such a great experience to discover and use such a gift from nature. It's like finding money on the ground, but way more useful. I later found out that a friend also knows about this tree, and so next autumn this will be a challenge for the both of us. Who will get there first?

I had a heap of green jalapeño chillies and I wanted to make something different from a Salsa picante (page 113), so I tried a fermented sauce. Sometimes when you have to use an ingredient you have lots of you're forced to learn a new skill. Fermenting chilli to make a sauce was never really part of the plan, but I think I'll make a batch each year now. I may even take it up a notch and smoke some chillies before fermenting them. Who knows what might happen? I love that about food – there are no rules, you just give it a go. This type of sauce will take a few days to make, as you need to allow fermenting time, but like all good things, it's worth the wait.

This sauce works just as well in food that you'd normally use store-bought sriracha for, but minus the preservatives. It works really well with Pork & ginger pot stickers (page 280). Next year, I'm going to try this recipe with red chilli and see if it makes a difference in sweetness. But for now, green will do the job.

Green Sriracha

MAKES ABOUT 1 LITRE (34 FL OZ/4 CUPS)

What you need

1 kg (2 lb 3 oz) jalapeño chillies, ends removed, seeds in

2 garlic bulbs, cloves separated and peeled

50–100 g (1¾–3½ oz/ ¼–½ cup) brown sugar

1 tablespoon salt

250 ml (8½ fl oz/ 1 cup) white vinegar

1 teaspoon xanthan gum

How to make it

Blitz the chillies, garlic, sugar and salt in a food processor.

Transfer the mixture to sealed glass jars, then once a day for 5–7 days, remove the lids to stir with a clean spoon.

Turn the mixture back out into the food processor and blitz again, this time adding the vinegar.

Strain through muslin (cheesecloth) into a saucepan, discarding the seeds and pulp.

Heat the strained sauce, add the xanthan gum and cook, stirring frequently until the sauce thickens. Pour into sterilised bottles and seal.

The sriracha will keep for a few months in the larder. Refrigerate after opening.

Melty Lamb Ribs

SERVES 4

What you need

1 garlic bulb, cloves separated and peeled

2–3 tablespoons olive oil

juice of 1 lemon

handful of rosemary, leaves picked

salt and pepper, to taste

1 kg (2 lb 3 oz) lamb ribs

I have no idea why these things aren't really popular to cook with. I've never seen them in the window of the butcher's – have I not been looking hard enough? In fact, I'd never cooked with them until I broke down a lamb with my mobile butcher. He cut up the flaps (belly) and ribs then said, 'Have you got a dog?' Bugger the dog! I was going to eat those ribs!

Slow-cooked ribs done right are a really fun meal. You feel like a caveman, holding that massive rib and gnawing off the meat. I think I must look extra Paleo when I eat these things. But don't be fooled, I'll probably eat bread and everything else non-Paleo soon after. Real food, dude, that's all we need to eat.

Once you've cooked this caveman-style meal, you'll never feed your dog lamb ribs again.

How to make it

Preheat the oven to 200°C (390°F).

Crush the garlic to a thick paste in a mortar and pestle. Add the olive oil and lemon juice, stir in the rosemary, then season with salt and pepper.

Rub this marinade all over the ribs, then wrap them in aluminium foil.

Transfer to a baking tray and cook for 30 minutes, then turn the oven down to 150°C and cook for a few hours.

Remove from the oven and have a sneaky look under the foil. Once the meat comes off the bone easily, allow the ribs to rest on the bench for 10 minutes.

Devour.

It's now cold enough to warrant the fire being lit. I'm wearing a few extra layers and the autumn rain has me dusting off my old Bean boots. It's a pretty wondrous time of the year. It's the season when I spend more time walking tracks in the forest, hunting for mushrooms. I make an effort to explore new territory, walking over hills I've never walked before, searching for new spots where the mushrooms are plentiful and the scenery pleasing. I love to take a rest on fallen logs blanketed in pine needles and browned oak leaves, and just sit and listen to the forest. The wind blowing gently high in the tree canopy above, the birds making busy all around – and the distant hum of two-stroke motorbikes completely ruining my serenity.

I love a good bruschetta with wild mushrooms, I love them stuffed and covered in melty cheese, in risotto and pasta, and especially in a heart-warming soup. When I'm out hunting autumn ducks and quail, a hot thermos of mushroom soup can brighten up a dreary autumn day. Just remember to pack the crusty bread to mop up all that goodness.

Peppered Wild Mushroom Soup

SERVES 4

What you need

2–3 tablespoons olive oil	1 litre (34 fl oz/4 cups) Home-made chicken stock (page 294)
3 onions, chopped	
4 garlic cloves, chopped	1 teaspoon freshly cracked mountain pepper berries
handful of either rosemary, sage or thyme (they all work well with these mushrooms)	1 teaspoon chilli powder
	salt and pepper, to taste
50 g (1¾ oz) butter	250 ml (8½ fl oz/1 cup) pouring (single/light) cream
500 g (1 lb 2 oz) saffron milkcaps (pine mushrooms), chopped	aged cheddar, grated, to serve
500 g (1 lb 2 oz) wood blewit mushrooms, chopped	freshly cracked black pepper, to serve

How to make it

Heat a generous glug of olive oil in a large saucepan over medium heat and brown the onion and garlic. Add your herb of choice and cook for a minute or two to flavour the onion. Melt in the butter.

Add the mushrooms and stir until well softened, adding extra olive oil if needed. Once the mushrooms are well cooked, add the stock, mountain pepper berries and chilli powder, then simmer over medium heat for at least 30 minutes, stirring occasionally.

Remove from the heat and allow to cool a little, then blitz to a soft purée with a hand-held blender. Season with salt and pepper, then add the cream, return to the heat and simmer gently for a further 5 minutes.

Serve with cheese and cracked pepper.

I never thought I'd love eating pink pasta. I like squid ink pasta, but that's acceptably way tougher, being black and all. But pink, come on! Just kidding, I'm totally fine with pink food, especially when it's pink because home-grown beetroot is involved. Like much of the food I make for the family, this meal came about from trying to use leftovers. I had some beetroot I'd poached with a salad in mind, but I'd cooked too much, so they were just lying around, waiting for me to do something useful with them.

I made the kids a pasta with mashed beetroot and it went down so well I've been making it ever since. It's got everything in it the kids like – lots of cheese, pasta and pink. Well, actually, not all four of the girls like pink things. In fact, only one does. I thought all little girls liked pink and princesses, and were tidy. I was way off!

Pink Pasta

SERVES 4 HUNGRY KIDS

What you need

4 garden-fresh beetroot (beets)	90–180 g (3–6½ oz/ 1–2 cups) grated pecorino
handful of basil, chopped, plus extra to garnish	salt and pepper, to taste
1–2 tablespoons olive oil, plus extra for drizzling	soft goat's feta, to serve
500 g (1 lb 2 oz) Pasta (page 295)	

How to make it

Poach the beetroot in water until they're mega-soft, so soft you can pierce them easily with a fork. Strain and allow to cool, then peel off the outer skins and pop the beetroot in a mixing bowl.

Add the chopped basil and a glug of olive oil, then blitz with a hand-held blender until you have a pink beetroot paste.

Meanwhile, cook the pasta until al dente, drain, then return to the saucepan it was cooked in. Add the pink sauce and the pecorino, and stir through.

Season with salt and pepper, then serve with soft goat's feta, a drizzle of olive oil and a garnish of basil. No Barbies at the table, please.

A dear mate of mine heads to western Victoria for a week each year with his .222 rifle and a set of empty iceboxes, hoping to stock up on wild goat. The animal is in plague proportions out west, where the resources are perfect for their prosperity. It's dry, rugged terrain with vegetation pasture-grazing animals like sheep and cattle aren't interested in feeding on. But goats are browsers – they eat down and up, which widens their range. Out west there are large farms with minimal fencing, which allows the goats to spread far and wide. Eventually, as the population rises, the farmers allow hunters to cull and harvest the goats.

This is where my mate comes in. I haven't yet been admitted into his wild-goat-hunting party, but in the meantime I'm happy to receive the odd leg of goat from him. The first time Kate cooked this meat we ended up in a bit of food hilarity. The leg slow-cooked all day, the aromatics sending us wild the whole time. When it was pulled out of the oven for dinner, the whole family gathered around in the kitchen and we feasted immediately, devouring the entire leg in moments.

Melty Goat Leg

SERVES 4

What you need

1 wild goat's leg	3 tablespoons ground turmeric
100–150 g (3½–5½ oz) butter	6 garlic cloves, crushed
3 tablespoons ground cumin	salt and pepper, to taste

How to make it

Preheat the oven to 120°C (250°F) and allow the leg to get to room temp.

Make a paste by mixing the butter, spices, garlic, salt and pepper.

Using a sharp paring knife, make many incisions in the meat. (You'll find the number of stabbing incisions will vary depending on your mood. Calm mood equals few incisions. Stressed mood resembles a Hitchcock murder scene. The idea is that the cuts will allow the butter rub to penetrate and add more flavour to your leg. Well, the goat's leg, anyway.)

Rub the leg all over with the garlic butter paste then wrap it tightly in aluminium foil, allowing no gaps or chance for moisture to escape. Sit the wrapped leg in a roasting tin.

Cook for 6–8 hours, or until mastication is optional.

It was like of a wolf-pack feeding frenzy. The food didn't even make it to the table. Each time we're lucky to receive a goat leg, we reminisce about our first moment in the kitchen stuffing our faces with tasty wild goat meat. The legs are cooked the same way every time still, but we try to serve the meal at the table now instead of feasting at the door of the oven.

This recipe is so easy I reckon any idiot can make it! Now I'm not saying you're an idiot, I'm just saying that for anyone out there lacking confidence in cooking wild meat, this is the doorway to wild food pleasure land. It's a land where meat is so tender it falls from the bone and melts in your mouth. It's a happy land where dentures are welcome, because mastication is optional. This meat is so tender you could tongue it down to your gut. Some folks out there are sceptics when it comes to getting wild meat tender, and this meal – well, it will open their minds like a weekend hunting trip with Hunter S. Thompson.

Hare is fine meat. It's royal. It's red, dark red like lamb or venison. And the taste sits comfortably between those two meats too. There's a gaminess to the meat, so it tends to hang well with some fruity action, hence my use of cinnamon and nutmeg here, which are also a little fruity – and let's face it, there's nothing wrong with being a little fruity.

This is a perfect feed for when the nights become cooler. It's great for those days when I'm out in the field working on some annoying physical job that leaves me stuffed and hungry by the end of the day. I can drop the stew on around mid-morning and return to working. By evening, when the sun has dropped over the hills and my muscles ache, I can enjoy dinner with no immediate effort other than spooning it into a bowl. That's what I call easy takeaway! I'm usually so lazy I'll just slice bread and dip it into the stew instead of making rice or couscous. So if you have a bit more energy, go ahead and add your favourite carbs. I'll stick with crusty bread and a beard full of man stew. That sounded better in my head.

Idiot Hare Stew

SERVES 4

What you need

1 hare

plain (all-purpose) flour, for dusting

60 ml (2 fl oz/¼ cup) olive oil

2 large carrots, chopped

3 onions, chopped

10 garlic cloves, chopped

1.5 litres (51 fl oz/6 cups) Home-made poultry stock (page 294)

1 cinnamon stick

2 teaspoons ground nutmeg (grate it yourself, you lazy bastardo)

5 garden-fresh rosemary sprigs, chopped

handful of garden-fresh thyme, leaves picked

salt, to taste

small bowl of whole new potatoes, washed (the first spuds of the season – cute little babies they are, too)

parsley, to garnish

crusty bread, to serve

How to make it

Quarter the hare. Don't get the butcher to do it. Do it yourself. It's easy. Just cut around the meat of the legs where the leg joins the body, all the way down to the bone. (Stop cutting at this point otherwise you'll blunt your knife.) Snap the leg off from the joint. See, easy! Apply the same process to the other legs. (While you're there, cut out the backstraps by slicing along the spine and then scraping the meat off the ribs with your knife until you have a tenderloin fillet. Use the fillets in another dish, such as Herby hare & a naughty gravy on page 169.)

Dust the hare legs in flour. Heat half the olive oil in a large saucepan over medium heat and brown the hare legs, then set aside to rest in a bowl, saving any juices that leak out while they rest.

In the same pan you browned the hare, heat the remaining olive juice over low–medium heat, then soften and brown the carrot, onion and garlic. You want the veg just to soften and you definitely don't want to burn that garlic, so keep an eye on the heat. After about 10 minutes, once the veg has changed colour somewhat and softened, add the stock and bring to a simmer.

Add the hare legs to the pan, then stir in the cinnamon, nutmeg, rosemary and thyme, and season with salt. Return the pot to a gentle simmer, not a mega-boil. Simmer for 3 hours, then add the potatoes.

Check every hour for meat tenderness with a fork. If that meat falls off easily then she's done like a dinner.

Garnish with parsley and serve with crusty bread.

Winter

Winter

It arrives one of two ways, either ever so slightly sneaking in the back door, or as subtle as a freight train. This year it was the latter. With gusto and conviction, the wildness of the Central Highlands winter abruptly appeared on our doorstep. On the hill it's either all wind or all calm; rarely is it an even balance of the two. The winter wind can be icy and cruel. It blew fierce for days, removing all but a handful of leaves from the old walnut tree. When the last leaves drop off that tree, we have no option but to accept the inevitable – autumn is over and winter is here.

There are signs everywhere that Jack Frost has moved back in. The cold evenings have killed off all the field mushrooms, which have retreated back into the soil until the following autumn. The chickens have gone off the lay, as they too can sense the change of season and spend most of their days huddled inside their wooden shack, sheltered away from the cold. The garden is again in an obvious state of transition, with some remnants of summer crops looking quite dismal and shambolic, while new crops pop their delicate heads from the soil, green, fresh and ready for a life of cold-season growing. If you've a keen eye you can notice the changes in the paddocks, the sky and the bush. Rabbits start getting frisky, bouncing around each other in mating displays that look more playful than serious. Robins fly down from the colder hills and prance and chirp in our farmhouse garden. The frog calls of winter become more of a ruckus, and frog foam appears sporadically on the still water of the dams. It's a pretty nice time of year.

Although there's a lot of activity for much of the animal world, this here animal uses winter to slow down, recuperate and enjoy the spoils of previous seasons.

I've worked hard for this time. My larder is stocked, my freezer is full, and my kitchen is primed for months of hearty-style cooking. I've spent the previous nine months growing, hunting, harvesting, foraging, preserving, pickling, drying, bottling, saucing, curing, smoking and sorting. Now's the time to enjoy all these food assets I've worked for.

My firewood cache is bulked up with seasoned firewood, which will keep the house fire burning away and the house warm. My boots have a fresh layer of beeswax and new woollen liners. My jackets are dusted off and waxed to offer protection from the elements. Winter is finally here. It's a great time of the year on the hill. I love and appreciate every minute of it.

Little bastards

Almost every day I check on the veg patch. Even in the dead of winter there always seems to be some action going on. To be honest, though, I think the only reason anything grows this time of year is that I'm mentally willing it to grow. It's ridiculously cold on the hill. Cold enough that the frigid wind has blown the leaves off my poor lemon tree. That's not supposed to happen. I have all my garlic in, which has sprouted those little green stems of hope. The onions are in the ground, although I'm pretty sure they'll show zero activity until springtime. The broad (fava) bean crop is ticking along – there's growth but it's at a snail's pace. All the leafy stuff like kale, rainbow chard, rocket (arugula) and silverbeet (Swiss chard) seems to thrive in these conditions, and gets a hammering in the kitchen.

But what I'd really like to see thriving at this time of year is the broccoli. Sure, it's nice to eat the fresh leafy greens, but broccoli feels more like a vegetable, and its arrival hints at the recurrence of slightly warmer spring weather.

Broccoli is one of those vegetables that I seem to plant more of each year. It's a great ingredient that's welcome in pasta and fritters or grilled with chilli for a warming salad. I'm a big fan of the sprouting broccoli because it allows you to harvest a little at a time without killing the plant, as it resprouts and continues to provide food. I do still grow the big boys, though; I can't give up those jumbo florets that are a meal in themselves. My crop has got off to a great start. The seeds all germinated and transplanted happily into the garden. Within those last few weeks of autumn the plants thrived, with new green leaves promising future food for the family. I could almost taste those fritters dipped in a chilli aioli. Then disaster struck. One morning after feeding the chooks I did my rounds and inspected the veg patch. Most of that thriving broccoli crop had been nibbled to the stem, all those leaves needed for photosynthesis now completely destroyed. It's such a shit feeling, a feeling not only of failing the family but missing out on the joy of eating such a great gift from nature.

I got down on my knees for a closer inspection, my jeans soaking up the moisture of wet grass. Fuming with a mixture of anger and sadness I saw the tiny teeth marks of the culprit – a yet-to-be-identified mammal. I know this might not seem like something worth making a fuss about, but in my world it's a big issue. It's bloody devastating. All that effort of propagating the seeds, thinning them out and transplanting them, all so that I have access to pure, chemical-free broccoli. Now it's all gone. I have to start from scratch. But if I planted new seedlings, surely they'd just get hammered again – an exercise in futility, perhaps. And what animal was it that had feasted on my broccoli? I've built the garden with a rabbit-proof fence, so surely they couldn't get in! I checked the entire perimeter like a special forces agent at the White House. No cracks in the perimeter wall, so how was it breached? Maybe the culprit was already inside the 'compound'? Maybe it wasn't a rabbit. My other options were possums, rats or mice. How can I protect my garden from these guys? Impossible! For possums I'd need to fence the entire structure, floor to ceiling! That would cost me a fortune in wire. I'd never seen any possum scats there, nor had I heard them of an evening so, throwing caution to the wind, I placed my bet on rodents. Determined that those little bastards wouldn't get the next round of seedlings, I went and collected a bunch of plastic soft-drink bottles and cut off the bottoms. The bottles could now be placed over the seedlings, allowing air to get in but not mice or rats. I set traps all over the garden in the hope of making a dint in the population of the perps. I kept an even closer eye on the next round of seedlings. I was a veggie-garden security hawk. Over a few weeks I trapped a heap of rats and mice, confirming my suspicions of their heinous crimes. The seedlings are doing just fine in their little plastic bottle enclosures, and although the crop will be slightly delayed, I'm hoping to feast on those broccoli fritters sometime soon. I did wonder briefly what trapped rodents taste like, but it was a fleeting thought.

The mighty wind

My landlady once said to me, 'There's two types of weather here: calm and uneventful or wild and windy.' She should know; her family has owned the land for more than a hundred years. It's true most of the time. I guess that's what you have

to expect, living on a hill that's part of the Great Dividing Range. I can't say for sure which season is the windiest – it seems to be windy when it wants to be windy, which is most of the time – but winter has brought some pretty wild weather this year, wild and scary at times. The last few nights have been particularly bad. I lay in bed listening to the old cedar and oak trees bend backwards and forwards in the fierce wind. These trees are both old and enormous, having been planted more than a century ago. I wonder if one will ever blow down and crush the house. I guess the house has been here since the mid-1940s, but maybe it's just had good luck. There's always a chance, though, and maybe it won't be the whole tree, maybe just a huge limb. Whatever the case may be, it's enough to keep me awake and alert on those extremely windy nights.

When I woke early in the morning, a hot cup of coffee had been placed on my bedside table, steam drifting up from the cup like a ghostly figure. It's amazing how a cup of coffee in bed can make the start of the day more excellent than ever. Only one other thing can make the start to the day perfect. Today I missed out, but the coffee was much appreciated. I rubbed the sleepiness from my eyes and slurped up that warm brew. Before anything was done this morning I had to inspect the carnage from last night's storm. The weather report said we'd had strong wind gusts, but it's always more severe up here. Outside I went, checking both sides of the old farmhouse. A few little branches were down but, again, this house was lucky.

Out into the backyard I went to check the chooks, and it was then that I was greeted with the view of destruction. My beloved new poly tunnel, flattened. The northerly wind had found the weakest part of the structure and after one tube snapped,

others obviously followed and the frame came down. Just devastating. I'd worked hard on that construction, but now it looked like an installation at Tate Modern. I was really proud of what I'd made, but now it was a pile of broken PVC pipe and clear plastic flapping in what remained of the storm's wind. Upon closer inspection, any hopes I had of a patch-up repair were dashed. Too much of the framework had been compromised, and there was a huge rip in the clear plastic. Even if I did repair the frame, I'd have to replace the plastic, as a rip that large could never be held back together with tape.

I had to admit to myself that the gamble of the cheaper PVC version of a poly tunnel was a bad choice. It was one of those moments where there's no point getting angry at yourself, you just have to accept the failure and plant it firmly in your memory so you don't do it again. There was no way I'd rebuild with PVC; my next version would have to be steel. At least that way, when I move sometime in the future, the next poly tunnel will be easy to disassemble and transport to our forever house.

I've not yet pulled the tunnel down. It's still there, taunting me every time I visit the garden. All I've done is crawl inside and harvest the last of the jalapeños and capsicums (bell peppers). I was going to grow broccoli and peas in it over winter, but that experiment will have to wait until next winter.

Got wood?

We have plenty of firewood for now, but I have to admit I'm worried about getting through to spring. For every house I've lived in that's had to rely on a house fire for warmth, I've fretted about making it to spring. It's natural to worry about such things. The very thought of not having a supply of firewood to heat the house on those cold winter days is, quite frankly, frightening. Even when the fire is roaring, it's still cold in some parts of this old farmhouse.

I used to think that it was sufficient to have one year's firewood in stock, but I've changed my view on that. I now like to have two years of stock. I think it's a good approach to have one year's worth of firewood ready to go, all stacked up, dry and neat, and another pile of wood seasoning away a few years in advance. That's what I've been working on lately. There are domestic logging coupes open to the public that have at some stage already been logged and are now thick with copious regrowth. The Forestry Department crews thin out the weak trees to allow the stronger ones to thrive. People like me benefit because we're permitted to go in and clean up the fallen timber. There aren't many of us left who rely totally on firewood for heating, but enough of us still exist for this system to remain in place. There's a town not far from us that only just got connected to the gas mains after all these years. Imagine that in this day and age. Our house is still too far away from gas mains, so we have no option but to rely on a fire for heating.

There's something I love about relying on a roaring fire for warmth. The sounds, the glow and the smell of certain timbers as they blaze away – it's primitive and nostalgic and it's grand. I don't mind burning wood – it's a renewable resource, and if I lived in the city I'd be using gas heating. But I'm not. I'm out here, on a hill, in the sticks. So firewood it is.

This forest

This place hasn't always been my home. I've lived in a million other places – well, that's a slight exaggeration, maybe a few thousand. I was fortunate enough to spend the best of my childhood years living on a little farm at the base of alpine high country. There's no doubt in my mind that my time living there formed the basis of who I am today. I was ten years old when we moved there, and you can imagine how exciting the whole experience was for me. Real farm life! Raising animals, growing food, fishing the river and playing cowboy. I'm obviously not ten any more, but not much has changed; I still love the same things. These days, though, all cowboy action is reserved for the bedroom only.

But that alpine high country, it somehow got into my blood and became part of

me, or I became part of it. I remember fishing the creeks for trout before I was a teenager – the clear water, fresh from snow melt and mountain rain. The forest was actually temperate rainforest, loaded with delicate ferns, grasses and fungi of all shapes and sizes. In some parts the bush is so thick that visibility is limited to a few metres. Just magic. When you visit these places you need to go with your heart open, because one of its roles is to recharge the human soul. This bush and I have a relationship. It doesn't talk to me; it's a one-sided relationship, where I just admire its beauty.

If it were a thousand years ago and there were no cars, houses or iPhones, that forest would be everything to us. This bush has supported Indigenous people for thousands of years. They lived quite happily here. They took what they needed to survive and allowed it to repair itself. The water was pure and drinkable, the animals as they were meant to be – native, wild and free. Since we white people have been here, the bush has taken a bit of a beating. It's now plagued with weeds, it's filled with introduced animals and in places we harvest it for our needs, be it to manufacture toilet paper, house-building materials or woodchips. This forest, all the forests, all the remaining patches of land that have not

yet been molested by humans, are more precious than ever.

It was my affection for this forest, its secret valleys and clear waters that initially got me thinking about living lighter. When I was a kid I dreamt of building a tiny house in the bush and living off fish, mushrooms and wild game. It was the idea of that forest being the source of much of our existence that made me think with a greener attitude. Even years ago, when I worked a corporate job, I'd often pack up my car and camp out there for a few days. It was a recharge that kept me sane.

I know it's a cliché for me to be a lover of trees and forests, but I don't care. It's part of me. In the bigger picture, it's what drives me to step back from the wicked ways I lived, where little care was given to making an effort to live lighter. And yes, I'm aware that growing my own vegetables, blah, blah, blah, won't directly save the forest, but the mindset of living lighter, the concept itself and putting it into action, will reduce other environmental impacts. Having that picture of a pure temperate rainforest in my mind helps me make more deliberate choices in my consumer life. I wonder what difference we could all make if each of us had a forest in our life. Maybe take a walk in the bush and think it over.

White powder

The soft touch of her hand against my face woke me. She smiled that beautiful morning smile that makes the day start just right. 'I'll put a pot of coffee on,' she whispered as she climbed into one of her big woolly jumpers. The wall-mounted hand grinder rumbled through the walls, crushing the roasted coffee beans for the morning's brew. The grinder came to an abrupt halt. A shrill voice cried, 'It's snowing … really snowing!' I sprang out of bed, dressing quickly as if I was late for work. Outside the frosty kitchen window the white powder fell like confetti at a wedding. Thick and fast it was, too. It was just the two of us that morning – the kids were at school and just had to miss out. But we had cameras and we'd do the best we could to capture the moment. Rugged up in jackets, boots and hats, we walked over the property while the snow got thicker and heavier. Before long, the whole place was covered in a good few inches of snow. Everything was white. The light meter in the camera went into overdrive, trying to compensate for the brightness of the snow. We knew it wouldn't last long, maybe a few hours, which just made it so much more important for us to be out in it, enjoying it as a gift from the clouds above.

The hills around us had completely disappeared. I guessed they'd be copping a heavier fall of snow than us. Like ocean waves, the snow blew in, bending and swirling in the breeze. Trees turned white, sheep's backs were covered with icy flakes. My vegetable garden had almost disappeared, but thankfully it was protected somewhat by the large old cypress pines that stand tall in the adjoining paddock.

Although the snow didn't hang around for days, it was very much welcome. There's a purity about it. Everything looks beautiful covered in snow. Just like a Photoshop treatment, even things that weren't that pretty suddenly appear wonderful – a pile of logs, abandoned kids' toys and even a heap of rubbish, all now suddenly pretty. The most beautiful gift from winter.

Pulling the trigger

I've been cooking a lot of deer this winter. In years past I'd only get little trickles here and there from friends or from the local deer farm, but this year, having hunted them myself, I've been blessed with loads of venison. I know hunting isn't everyone's cup of tea, and I'm very thankful for that, but I must say that making the choice to eat mostly meat that comes from hunted animals is quite a deal. It's not the culinary side of things that's the raddest, although saying that I can inform you that venison, when cooked right, is a tasty feed. I'm talking more about the *process* of hunting, which has been the real surprise for me. These two deer in the freezer, for example, they took some work to get there.

Not being self-righteous here, merely hypothetical. What if you had to cut open a large animal's guts, place your hands in amongst the warm organs and rip the entire system out? What if you had your meat animal down the scope and you had to pull the trigger knowing all too well what the consequences would be? What if you thought about the concept that you're killing some creature's relative, a mother doe, a father buck? When we buy meat off the shelf, this hypothetical is nowhere to be seen. It makes buying 'flesh' an easy task, so easy that one could hypothetically buy loads of it without a thought in the world as to how and where said flesh came from. The thing most of us look at on the packet is the price. It's a price that shrouds all sorts of behind-the-scenes stuff, from agricultural chemicals and antibiotics to welfare issues and carbon-costly transport. Wouldn't it be a better system if we made more effort to know where our food came from? Do you think we would make better food choices? Is it even worth talking about? Or should we just allow the status quo to continue?

Some people say they've cooked venison and it ended up as tough as an old boot. Well, it's a wild meat and, just like a little wild bunny, it needs a bit of love in the kitchen. I cook more with wild meat than I do farmed meat, so I guess I'm used to it, but if you take up this approach to cooking with wild food or you just want to give it a try, then take the time to listen up and you'll get a mega-result.

I cut this tenderloin out from under the spine after I've gutted the deer. It's a muscle that probably doesn't do much of the heavy lifting, so it can end up pretty tender when cooked using this method. The flavour is rich, I won't deny that, but don't be put off, try it. You may fall in love with venison as I have. It's a more exciting option than beef – that's my take on it.

The key to this meal is the onion jus or gravy. It's a bitch to make, but I reckon it adds something really special to what's in reality a very simple meal. Meat on mash with a gravy – you can't get any simpler than that. But the flavours … Goosebumps!

This is one of those dinners to cook for a lover. Serve with good pinot, a warm fire and the mood for lovin'.

Venison Tenderloins

SERVES 2

What you need

2 venison tenderloins	100 g (3½ oz) real butter
salt and pepper, to taste	1 tablespoon full-cream (whole) real cow's milk
3 tablespoons olive oil	
2–3 onions, sliced	50 g (1¾ oz/½ cup) grated Parmigiano Reggiano
5 whole cloves	
1 teaspoon juniper berries	1 tablespoon fino sherry
4–5 potatoes, peeled and halved	
2–3 carrots, peeled	

How to make it

Take the tenderloins out of the fridge to bring them to room temperature. Trim away any obvious sinew, season all sides with salt and pepper, and set aside.

Heat about half the olive oil (a little glug) in a cast-iron frying pan over low–medium heat. Throw in the onion, whole cloves and juniper berries, and cook, making sure the temp never gets too hot. As the pan starts to dry up, add a dash of hot water, allowing that to reduce before adding a splash of water again, never letting the onions get dry and burnt or drowned in water. The idea is to get the onion sweated down until it's almost a brown sauce.

Meanwhile, boil the potato and carrots for 20 minutes, or until soft. Drain then transfer to a large mixing bowl and drop in about three-quarters of the butter (a few knobs), which will start to soften and melt straight away in the hot veg. Add a splash of milk and make a creamy mash using a potato masher. Grate in the parmesan and mix it through, then season to taste.

Preheat the oven to 200°C (390°F) and heat a chargrill pan with the remaining olive oil over medium–high heat on the stove top. Seal the tenderloin on the chargrill pan for about 2 minutes each side, then wrap in aluminium foil and bake for 10 minutes.

In the meantime, strain the onion through a metal sieve, pushing it through with a dessertspoon until your arm and hand feel like they're about to fall off. Scrape the underside of the sieve, as this is where the good stuff with all the flavour has been pushed through. Discard the bits of onion remaining in the sieve.

Return the sauce to the frying pan over medium heat, then add the remaining knob of butter, a splash of sherry, and a pinch of salt and pepper.

Once the venison is cooked, remove it from the oven and set it on a plate to rest for 5–10 minutes.

Slice the venison and arrange on top of the mash on a long plate. Drizzle over the rich gravy and serve.

I've had to find ways to use my food resources as cleverly as possible. I also want to be as practical and efficient with my time in the kitchen as possible, and this meal is a good example of how I get things done in kitchen town. When I cook a large cut of meat like a leg or a shoulder, I invariably have a lot of leftovers, even when there's a pack of hungry rats salivating at the dinner table. With excess cooked meat I can make a few really easy meals for days after. A slow-roasted leg of venison can be eaten for a meal straight away or I can turn it into something like a pasta ragu, a warm salad, a tasty taco or the meaty ingredient in a hearty bean stew.

The meat tastes good of its own accord, but there's absolutely nothing wrong with adding some additional flavours. At my back door is a herb garden I planted. I've positioned it close to the kitchen door so it forces me to not be lazy and to get out and pick herbs for cooking. Not only are herbs tasty, but many of them have medicinal value, too. So it's win–win.

Herbed Barbecued Venison

SERVES 4

What you need

100 g (3½ oz) lard	1 tablespoon freshly cracked black pepper
100 g (3½ oz) butter	
venison shoulder	250 ml (8½ fl oz/ 1 cup) red wine
handful each of sage, thyme and rosemary, very roughly chopped	roast veg, to serve
1 garlic bulb, cloves separated, peeled and crushed	

How to make it

Make a bed for the venison with large-sized aluminium foil, making sure the bottom is as watertight as possible and bending up the sides to make a rough bowl shape.

Allow the lard and butter to get to room temperature to soften (in winter I pop them next to our house fire for a spell). Rub the lard and butter all over the shoulder, leaving a chunk or two on top. Sit the venison on the foil, then spread the herbs, garlic and pepper over it, ensuring good coverage. Pour over the wine and wrap the meat up tight. The idea of the wine is to help keep the meat moist, and assist with steam-cooking.

Pop the roast in a hooded barbecue on the lowest setting and cook for 4–6 hours, or until melty and delicious.

Serve with roast veg or use in other dishes, such as the Broad bean & venison warm salad (page 141).

Living with an obsessive baker means that I need to schedule oven time. We often end up arguing over who gets to use it. For this very reason, I've taken to using the outdoors hooded barbecue as an oven replacement. It does a fine job of slow-cooking, except on really windy days when the low flame can be blown out. But on a calm day, everything is peaches.

Venison Port Pie

SERVES 4

What you need

1–2 tablespoons olive oil

4 onions, chopped

4 garlic cloves, sliced

1 kg (2 lb 3 oz) leg cut of venison

250 ml (8½ fl oz/1 cup) muscat

725 g (1 lb 10 oz/2¾ cups) tomato passata (puréed tomatoes)

10 whole cloves

5 whole allspice berries, crushed

4 fresh bay leaves

handful of parsley, including stems, chopped

salt and freshly cracked black pepper, to taste

2 × quantity (500 g/1 lb 2 oz) Shortcrust pastry (page 105)

1 egg, lightly beaten

poppy seeds, for sprinkling

a few sage leaves, to garnish

Having a freezer full of wild venison keeps us well fed over winter. The very concept of harvesting while the weather is good in order to prepare for when the season of rain and freeze arrives is a winning formula. An approach to survival that's served humans well for thousands of years seems like a good idea to me, especially given my disdain for the impact of the commercial food system in Western countries. None of this food politics is on my mind when I'm hunting deer, though. It's just me and the animal I'm hunting. I'm in that mode, hunting mode. If you've hunted, you'll know what I'm talking about. It's almost like a switch gets flicked – you focus and nothing else matters but the task at hand. I used to think too much when I first started hunting. I'd think about the ethics of what I was doing. Now I just focus on getting a clean kill and picking the right animal. It's one thing to pull the trigger and kill, it's another to hold back and let the right animal go. Deer is one of those animals this applies to. If a doe has a fawn in tow, for example, you let her go. That can mean days in the bush with no meat for the freezer. As frustrating as it might be at the time, it's just the right thing to do. Patience and sensibility are skills a good hunter requires.

A good hunter also requires a glass of port, and to relax in front of a warming fire after a hard day's work. And to make that moment even more enjoyable, how about a serve of venison pie with a hint of port? Life's pretty good, you know.

How to make it

Preheat the oven to 220°C (430°F).

In a large cast-iron casserole dish (or camp stove) over medium heat on the stove top, heat the olive oil (a generous glug) and brown the onion and garlic for 5–10 minutes.

Push the onion to one side and brown the venison for 1 minute on all sides. Splash over the muscat and add the passata, cloves, allspice, bay leaves and parsley, and season well with salt and pepper.

Add enough water to half-cover the meat, then pop the lid on and transfer to the oven. Turn the temperature down to 130°C (270°F) and cook for 3 hours, then turn the meat over and cook for a further 3 hours, or until the meat is falling from the bone.

Turn the oven up to 200°C (390°F) and grease four 250 ml (8½ fl oz/1 cup) ramekins.

Remove the casserole dish from the oven and allow to cool a little. Carefully take out the venison, then remove the meat from the bone, discarding the bone. Shred the meat and return it to the sauce in the casserole dish.

Reduce the sauce over medium heat on the stove top. Adjust the seasoning if required, then allow to cool.

Spoon the meat and gravy into the prepared ramekins. Roll out the shortcrust pastry and use it to cover each pie. Brush with the beaten egg and sprinkle with poppy seeds.

Bake for 30 minutes, or until the pastry is golden brown. Garnish with sage leaves.

Serve with a glass of port and a few good hunting tales.

Sand carrots

Unfortunately, I don't have a large vegetable garden. I'd love to have one, but I'm a renter. One day, I hope to buy a patch of land, build a small straw-bale cottage and spread my veg garden far and wide. But that's not the case for now. Due to my space limitations, I have to manage my garden like a game of Tetris. When the seasons shift, there's sometimes an overlap in crops. Carrots that have been growing over summer and autumn, for example, still occupy real estate that's now needed for winter crops like peas, broad (fava) beans and kale. It's a dilemma sometimes, because we can't possibly eat all the carrots at once, but I sure need to harvest them to make way for the incoming crop. Over the past few winters I've been trialling a possible solution, and it involves a tub of sand.

I'd read somewhere that root vegetables used to be stored in a sandy mix on boats for long-haul journeys. Surely this could work at my place, too! I must warn you though, you do require some specialist equipment, notably a tub and some sand. This technique works a treat. I've stored carrots in the sand for months, then pulled them out and they've been stiff as the day I pulled them from the soil. Parsnips, potatoes and turnips also store well for a few months, but I've found sometimes beetroot (beets) can get a bit woody if left too long.

What the?

Can you believe it? A rabbit in my 'rabbit-proof' veg patch! Man, I feel like a complete hack at times! Darting for safety this morning, as I toured the patch, was a tiny baby rabbit. So small was it that it literally dived through the rabbit-proof fencing, through the ringlet only a few centimetres wide. This thing must be tiny under that winter fur! And it's eaten some of my veg, too, that little mongrel! This is so embarrassing. A rabbit-hunting dude who can't control the rabbits in his own backyard. Nobody's perfect, eh?

I've made it my mission to catch this baby bunny. No matter how damn cute it appears, it's got the eating potential of a hungry teenager at dinnertime. Left to its own devices it's capable of doing some real damage, so it has to go. My first wave of attack was to send in the canine. Henry's a damn fine rabbit-hunter. He often catches them when we go for a walk in the paddock, so maybe he could be the cat to my mouse. It didn't take long for Henry to pick up the scent. For a bird dog he's more interested in rabbits, which makes hunting quail a challenge when we're in thick rabbit country! Straight away he's madly pointing under one of the fruit boxes, a perfect shelter for a tiny bunny. I get on my belly for a closer look and sure enough, looking right at me is a shit-scared bunny that picked the wrong garden to invade. With a bit of encouragement, it made a dash for freedom only to be chomped by Henry. A feed for the dog and I can rest a while, knowing my veggies are safe. For today, at least.

Crowd pleaser. That's what this meal is. It's not fancy or hard to make, but it's delicious and unashamedly a meat-lover's merry-go-round. If you're vegetarian, vegan or anything of the sort, please quickly turn the page, as this will either offend you or turn you to the dark side.

I started cooking this burger years back, for what reason I cannot recall – it may have been when I was going through my 'What else can I do with rabbit meat?' period. Mixing the lean wild rabbit with fatty and full-flavoured bacon or chorizo was part of the menu at home already, but for some reason I'd never thought of blending the three meat gems. I sometimes cook this meal at the end of workshops. One time, while I was preparing the meal and had blended bacon, chorizo and rabbit meat in the mixing bowl, one fella said it looked like the three colours of the flag of 'Meatopia'. Maybe I should get a T-shirt made.

These burger patties rely on the fat of the bacon for binding, the chorizo for the spicy flavours and the lean rabbit meat to convince yourself you're eating something slightly healthy. I like to serve the burger on toasted brioche, if possible, with some slow and gently fried onions, bitey cheddar and garden greens, with a little dressing for zing. Oh, and if you get to make the Chipotle sauce (page 187), it works well smothered over these patties.

I highly recommend cooking this on a barbecue. Start cooking on a flat plate then finish off on the grill, cooked really well with an ice-cold beer in hand.

Rabbit & Chorizo Burgers

MAKES 4 BURGERS

What you need

4 rashers (slices) smoky loin bacon (page 189)	bowl of garden greens, such as chicory (endive), rocket (arugula), mizuna and cos (romaine) lettuce
3–4 rabbit backstraps	
150 g (5½ oz) chorizo (page 49)	1 teaspoon balsamic vinegar
plain (all-purpose) flour, for dusting	Chipotle sauce (page 187), to serve (optional)
3 tablespoons olive oil	aged cheddar, sliced, to serve
4 onions, chopped	
4 brioche buns, halved	

How to make it

If you've home-cured the bacon, the skin will most likely already be cut off. If you're using store-bought, cut the rind off. Chop roughly, then whizz in a food processor and transfer to a mixing bowl.

Trim any sinew off the rabbit backstraps and chop roughly, then whizz in the food processor and transfer to the mixing bowl with the bacon.

Roughly chop the chorizo, then whizz in the food processor and transfer to the mixing bowl with the other meats.

Hand-mix all three colours of the Meatopia flag, then form portions into burger patties. Refrigerate on a flour-dusted tray for 30 minutes.

When ready to cook, heat 2 tablespoons of the olive oil on a barbecue hotplate and fry the onion for 20 minutes. Add the burgers and barbecue evenly, finishing them off on the grill. Toast the brioche halves on the grill.

Wash the greens and toss with the vinegar and the remaining olive oil.

Serve the burgers on the brioche, with dressed salad, chipotle sauce (if using), onions and a few slices of aged cheddar.

Rabbit Jamon Logs

What you need

8 rabbit backstraps of equal size

12 long slices jamon

100–200 g (3½–7 oz) blue cheese

cooking twine

1–2 tablespoons olive oil, plus extra for drizzling

a few handfuls of white asparagus, blanched for 5 minutes

peppercress, to serve

freshly cracked black pepper, to taste

There are two cuts of wild rabbit meat: the legs, which require a few hours braised over low–medium heat; and the backstrap tenderloin, which can be tenderised and cooked quickly in a frying pan. If I have a successful night hunting, I'll butcher out the tenderloins and reserve them for a meal such as this. I'm so used to rabbit meat that I like to add flavour to make it a bit more exciting. I don't think they taste gamey at all – in fact, they can be a bit bland, like a chicken breast – so adding some flavour is common when cooking the backstraps. I cure a pork leg every year and thus have a decent supply of finely sliced jamon that's been cured for at least 12 months, if not longer. We're also blessed to have a small cheese-making company nearby that makes some killer cheeses, notably a strong blue cheese that I like to use in this dish. Something strong like a Roquefort or even Gorgonzola would work well.

It's a delicate meal – rich but not stodgy – and makes a fine starter.

How to make it

Preheat the oven to 180°C (360°F) and grease a roasting tin.

Trim any sinew off the rabbit backstraps, then cover with plastic wrap and gently tenderise with a rolling pin (that means tap them firmly but don't squish them to a pulp). For each log, lay three jamon strips on the bench, then gently lay two tenderised backstraps on top of the jamon, side by side, and finally crumble over a quarter of the blue cheese. Roll up into a log and tie with cooking twine to hold it in place.

Heat the olive oil in a frying pan over medium heat and brown all sides of each log for 1 minute each side. Transfer the logs to the prepared roasting tin, cover with aluminium foil and roast for 15 minutes.

Meanwhile, heat a chargrill pan over medium heat and grill the asparagus.

Remove the rabbit logs from the oven and gently slice into portions. Serve on the grilled asparagus with a generous scattering of cress, a little pepper and a drizzle of olive oil.

Three times a charm

It's the middle of winter. The sky isn't just grey, it's covered in cloud, no sun to be seen. The old farmhouse on the hill is often in cloud during winter. We've already had snow twice this winter, and I wouldn't be the slightest bit surprised if we get more. The food I've squirrelled away from last spring, summer and autumn is getting well used in the kitchen. A lot of meals start with the gentle sweating of onions, carrots and celery, then in goes the meat to brown, topped up with lush red tomato passata (puréed tomatoes). The weekly winter bean stew bubbles away on the gas hob and feeds us for easy meals, for at least a few days if not a week. It's a season of hearty meals that bring us joy when the grey skies do not.

The veg garden has slowed right down. Nothing appears to be happening. In the forest, however, there's still activity, and it's a welcome surprise. You'd think the freezing winter conditions would bring the fungi to a grinding halt. For the most part it has, but a few mushrooms have popped up that I call 'the confused mushrooms'. One variety, though, is actually more of a winter species, and it's fast becoming one of my favourite mushrooms to hunt for. The wood blewit (*Clitocybe nuda*) is a beautiful species. It's not much to look at from above, but once turned over the gills are an iridescent lilac. It's one of those absolutely stunning forms in nature that we humans can only dream of creating. These winter beauties seem to grow in the rotting leaf litter of oak trees, sometimes under pines, and I've once found them in grass, but usually they're a forest species. They have an unmistakable mushroomy smell, which is a good sign, because often if a fungus smells distasteful it's not safe to eat. That's a loose rule, by the way.

I'd read about wood blewits in books, but I'd never spotted one in the forest until this season. It's been a bit of a game-changer, too. I have to admit I may have become a little obsessed with them. Every time I spot a bunch of old oak trees I pull over and scout around for some food, whereas for years I'd been avoiding oak trees because of their symbiotic relationship with the death cap mushroom (*Amanita phalloides*) – yes, it's deadly toxic, so don't eat it. But wood blewits are friendlier. They can be toxic if eaten raw, so the idea is to cook them before eating. Who likes raw mushrooms anyway?

The wood blewit is very mushroomy, not only in smell but in taste. Its texture is a little soft, but not like the squirmy slippery Jack (*Suillus luteus*). Fried in butter and olive oil with a few sage leaves and garlic, it's delicious. I've been so obsessed with trying to locate more picking spots that I'm spending time in the forest like it's still autumn. What a great excuse to get back among the pines and oaks. Better than being cooped up at home in front of the fire all day. I was already starting to get cabin fever. Thankfully, the wood blewits saved me – they've got me off my arse and back in the bush, no matter how cold it is.

In my winter-mushroom basket I have the three forest mushrooms I love: the slippery Jack, saffron milkcap/pine mushroom (*Lactarius deliciosus*) and wood blewit. And I have them in good numbers, too! Enough so that I've been able to experiment with a recipe idea that I think will bring some stunning results. I've fried up the medley of mushrooms and been adding a little ricotta and then rolling out tasty ravioli (see page 233). And when one type of cheese isn't enough, I add two more. I cover the cooked mushroom ravioli in mascarpone and grate over some pecorino. Each delicate parcel of pasta and mushroom is gently placed in my mouth and softly masticated where mushroom meets pasta and cheese alike. It's a recipe I'll be making year after year.

There's something special about the mushroom season. You tolerated the heat of summer, you got excited by the autumn break, and you worked your butt off preparing for winter – then it finally arrives. It's time to rest and eat well. The forest mushrooms still hang about well into winter – heck, I've even picked some in early summer. It isn't the season itself that determines the mushrooms' arrival, it's the weather conditions. One autumn when rain was absent our mushroom season arrived very late and it was a poor year for mushroom meals. Some years the conditions are just right and we get most of our favourite varieties in the bush well into winter. One of the three mushrooms in this recipe, the wood blewit, is actually more of a later variety, which typically arrives when the temperature is colder and there's plenty of moisture about.

If you're lucky enough to have a successful mushroom hunt and find all three species, then try this recipe, but it works equally well with just slippery Jacks and saffron milkcaps (pine mushrooms). If you're in the right place at the right time, do try the three-way.

Three-way Wild Mushroom Ravioli

SERVES 4

What you need

50 g (1¾ oz) butter	90 g (3 oz/1 cup) grated pecorino
1–2 tablespoons olive oil, plus extra for drizzling	300 g (10½ oz/1¼ cups) fresh ricotta
90 g (3 oz/1 cup) chopped saffron milkcap (pine) mushrooms	a dollop of mascarpone
	freshly cracked mountain pepper berries, to taste
90 g (3 oz/1 cup) chopped wood blewit mushrooms	
90 g (3 oz/1 cup) chopped slippery Jack mushrooms	**Ravioli**
4 garlic cloves, finely chopped	300 g (10½ oz/2 cups) organic plain (all-purpose) flour, plus extra for dusting
handful of thyme sprigs, leaves picked	4 large eggs (from the backyard chooks)
125 ml (4 fl oz/½ cup) white wine	
salt and pepper, to taste	

How to make it

Start by making the filling. Heat the butter with the olive oil in a frying pan over medium–high heat. Fry the mushrooms, garlic and thyme for 10 minutes, or until the moisture has evaporated, then splash over the wine and reduce. Season with salt and pepper.

Remove from the heat, transfer to a mixing bowl and add half the pecorino. Blitz using a hand-held blender, then fold through the ricotta. Cover and set aside while you make the pasta.

Now make the ravioli. Pour the flour into a large mixing bowl and make a well in the centre. Break three of the eggs into the well. Using an expensive kitchen device (i.e. your clean hands), mix and twirl the egg around in the flour until completely mixed, then knead on a floured bench for 5 minutes, or until a smooth dough forms. Wrap in plastic wrap and set aside to rest at room temperature for 1 hour.

Roll the dough into a sausage-shaped log and cut it into small chunks. Run each chunk of pasta dough through a hand-cranked pasta machine, first on a wide-open setting, then slowly progressing to a tighter setting. You might put each piece of pasta dough through six to eight times, until you have a large strip of flat pasta. Lay the pasta on a flour-dusted bench.

Beat the remaining egg in a small bowl and grab a small pastry brush. Arrange a few spoonfuls of the filling at regular intervals on one half of the pasta. Brush the egg wash over the exposed pasta, then fold over the half without filling to cover the filling, and seal well, pushing any captured air out of the pocket of filling. Use a pasta cutter to cut out the pretty little gems. Repeat with the remaining pasta strips and filling.

Bring a saucepan of salted water to the boil. Cook the ravioli for 5 minutes, or until al dente. Remove from the hot water with a slotted spoon and pop straight into a mixing bowl. Add the mascarpone and the remaining pecorino and toss gently to cover.

Drizzle over some olive oil, and season with salt and mountain pepper berry.

Now with a brand-new flavour

A mate of mine always shares stuff. Almost without fail, just before I leave his place, he'll take me aside and pass me some form of produce. Sometimes it's honey from his bees, sometimes it's a nice chunk of wood, but there's always something. I feel awful because I didn't come prepared with anything in return for a trade. I don't believe for a second that his motivation is trading. He's just a nice bloke who loves to share. His honey is something else, let me tell you! It's quite different from the honey from down our way, which seems to be slightly sweeter. But Hatto, he lives over the divide, the large range that slices from the south to the north of the state. We affectionately call it 'up there'. It's country that's drier and the vegetation is matched to the climate. It's box bark eucalyptus country, and this is where the bees get the nectar to make their unique honey.

So why am I telling you about some guy's honey from his backyard bees? Well, one thing I absolutely love about this 'practiculture' lifestyle is that I'm surrounded by many other people who kinda live in a similar way. They may grow veggies, they may raise animals, but in some way or another they take care of producing some of their food. It may be a little, it may be a lot. Regardless, the beauty is that we all share, give and trade. What's so good about that, I hear you ask? Well, besides the obvious facts of local, organic, blah, blah, think about the flavours! Everything is unique. Every time you put something in your mouth it's a potential new experience. New! Exciting! You picking up what I'm putting down?

Man cannot survive on bread alone. It would be too boring, although some breads are pretty delicious. But seriously, imagine a life of food that gives you that little rush of sensation every time you try it. Year in, year out, food shared this way always tastes different. Olives can struggle with drought one year and be waterlogged the next, affecting the yield and flavour of the oil. Variation in food is something I've embraced over the years. My expectations are zero. I never expect anything to taste a particular way – it's best just to lie back and enjoy the ride.

This is another mistake/experiment/leftovers meal that worked so well I now cook it over and over again. I can't stand food wastage. I get really mad when my kids don't finish their dinner. I'll sit and wait alone with them at the dinner table until the meal is finished. It's not like I'm force-feeding my kids, I'm just persevering with them, opening them up to eating different types of foods, especially vegetables. Man, that's often a challenge with my kids! I hope they read this one day and realise that all my hard work getting them to try different foods might have been worth it.

Because of this, I've got into the habit of serving smaller meals at dinner, which means I often have leftovers that end up in the fridge. Polenta is one of those things that if I'm going to stand at a stove for 45 minutes stirring what's basically a big pot of corn glue, then I'm going to make a decent batch. I love polenta the day after. I ladle the leftovers onto trays and they cool overnight. I can then cut them into chunks and fry them until golden and crispy. They can be served with almost anything, meat or veg, but here I'm going to include a hare recipe that worked really well. It's a bit sweet and a bit hot, but a lot yum.

Hunting hare should be described as accidental hunting. I rarely go out targeting hare. I'm always just hunting something else and then I see a hare and take the gift from nature. It's a stunning wild meat. Tastes almost like a deer crossed with a lamb. I'd buy that for a dollar!

Sweet & Hot Braised Hare with Fried Polenta

SERVES 4

What you need

oil, for shallow-frying	**Braised hare**
polenta squares (made using yesterday's left-over polenta)	1 hare
	60 ml (2 fl oz/¼ cup) olive oil
sour cream, to serve	7 onions, chopped
habanero sauce, to serve	125 ml (4 fl oz/½ cup) fino sherry
	1 teaspoon juniper berries
	1 tablespoon whole cloves
	1 tablespoon smoked pimentón (Spanish paprika)
	1 teaspoon chilli powder
	4 bay leaves
	4 rosemary sprigs, leaves picked and chopped
	3 tablespoons honey
	30 g (1 oz) butter

How to make it

Preheat the oven to 200°C (390°F).

Quarter the hare (see page 209) and keep the legs for making this dish.

Heat half the olive oil in a heavy-based flameproof casserole dish over medium heat on the stove top and brown the onion.

Heat the remaining olive oil in a frying pan over medium heat and brown the hare legs on all sides for a minute each side. Transfer the hare to the casserole dish.

Deglaze the frying pan with the sherry and pour it into the casserole dish, followed by the spices, herbs, honey and enough water to half-cover the meat. Pop the lid on, place in the oven, turn the heat down to 150°C (300°F) and cook for 2 hours, then turn the meat over and cook for a further 2 hours. This will ensure the meat not initially in the water doesn't dry out. The meat is done when it comes away from the bone.

Remove the meat from the dish and cool a little, then remove the meat from the bones, discarding the bones and setting aside the meat.

Return the casserole dish to the stove top over medium heat and reduce the gravy.

Remove the bay leaves and melt in the butter, then return the meat to the dish.

Heat some cooking oil in a frying pan and fry the squares of polenta in batches until golden brown on both sides. Lay the polenta on paper towel to drain off any excess oil while you cook the next batch.

Divide your polenta among the plates, ladle over the meat, and top with a dollop of sour cream and a drizzle of your finest habanero sauce.

Do the right thing?

There was a slight breeze, the clouds had rolled over, bringing with them a cover of darkness, and although there was a crispness in the air it wasn't too cold to hunt in the evening. I sent a message to Jack and we met up at our closest spot for a shoot. We've got permission from a nearby farmer to help out with the rabbit numbers. I'm not sure we make any sort of dint in the population – they just keep coming back! – but we get a feed and the farmer gets some crop saved, so it's a practical arrangement.

We walked the fields, up the rise and down into the wet gully, where the grass is long and damp. Not only are there plenty of bunnies, but there's everything else down in this patch. Possums in trees, sneaking foxes, hares, wallabies, kangaroos, and the owls that keep a watchful eye on us from the safety of their high top perch. We bagged a few rabbits, enough for a feed the following day and a few to freeze for storage.

On the hike back up to the truck, we noticed a few more roos jump over the fence into the bush for safety. All but one. This kangaroo had one hell of a limp. In fact, it wasn't a limp, the foot looked like it had been snapped at the joint and was just being dragged along. That roo must have been in a lot of pain. My heart sank, knowing that this fella was dead meat. With an injury that bad there's no surviving. It's not like a vet will suddenly arrive with lights flashing and operate and repair this animal. This guy was destined to limp around and end up possibly infected, dehydrated and most definitely food for foxes or wild dogs. If I were to follow the law, I'd walk away and leave the animal to die a slow death. It's illegal to shoot kangaroos in Victoria unless you've been issued with a destruction order from the Department of Environment, Land, Water and Planning.

The sad truth is, a lot of farmers, frustrated with the amount of crop loss they have, bypass the red tape and simply shoot the kangaroos in big numbers. Even for the people who do follow the law, the number of kangaroos that are culled is staggering. According to the ABC's *Bush Telegraph*, an estimated 70 000 kangaroos are culled every year. Not eaten. Culled. Shot and buried to simply rot away. Isn't that just madness? Here's an animal that has evolved with the environmental conditions of this land; it's the most sustainable red meat, requiring no fences, no stock feed, no agricultural antibiotics, no management other than to be shot and butchered.

It's illegal for me to hunt this animal, which is in almost plague proportions here. Instead, like everyone else, I'm expected to go to a supermarket and buy meat that's travelled miles to get to me, from an animal that's been given supplementary feed over winter (which has a high carbon cost). It's most likely been in a truck travelling a good distance and has been packaged in plastic and sat in a supermarket fridge waiting for pick-up. There just doesn't seem to be any logic to this system. Wouldn't it make more sense for me to drive down the road, shoot a kangaroo and harvest all the meat for the family to eat?

I'm not suggesting that everyone go out and hunt kangaroos to extinction – that's madness, and I'm sure it will never happen – I'm simply asking if it's time to look at what we have around us. Maybe it's time to look at more truly local native alternatives instead of relying on the commercially traditional ways that require a lot of agricultural resources. It's just something to ponder.

Kangaroo is as local as I can get. If you want to use the term sustainable, I reckon this animal is my best sustainable option. They're native, which is important, as it means they've evolved to live in harmony with the natural environment and the conditions of where they live.

Kangaroos have an ability to live within the carrying capacity of their ecosystem. They tend to reproduce based on the current supply of resources. This is a fantastic system for them, but it's not so rad for the farmers trying to grow grain crops, which the kangaroos love to feast on. There are more kangaroos in Victoria now than there were before European settlement, because the landscape has been altered through land-clearing for agricultural purposes. More fields of green tended for sheep or cattle means more food for kangaroos, which ultimately means a healthy roo population. The roos have become an agricultural pest, and are therefore shot by the farmers in an effort to manage their numbers.

In reality, we could dispense with the sheep and the cattle and simply harvest the kangaroos. Their meat is lean, they don't require fences (they simply jump over them), they don't need vet visits, drenching or mustering to fresh pastures. They just need to be harvested, butchered and packaged. But it's against the law to hunt them for

Roo Tail

SERVES 4

What you need

1 kangaroo tail	2 teaspoons whole cloves
1–2 tablespoons olive oil	
1 large carrot, sliced	4 dried hot bird's eye chillies, crushed
2 onions, sliced	roast pumpkin (winter squash) mash, to serve
50 g (1¾ oz) lard	
500 ml (17 fl oz/2 cups) red wine	thyme sprigs, to garnish

How to make it

Preheat the oven to 180°C (360°F).

Cut the tail into a few pieces.

Heat a glug of olive oil in a heavy-based flameproof casserole dish over medium heat on the stove top. Add the carrot and onion and cook for at least 10 minutes. Add the lard. Once the lard has melted, add the meat and brown on all sides. Splash over the wine and 250 ml (8½ fl oz/1 cup) water, then add the cloves and dried chilli.

Put the lid on the casserole dish and transfer to the oven. Cook for 30 minutes then turn the heat down to 130–150°C (270–300°F) and cook for another 3 hours, or until the meat is as tender as a middle-aged bum cheek.

Serve on a bed of roast pumpkin mash and garnish with thyme sprigs. Heavenly.

my family, so when I find a roadkill I check it for freshness – which is probably also illegal, but hey, we can't all be perfect citizens, can we? Kangaroo isn't available everywhere, but wherever we live, there are some more sustainable forms of protein for us. It's just a matter of identifying them and tapping into the supply.

Kangaroo tail is a great cut. It's gelatinous and tender, and if treated the right way it makes for an amazing meal. I've had a tail cooked with Chinese flavours and it was mind-blowing, so I guess the general gist is to experiment and find what works best for you.

Kangaroo Ankles aka Kankles

SERVES 2

What you need

1–2 tablespoons olive oil
50 g (1¾ oz) lard
5 onions, sliced
5 garlic cloves, chopped
1 tablespoon cumin seeds
2 kangaroo ankles (or ankles from other wild meat)
500 ml (17 fl oz/2 cups) red wine
herbed roast potato wedges, to serve

When I cook shanks, my kids ask me, 'What's that we can smell cooking?' For years I'd reply with 'Shanks', and I'd always get a blank look in return. So I started pointing to my ankles. This seemed to get the message across. The kids would then bugger off to whatever it was they were doing, and I'd return to my earthly role as chief food-delivery service for my offspring. I'm sure most countries would have some animal with a few ankles worthy of cooking. In lieu of kangaroo you could use lamb, deer, goat and even wallaby – feel free to experiment. The beaut thing with ankles (shanks) is that all mammals share the same basic anatomy. These are muscles that work hard for the animal, so they need to be cooked slow and low. They also have a few gelatinous bits, which makes them super-delicious.

If you're going to use this recipe as a suggestion only and you're not using roo meat (especially if you live in Wyoming and don't have kangaroos hopping around), I suggest you use the base spice that works well with that meat. Cloves or juniper berries work well with venison, rosemary and thyme work well with lamb, etc. I like to use cumin. It's great with kangaroo and goat. Hell, it's good with almost anything.

How to make it

Preheat the oven to 180°C (360°C).

In a large flameproof casserole dish, heat a generous glug of olive oil with the lard over low heat on the stove top. Gently cook the onion and garlic with the cumin seeds for 10 minutes, or until they colour.

Add the meat and brown on all sides. Add the wine and 500 ml (17 fl oz/2 cups) water, put the lid on and cook in the oven for 40 minutes.

Turn the heat down to 150°C (300°F) and cook for 5 hours, or until the meat is tender and falling off the bone.

Serve the ankles with herbed roast potato wedges, and spoon over the sweet cooked onions – this is what pulls the meal together!

Bean cooking

The romantic notion of living the simple life has been stuck in my mind since I was a kid on the farm.

Maybe I watched too many episodes of *Little House on the Prairie*. But seriously, how amazing, sweet and beautiful is the idea of living simply from what you've worked hard for, a life full of great food, experiences, traditions and nature stuff? This lifestyle is summed up in a few meals that consist mostly of ingredients for whose production I've been totally responsible. This is why I love beans so much. The idea that I can add things to beans in any season is brilliant. They're as versatile as a desperate actor. I can make a cool bean salad in summer or a hearty bean stew in winter. Any which way you like it.

This winter, though, I've loved the beans more than ever. I've 'bean' having so much fun cooking different meals with the beans, and I've even got the kids to like a few bean meals! This winter I've discovered that you can make an amazing pâté de tête by boiling the head of a pig and removing all the good meaty bits. But then you're left with pig's-head stock. What to do with it? Well it makes an excellent broth for a bean stew. It's rich in flavour so beware, el blandos. I ate this bean dish for days. French white beans simmered in pig's-head stock with rosemary, garlic, butter and pecorino. I may have added a splash of white wine, too.

Still one of my best go-to bean dishes is the combination of dried beans, winter green crop and hunted or home-reared meat – all things I can be responsible for. For example, I had some of the slow-cooked venison left over in the fridge that I needed to eat. I also had a winter veg patch loaded with blue kale. So I boiled the beans, fried the kale and then added the roast venison. Some wine, herbs and a knob of butter, and a hearty bean meal is created. These meals can be for any time of the day. Before I start my day of work I have beans with toast; I can even stomach it for lunch and dinner, too. And that's why beans are a staple for this way of living. They're reliable. They store indefinitely and they can be added to most ingredients you have on hand, making them perfect for frugal living.

Staples

It's so damn grey here it could make most people as blue as a Howlin' Wolf tune. But the house fire is crackling away, my legs are covered in my Pendleton woollen granny blanket, and I'm as comfortable as a pig in poo. This is the end of my yearly cycle and I'm not making any excuses for the fact that I'm putting my feet up in front of the fire. I've worked for this, and to be honest there isn't much else for me to do right now other than supply split firewood and cook food for the family. It's the quiet months of winter that I adore, and sometimes it feels a wee bit extravagant. My larder is loaded with provisions; I simply need to walk in, open the freezer, grab some meat, dig in the sandbox for some root veg, grab a bottle of passata and some herbs from the garden, then go inside and cook.

I could only have imagined a lifestyle like this years ago, but here it is, in full form, keeping me content just as I imagined it would. Every bit of effort I make for us, to keep us fed, is very much appreciated. Well, at least by me. When you grow, raise and hunt your own food, nothing goes to waste. Every food ingredient has so much more value – it becomes precious. To eat meat I have to do the dirty work of killing – and it *is* dirty, it's bloody and sometimes it's confronting. For the food I grow, I must get my hands dirty, I often sweat and yes, when things don't work out, there may be some salty discharge from the corner of my eye.

In the kitchen, prepping and preserving takes patience, hard work and organisation. Everything takes some form of effort, be it physical, emotional or mental. And how does that affect us? It makes everything we work for more valued. It gives the doer a sense of pride and achievement, and of doing things with a practical purpose. There's little or no time for folly, for worrying about appearances, for doing things to appease others. Most tasks have a very real purpose. If I don't do task A then I don't have a warm house in winter. If I don't do task B there'll be no bread for the school lunches in the morning. You need to have your eyes on the ball at all times.

For three seasons I've kept my eyes on the ball. If I hadn't, then we'd have a pretty lean winter and, to be honest, that scenario has no appeal whatsoever. This morning, as for many other breakfasts in winter (and lunches and dinners), I sparked up the gas hob and warmed up a big pot of chilli beans. It's such a peasant meal, one that represents the entire system I live by. The beans I grew back in summer, the passata was made in autumn, the parsley, garlic, chilli, onion, carrot, kale and chard were all picked from the backyard garden. The cured chorizo I made from a pig that was raised on a mate's farm, and the olive oil was bartered for with wild mushrooms foraged from the bush. This meal is what it's all about – a range of base ingredients that I've either worked for or wrangled, and not a supermarket ingredient to be found.

I know I'll always need to buy a block of cheese, butter or any other staple ingredient I can't physically produce myself (although I do intend one day to milk a goat and make cheese). I don't expect myself to make everything. I don't expect anyone to be able to be that 'self-sufficient' unless they're superhuman. The reality is we all need each other for our species to continue. By living in 'practiculture', I reckon I've made a rather large dint in my reliance on what I see as a flawed food system. Practiculture isn't an extreme or all-or-nothing approach, it's about doing practical things with the goal of finding an alternative to the standard option (which by now we all should agree is not rad for us, and nor is it rad for the natural world).

All this talk of ethical food is making me hungry. I might go toast some sourdough and warm up some chilli beans.

Secrets of Sourdough

Sourdough used to be such a mystery to me, as it is to a lot of people, I imagine. I'd look over thick books on the subject, I'd peruse endless pages of sourdough recipes, have some sort of mini anxiety attack and close the book, never to look at it again. We love to over-complicate things, don't we? I'm not sure why, but I see it in all facets of life. The result of the over-complication of sourdough is that most people who initially show an interest in the subject eventually shy away, believing it's too technical. It's similar to cooking in general. The more people make things look difficult, fancy and over-complicated, the less interest we'll tend to show. The inevitable side effect is that people opt for the convenient processed food, which we all should know by now isn't doing anyone any favours in the health department. The same can be said for bread. If you look at the ingredients list for processed bread it's as long as your arm. But home-made sourdough has the same three ingredients it's had for centuries: flour, water and culture.

I'm no doctor of medicine or nutritionist, nor am I a researcher in food science, but I can't help wondering what all those ingredients in supermarket bread do to our bodies. I wonder why so many people have bread issues these days. I don't remember anyone having bread allergies or being gluten intolerant when I was at school. Maybe bread is doing something to us that it didn't thirty years ago. Has the way bread is produced changed so much that it's making us sick? Like I said, I don't know the answer, but I did know I wanted to stop eating processed breads, so years ago I started to make my own. Initially I used dried yeast, then I moved one step further to independence and took up sourdough. I haven't looked back.

THE STARTER

To make any sourdough bread you'll need a starter. A starter is a live culture that thrives on a mixture of flour and water. It's smelly and bubbly and it's a bit of a fun science experiment. It's super-easy to get one going, but some people with busy lives find it hard to keep them alive. If you want it badly enough you'll keep it alive. If not, then maybe give up and try again when you're ready for the commitment.

You'll need super-specialised, hard-to-acquire equipment to make a sourdough starter, namely a smallish bucket with a lid. Here's a basic method for creating a starter.

Day 1 – Combine 100 g (3½ oz/1 cup) organic rye flour with 250 ml (8½ fl oz/1 cup) water in your starter bucket and stir until well mixed.

Day 2 – Add the above to your starter bucket.

Day 3 – Add the above to your starter bucket.

Day 4 – Check for any bubbles. If you have bubbles this means you have fermentation occurring. You hip dude! Fermenting is, like, so hot right now. Discard about half the contents, add your usual 100 g (3½ oz/1 cup) rye flour and 250 ml (8½ fl oz/1 cup) water, and stir well.

Days 5–8 – Each day, take out half the contents and feed your starter as usual. Once the starter has a sour smell and fermenting bubbles, you can start removing half and feeding it every second day.

After a few weeks of looking after your starter and keeping it alive by feeding it every second day, try making a loaf (see overleaf).

Tip: Leave your specialist sourdough bucket in the warmest room of the house, especially if you're trying to develop a starter in the middle of winter. Summer just happens to be the best time to get a culture going because the starter is more vigorous in warm temperatures, but anything is possible. And don't forget, when you take starter out to make a loaf, feed it to keep the level of starter constant.

The Bread

In our kitchen we bake two types of bread: a weekday loaf and a weekend loaf, one easy and one slightly less easy. The weekday loaf, baked in a loaf (bar) tin, requires absolutely no kneading, and takes only a few minutes of effort (see photo opposite). The weekend loaf, baked in a casserole dish, requires a little bit of kneading and shaping, and looks cooler (see photo page 247). But essentially it's the same ingredients in both, just a slightly different process.

1. The weekday loaf

What you need

125 ml (4 fl oz/½ cup) vigorous and happy Sourdough starter (page 246)

450 g (1 lb/3 cups) organic plain (all-purpose) flour

olive oil, for greasing

poppy seeds, for sprinkling (optional)

How to make it

Mix the starter and flour in a large bowl with 375 ml (12½ fl oz/ 1½ cups) water to form a thick, sticky dough. Cover the bowl with a tea towel (dish towel) and leave to brew for at least 12 hours (I normally make the mixture in the morning and bake the bread at night, but you could mix at night and bake the next morning). In winter I leave the mixture in our one heated room to assist in fermentation.

Preheat the oven to 240°C (470°F) or 220°C (430°F) fan-forced if you have it, and brush a 24 cm × 13 cm × 7 cm (9½ in × 5 in × 2¾ in) loaf (bar) tin with olive oil.

Manoeuvre the wet mixture into the prepared tin using a spatula. Sprinkle over poppy seeds, if using, then cover with aluminium foil and set aside for 30 minutes to settle.

The oven will be super-hot now, as it's been preheated for 30 minutes. Bake the bread with the foil on for 30 minutes, then remove the foil and bake for a further 20 minutes to form a nice crust. Remove from the tin and allow to cool on a wire rack.

Sit back and ponder why it's taken you this long to try making the easiest loaf of bread ever.

2. The weekend loaf

What you need

125 ml (4 fl oz/½ cup) vigorous and happy Sourdough starter (page 246)

450 g (1 lb/3 cups) organic plain (all-purpose) flour, plus extra for dusting

pinch of salt

How to make it

Mix all the ingredients in a large bowl with 375 ml (12½ fl oz/ 1½ cups) water to form a thick, sticky dough. Cover the bowl with a tea towel (dish towel) and leave to brew for at least 12 hours (I normally make the mixture in the morning and bake the bread at night, but you could mix at night and bake the next morning). In winter I leave the mixture in our one heated room to assist in fermentation.

Preheat the oven to 240°C (470°F) or 220°C (430°F) fan-forced if you have it, and place a casserole dish in the oven to warm up.

Get the bread dough out of the bowl and onto a floured bench using a spatula. Dust your hands with flour and knead the dough for a few minutes, to stretch the gluten. Form into a rounded loaf, use a serrated knife to cut a cross on top of the loaf, then cover the dough with the bowl the mixture was brewed in, and leave to rest for 30 minutes.

Dust the now-very-hot casserole dish with flour and place the formed bread loaf in it. Dust the top of the loaf with flour, then pop the lid on and bake for 30 minutes.

Remove the lid and bake for a further 20 minutes. When done, remove the bread from the dish and allow to cool on a wire rack.

Beer Bread

What you need

450 g (1 lb/3 cups) self-raising flour

375 ml (12½ fl oz/1½ cups) beer

3 tablespoons dried oregano or thyme, plus extra for sprinkling

1 tablespoon olive oil

pinch of semolina

30 g (1 oz) butter

Isn't it usually the case that you have a supply of beer when you're also sitting around a campfire? It's almost like beer bread was meant to be made when camping. It's super-easy to make and produces a lovely loaf. When you're heading out bush for a few days, some beer and self-raising flour can make you fresh bread and make your camp feel a little more homely. Beer with no added sulfites makes a nice bread, but most beers would do the job. I've never made it with a heavy beer like a stout; I just use what I drink, which is a dry lager. Unless it's whisky. Which isn't beer.

How to make it

Mix the flour, beer and oregano in a large bowl until they form a dough.

Splash a glug of olive oil in the camp pot, add the semolina, and rub the mixture all over the inside of the pot.

Pour the bread mixture into the oiled pot. Sprinkle over the extra dried oregano. Pop a knob of butter on top of the loaf and put the lid on the pot.

Sit the pot on a bed of hot coals and cook for approximately 35 minutes, or until a nice crust has formed on the outside but the inside is soft and fluffy.

'Support your local pig farmer'. I want to get a T-shirt made with this slogan, because over the past decade more and more small-scale pig farmers have popped up, and we need to continue to support them. What's been happening is a beautiful reversal of a food-production system. Years ago, pig farms were numerous and small in scale. Then they became industrialised and factory farms dominated the market. We all know the conditions in which the pigs are kept at a factory farm, not to mention the problems with pathogens and application of agricultural antibiotics. But there's been a wonderful shift away from this system, and the old ways have been embraced once more.

The new small farms are mostly free-range, with the pigs outdoors, and some are organic. It's a bit of a victory, I reckon, but these farmers need our continued support. Many of the farmers have been bullied by the larger companies in the industry, which are now feeling threatened by the consumers' move towards free-range. I've heard all sorts of nasty stories about the industry coming down hard on compliance and regulation for the small farmer, which makes their life miserable when they're trying to do a good service for people who are keen to change their consumer habits.

Pâté de Tête

MAKES 4 × 330 ML (11 FL OZ) JARS

What you need

2 onions, peeled	1 teaspoon ground allspice
2 heaped tablespoons whole cloves	1 tablespoon black peppercorns
1 whole pig's head, skin removed	8 fresh bay leaves
2 carrots, roughly chopped	1 tablespoon salt
4 celery stalks, roughly chopped	1 tablespoon Red wine vinegar (page 293)
large handful of parsley, roughly chopped	

How to make it

Stab each onion all over with 1 tablespoon whole cloves.

Sit the pig's head in a large stockpot. Add the onions, carrot, celery, parsley, spices, bay leaves and enough water to cover.

Bring to the boil, and simmer over medium heat for 4 hours. Keep an eye on the water level, adding more water if needed.

Remove the head from the water and allow to cool. Remove anything from the skull that looks like meat and transfer to a large mixing bowl. Peel the tongue and use that meat, and be sure to grab some of the fatty, gelatinous meat (all the left-over unidentifiable stuff I usually feed to my dogs), which will help set the pâté.

Strain the stock and store for other meals.

You can either use your hands to mulch the processed meat into smaller shredded pieces or you can chop it in small batches with a kitchen knife. I like mine to be well chopped, as it helps with spreading on bread. Add the salt and vinegar – the idea is to get it slightly salty with a little tang.

Spoon the processed meat into sterilised jars, ensuring a good mix of meat and fat in each. Seal with lids and boil the jars in a large stockpot of water for 1 hour. Allow to cool overnight.

It will now keep in a cool larder for months. Refrigerate after opening.

One of my beautiful pig-farming mates put me on to this recipe as a way to use a part of the animal that would normally have been disposed of – the head. If I were to serve this pâté on toasted crusty bread before telling you what it was made from, you'd have no problems eating it. But as soon as I mentioned that it's made from the head of a pig, you might feel somewhat iffy about it. Trust me, it's just meat. If you have a spare pig's head floating around, try this recipe.

This is a real homesteaders' meal if I ever saw one. Roosters are definitely not unwanted in our backyard. We only need to keep one, but the rest we love to raise for their meat. We only get a few each year from what we raise ourselves, but thankfully we have a mate with an incubator, so we pass our eggs on to him to be cooked. Sounds weird, doesn't it, but it's a good system, and it's been working well for a few years now, so I think we'll just continue.

When the roosters are teenagers, they start getting all huffy with each other, trying to sort out who's boss. 'It's hard on the peace, and it's hard on the furniture' – John Cleese, Silverado. Classic. The day comes when I've had enough of cockfighting, and I'll process all the birds at once. It's a gross job, but I eat meat so I have to kill the animal to cook it. I wish more meat-eating people would experience this process. It sure makes you appreciate your food.

This meat keeps well in the chest freezer. We bring it out for special occasions and when we're totally sick and tired of cooking rabbit. I have to tell you, though, never in my life have I appreciated variety the way I do living this way. I have pork, venison, rooster, goose, quail, duck, teal, trout, eel, hare, kangaroo and even lamb. We don't eat meat all the time, but when we do it's really nice to have a range of different types to cook with. Only since I've been doing the dirty work myself have I eaten such a diverse selection of meats. It's nice. Should have done it years ago.

Rooster, Beans & Greens

SERVES 4

What you need

1–2 tablespoons olive oil	480 g (1 lb 1 oz/2 cups) cooked dried beans, such as cannellini, scarlet runner or borlotti beans
1 garlic bulb, cloves separated, peeled and chopped	
1 tablespoon cumin seeds	2 cups finely chopped rainbow chard or silverbeet (Swiss chard)
1 tablespoon dried rosemary	50 g (1¾ oz) butter
1 naughty teenage cockfighting rooster, quartered	90 g (3 oz/1 cup) grated pecorino
250 ml (8½ fl oz/1 cup) pinot grigio	

How to make it

Preheat the oven to 180°C (360°F).

Heat a glug of olive oil in a flameproof casserole dish over medium heat on the stove top. Cook the garlic, cumin seeds and rosemary (smells amazing), moving them around for a minute or two. Add the rooster and brown on all sides. Pour over the wine and allow some to cook off. Pour in 250–500 ml (8½–17 fl oz/1–2 cups) water and bring to the boil, then remove from the heat, pop on the lid and transfer to the oven for 30 minutes.

Turn the heat down to 130°C (270°F) and cook for a further 3–4 hours, or until the meat is tender. Remove from the oven, allow to cool, then take out the rooster, remove the meat from the bones and shred, discarding the bones.

Strain the stock and transfer to a clean large saucepan over medium heat with the beans, chard and shredded meat. Cook for 5–10 minutes, or until the chard has softened.

Stir in the butter and pecorino until melted, then serve.

Spit Goose

What you need

5 large garlic cloves, peeled

3 tablespoons olive oil

1–2 tablespoons smoked pimentón (Spanish paprika)

3 tablespoons dried thyme

juice of 1 lemon

salt and pepper, to taste

1 whole goose

Goose is something relatively new to me, but I reckon it's now going to become an annual food tradition. An old acquaintance of mine asked for some help killing a bunch of birds, and for my troubles I was paid with a handful of the spoils. With all those geese in the freezer, I had plenty of opportunities to experiment with this tasty bird. I slow-cooked them, roasted them and finally got brave enough one day to put one on the spit-roaster.

The family and I just devoured that goose. Not only was the bird succulent and full-flavoured, it was lifted a notch or two by the smoky flavour imparted by the hot coals that roasted it.

How to make it

Crush the garlic in a mortar and pestle to form a smooth paste. Add the olive oil, pimentón, thyme, lemon juice and a pinch each of salt and pepper, and mix well. Rub the marinade mix all over the bird, then and refrigerate in plastic wrap overnight.

Set the fire going using either heat beads, wood or briquettes – it doesn't really matter what you use, as long as there's a solid base of hot coals under the spit-roaster. Take your time getting the fire going – I advise beer and a long hour of fire-poking before you start cooking. In fact, it's mandatory. Before you spike the bird with the metal spit-roasting rod, you should have the temperature just right. If you can hold your hand above the coals for 5 seconds or so without screaming like a small child, you should be right. Remember, we want to slow-cook the bird, not burn the outside!

When you're happy with the temperature of your coal base and the coldness of your beer, set that bird a spinnin'. It takes about an hour and a half, depending on the size of your goose. Keep a close eye on that coal base – if the temp drops, add a little fuel. No, not petrol.

If you think the bird is ready, stop the machine and pierce the bird with a skewer in a few places. If it's still dripping red, return it to the heat for a little longer, until it drips a bit clearer when pierced. You can also use one of those fancy meat-temperature gauges, but I'm still a little bit prehistoric when I cook with my outdoor fire.

Now eat that bad boy like a caveman. Or cavewoman.

It doesn't really feel right having a salad in the middle of winter, but it's all thanks to the magic of the poly tunnel. The tunnel protects the plants from cold wind and freezing temperatures. I can grow spinach and rocket outside in winter, but mizuna is a little bit more delicate. I tend to use it more and more to extend the seasons and provide the family with a good mix of vegetables the whole year round. I've been known to have a vegetarian salad on occasion, but I don't mind sneaking a bit of meat into a meal. Hell, I've usually raised it or hunted it, so I'm cool with eating it! This year has been a bit of the year of the goose and I prefer it to chicken now. It's unique in flavour and there's

plenty of meat on a bird. But that's not the best bit. The geese now live at my place and are the best damn lawn mowers you ever did see. They nibble the grass down and even do a fair job on the weeds. They don't require much attention other than some supplementary grain and plenty of water. There's a bit of an odd Western obsession with lawns but I can't stand them. They're a waste of resources, similar to the lavishness of a golf course. They're a Western privilege that starving people in developing countries must be scratching their heads over. Go the geese. Edible lawn mowers.

Braised Goose Warm Winter Salad

SERVES 4

What you need

Braised goose

60 ml (2 fl oz/¼ cup) olive oil
1 goose
250 ml (8½ fl oz/1 cup) white wine
1 garlic bulb, cloves separated and peeled
2 rosemary sprigs
handful of thyme
50 g (1¾ oz) butter
½ teaspoon chilli powder

Salad

handful of mizuna
handful of rocket (arugula)
handful of baby spinach
olive oil, to dress
balsamic vinegar, to dress
60 g (2 oz/½ cup) slivered almonds, toasted
goat's feta, to serve
Pickled jalapeño (page 293), to serve

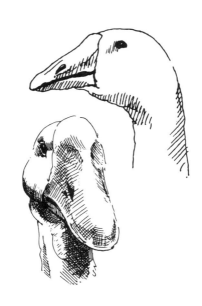

How to make it

Preheat the oven to 200°C (390°C).

Heat half the olive oil in a large flameproof casserole dish over medium heat on the stove top and brown the goose on all sides as best you can. Pour the wine over the bird and reduce.

Remove from the heat, stuff a few garlic cloves in the goose's back end and the rest around the dish. Scatter over the rosemary and thyme, pour in 250 ml (8½ fl oz/ 1 cup) water, pop on the lid and transfer to the oven.

Turn the oven down to 150°C (300°F) and cook the goose for 3 hours, or until the meat is melty.

Allow the bird to cool, then remove all the meat from the bones, discarding the bones or saving them for stock. (I tend to pop half the meat in our fridge for a future meal and use the other half for this dish – more greens, less meat.)

To prepare the salad, rip the greens roughly with your hands and pop in a salad bowl. Dress the leaves with a 2:1 mixture of olive oil and balsamic.

Shred the goose meat, then melt the butter in a frying pan with the remaining olive oil and warm up the meat. Sprinkle over the chilli powder then add the meat to the salad bowl and toss through.

Serve with a scattering of almonds, a crumble of cheese and a generous amount of pickled chillies.

Old soles

It's either mud, snow, dirt, blood or shit. Out here you just have to get used to walking through it all. Every frigid winter morning, as I head out to start my day, I slip my boots over my feet and I don't even think about them. I just expect them to work, to do what they were made to do. To keep my feet dry and safe.

It's amazing how we can get into a daily habit where we become almost robotic in our actions. We end up unintentionally dismissing the things around us, the things that support us day in, day out.

I find myself falling into this pattern often. It's this DIY lifestyle, you see. I have a busy schedule. There's always something that needs attending to. This time of year, many of my chores and responsibilities wait for me outside, which means that this old boy must contend with the winter elements. All the tracks, fields and paddocks are either soaking wet or muddy. Whatever conditions I face, my boots face them too. These guys look after me, so I must look after them. Every few weeks I dry them by the fire then rub them with beeswax, which keeps the leather in good shape and more importantly offers a little more waterproofing for my precious feet.

I've learned one great lesson from this lifestyle, and that is it pays to look after the things that look after you. My old boots, they sure look after me. We've spent evenings together walking up hills searching for rabbits and hares, and days together quietly stalking forests, hunting deer. We've cut firewood together and spent hours under an old car getting soaked in oil and dirt. My shoes and I spend more time together than I do with my loved ones. It's not like I have a 'special' relationship with my boots, it's more that I realise how important they are to me. You know, it's like a good pair of jeans you wear all the time. In time they develop a character. You love slipping them on; they make you feel comfortable. I like that we humans have these items that are so dear to us. I also like wearing jeans, for without them I'd get arrested.

In my previous life I owned many shoes. I'd say at one point I'd had thirty pairs floating around the house. Too many shoes, not enough feet. So as part of my downsizing and minimisation, I gave most of them away to charity. I kept a few pairs, some for hunting, for working and something fancy for going out on dates. That's it. And remarkably, my life feels much clearer because of it. I loved the process of clearing out excess clothes, shoes and household stuff. It tends to lighten my mental state. Odd? Maybe.

But I'll never be able to get rid of my old boots. They've lasted me a long time, even though I've put them through some hellish conditions. They're the metaphor for how I view a lot of stuff now. They're well made, practical and hard-wearing. Anything else just doesn't get the job done.

Kale, chard and spinach are the three crazy leafy greens mad enough to grow in winter, and I love them all for it. For most of winter and into spring I cook with all three of these vegetables. I'll be honest, though: sometimes I hear a voice in my head screaming, 'No more fucking kale!' But I don't have many other options this time of year, so it's just something I must accept. Well, I do have lots of meat in the freezer, but man, you need a break from meaty meals in winter. Often I find

myself longing for anything but meat. I dream of our summer vegetable diet, and I'll eat anything that resembles plant matter over meat. Over the years, I've tried to come up with creative ways to eat these greens, and I often turn to this meal for my lunch break. I can use any one of the three leafy veg, and they all have their unique result. It's a good way to get some greens into you while feeling like you're eating something a bit naughty.

Bruschetta of Kale

SERVES 2

What you need

1–2 tablespoons olive oil	100 g (3½ oz) blue cheese
5 garlic cloves, finely chopped	30 g (1 oz) butter
2 cups shredded, stalks-removed kale, silverbeet (Swiss chard) or rainbow chard	freshly cracked black pepper, to taste
	crusty bread, toasted, to serve
60 ml (2 fl oz/¼ cup) dry white wine	kale flowers, to garnish (optional)

How to make it

Heat a glug of olive oil in a frying pan over medium–high heat and fry the garlic for 1 minute. Add the kale and cook for around 5 minutes, or until it starts to soften. Then splash over the wine and reduce for a further 5 minutes. (If you're using silverbeet or rainbow chard it will cook down much faster.)

Add the blue cheese and butter, and stir until they're melted. Stir through the pepper and serve on toast. Decorate with kale flowers, if you like.

Corn Fritters

SERVES 4

What you need

2 eggs

400 g (14 oz/2 cups) corn kernels

75 g (2¾ oz/½ cup) plain (all-purpose) flour

1 tablespoon garam masala

15 g (½ oz/¼ cup) snipped chives

salt and pepper, to taste

oil, for shallow-frying

goat's feta, crumbled, to garnish

olive oil, for drizzling

Salad bed

handful of rocket (arugula), plus flowers to garnish (optional)

1 tablespoon balsamic vinegar

1 tablespoon olive oil

salt and pepper, to taste

Corn isn't a winter crop, but it's one of those crops that I can grow a lot of over summer and freeze the excess for winter meals. In the horrible freezing depths of winter, one can simply remove a bag of home-grown kernels from one's freezer then one can make a delicious meal with them. It's all rather proper and convenient. To store the corn in the freezer, it needs to be snap frozen to keep its freshness and retain all the sweetness. In summer, when I have excess corn, I peel the corn and boil it for 7 minutes. When done, I transfer it to a large pot of iced water to stop the cooking. I leave it in the water for 7 minutes then slice off the kernels and distribute in re-usable zip-lock bags. Like a drug dealer, my stash is everything to me. It's comforting to know I have some summer veg stored in the freezer to raise our spirits on a rainy winter's day.

How to make it

Make a batter by mixing the eggs, corn, flour, garam masala, chives, and salt and pepper. Stir like crazy – you need the batter to get a bit gluggy.

Heat the oil in a cast-iron frying pan over medium–high heat and, working in batches, spoon in dollops of the batter. Cook until golden brown on both sides, then lay on paper towel to soak up any excess oil while you cook the next batch.

Toss the salad ingredients in a bowl, then arrange on a serving dish. Sit the fritters on the salad bed and garnish with the goat's feta, a drizzle of olive oil and rocket flowers, if using.

It's really exciting when one of the kids takes to a meal you've cooked and it becomes their favourite. When the broad beans are in season, I tend to make quite a few meals with them, then blanch and freeze the excess beans for future food. I do like to make this meal while the beans are in season and fresh, but in the middle of winter, when you're longing for something to remind you of sunnier days, a meal like this can really lift your winter spirits. Although this could be a vegetarian dish, I do like to add the smoked bacon if I have it. I think beans and bacon work really well together. It's a clash of fresh and healthy versus fatty and smoky. And isn't that what most of our food lives entail?

Broad bean freezing tip: Harvest your excess beans in spring. Blanch them for 5 minutes, cool them in iced water for 5 minutes, then portion into zip-lock bags and freeze.

Broad Bean Risotto

SERVES 4–6

What you need

2 litres (68 fl oz/8 cups) Home-made meat stock (rooster, lamb or pork; page 294)

1–2 tablespoons olive oil

2 onions, finely chopped

2 large celery stalks, finely chopped

4 garlic cloves, finely chopped

500 g (1 lb 2 oz) risotto rice

250 ml (8½ fl oz/1 cup) pinot grigio

350 g (12½ oz/2 cups) podded broad (fava) beans, blanched and skinned

5 rashers (slices) smoky bacon (page 189), chopped

handful of parsley, finely chopped (optional)

salt and pepper, to taste

180 g (6½ oz/2 cups) grated sharp pecorino, plus extra slices to serve

50 g (1¾ oz) butter

How to make it

Heat the stock in a saucepan over medium heat and keep it hot.

Meanwhile, heat a glug of olive oil in a large saucepan over medium heat and fry the onion, celery and garlic for 5 minutes, or until they colour and soften. Add the rice and stir through for a few minutes, or until it begins to look translucent. Add the wine and allow mostly to evaporate.

Ladle in the stock one ladleful at a time, allowing it to be absorbed into the rice as you stir each time, then adding another ladleful. After 10 minutes of this process, add the beans, bacon and parsley, if using.

Continue the process of adding stock until the rice is almost cooked through – tasting it is the best way to tell. Season well with salt and pepper.

When the rice is cooked through, remove from the heat and stir in the grated cheese. Add the knob of butter, pop on the lid and allow to rest for 5 minutes.

Serve topped with the sliced cheese and a sprinkle of black pepper.

Change

Once you become aware of certain information, there's no way to 'unknow' it. You're stuck with it, and if it's crucial information there's a fair chance it may change the way you see things, the way you think and your opinion. I recently discovered how much methane cattle and sheep add to our global-warming woes. On top of that I discovered the amount of resources required to raise each animal. I'm not going to state all the scientific figures, but let me assure you, it's not a very environmentally friendly way to get meat.

The process cows and sheep use to break down grass in their stomach oozes methane. Like a *lot* of methane. And on top of that, it takes a heap of resources to raise and then transport them, not to mention the resources needed to manufacture the chemical and medical treatments administered to them. According to the Food and Agriculture Organization of the United Nations, on a global level, livestock accounts for 18 per cent of greenhouse emissions. Knowing this, with a desire to contribute less to global environment issues, I think I won't ever be buying a sheep off any farmer, no matter how close their farm is. I'll still eat some lamb, and a burger *every* now and then. It's just that I have other sources of meat that are slightly more climate-friendly.

I consider myself a relatively forward-thinking person. That's not to say that I think I'm better than anyone. Jeebers! I'm just saying that I like to be aware of the impact my daily choices have on a range of different problems. So I keep my ears to the ground and pick up bits of info that can 'improve' the way I live. But sometimes I think – if I keep hearing depressing news about how certain types of food are bad for the planet or bad for our health – that one day I'll opt to not eat at all!

That's never going to happen, but you get what I'm saying? Our food will always have some impact on the natural world. I think the best thing we can do is identify where we can reduce our impact, be honest with ourselves, actively make positive changes to reduce where we can, and strive for some balance that's right for us and our families. I've clearly said before that what I do, the way I live, the way I acquire my food, isn't the answer for everyone and nor will it solve the world's problems. But I've found that it works for my family, it's practical and it's had a positive impact on my health. I've changed a lot over the years, and I'm now enjoying this second chance at life. Sure, on the outside I've lost a few pounds, but it's the insides that seem to be back in order now.

Ideally, we should all eat less meat. Ideally, we should all shop direct from farmers. Ideally, we should buy free-range, organic, chemical-free, antibiotic-free and every-other-bad-thing-free. But that's never going to happen. There are many social and individual reasons for this. But many of us can make some little changes, and together they could make a big difference.

For any real impact to occur, we need us Westerners, those of us with the ability to change some of our food-buying habits, those of us willing to be more aware of the impacts of our consumer choices, to influence some societal shift. It's just a case of identifying and acting. I'm not suggesting that it's super-easy, either. It takes true grit and determination. It doesn't mean we all need to put our hands inside rabbits or rip the heads off backyard chickens. There are plenty of food choices that can make a difference. It's the twenty-first century: if you're not aware of those choices, then we've failed ourselves somewhat.

Rest

Winter is such an important time for me to rest. I've worked my middle-aged butt off for three seasons and I don't feel a bit of guilt taking it easy for a while in winter. Let's be honest, it's so crappy here, there isn't much to do anyway. I could spend all winter drinking wine and making love but there are some things that need to be done outside the warmth of a cosy bed. Not that I drink wine in bed (any more). Winter on the hill is about taking it easy. It's about as clichéd as you can imagine: warm jackets, wool-lined boots, knitted gloves, roaring fires, hearty meals and the chance of snow. I love it. Each season I can be caught saying, 'This is my favourite season.' Maybe I just like being alive no matter what the season.

It's not only us hill-living humans who take time out to rest in winter. The veg garden doesn't mind a little rest over winter either. The past three seasons will have taken a great deal from the soil, and winter is a good time to allow some rest. Each year, I choose a row or two that will remain dormant over winter. I don't plant a crop as such, but sometimes I plant a green manure or allow weeds to take over for the winter. When spring arrives I dig in the weeds and allow them to rot down, returning some goodness to the soil.

Winter is also a great time to collect manure from the surrounding paddocks and spread it out over the soil. I don't bother digging it in, as nature will do some of the work for me. The rain and elements will help break down the manure, and the goodness will be slowly released and filter down into the soil, eventually making its way to the roots of my plants. By the time spring comes around the soil is full of natural energy and summer crops will have a better chance of success.

If I don't put love back into my soil and push it to be productive year in, year out, it tends to get a little grumpy and my crops aren't as prolific as I'd like. I've found this to be the case with broad (fava) beans this year. Their germination rates seemed fine, but the number of beans was down on last year. I didn't plant the crop in the same row, I just didn't let that bed rest over winter. It's a good reminder of the importance of allowing the natural world to recover from what we take from it. The same approach is scalable, too. The demands our Western lifestyle places on the natural world are high. It's important that we allow nature to recover. How we do that on a large scale I don't know. I guess it would be something like live lighter, live with less in the hope that we're personally using fewer natural resources. Is that too simple?

Blewit & Bunny Bows

What you need

1 whole wild rabbit
1–2 tablespoons olive oil, plus extra for drizzling
50 g (1¾ oz) butter
4 garlic cloves, crushed
180 g (6½ oz/2 cups) chopped wood blewit mushrooms
180 g (6½ oz/2 cups) sliced field mushrooms
125 ml (4 fl oz/½ cup) white wine
3 tablespoons chopped thyme
500 g (1 lb 2 oz) Farfalle (page 277)
55 g (2 oz/¼ cup) mascarpone
135 g (5 oz/1½ cups) grated pecorino, plus extra slices to serve
salt and freshly cracked black pepper, to taste

My ex-father-in-law used to say that if he ever put an ad in the wanted pages of the local newspaper he'd call himself 'Triple B' (BBB) for bald, beard and bifocals. That has absolutely nothing to do with this recipe but it still makes me chuckle every time I think of it. This meal is my triple B, made with three ingredients I love in winter – blewit mushrooms, bunnies and pasta bows (Farfalle, page 277). The three ingredients marry well to make a creamy and saucy pasta. This is the prime time of the year for hunting wild rabbit, as the fields surrounding the old farmhouse are teeming with the pesky beasts. They like to sneak into my veg garden and munch on food I'm trying to grow for my family. So I like to eat them before they eat our food.

In the winter forests, the leaf litter under the oak trees provides prime growing conditions for the spectacularly beautiful wood blewit. The colour underneath these mushrooms is mind-blowing, especially if you find a specimen at that perfect age when the lilac colour is at its peak. But make sure you've been taught by an experienced guide before picking and eating wild mushrooms, especially under oak trees, where the death cap likes to grow. That's a mushroom that will surely ruin a perfectly good day. The wood blewit, on the other hand, is less dangerous, but still must be cooked, as it's a bit toxic raw.

How to make it

Poach the whole rabbit in salted water for 2 hours, or until the meat falls from the bones. Set aside until cool enough to handle, then remove the meat from the bones and shred it with your hands into a bowl.

Heat the olive oil (a glug) in a frying pan over medium–high heat. Add the butter and garlic and stir. Once the butter has melted, add the mushrooms and fry for about 5 minutes. Splash over the white wine, add the thyme, and reduce for a further 5 minutes.

Meanwhile, cook the farfalle in salted water until al dente.

Drain the pasta, then return it to the saucepan you cooked it in. Add the shredded rabbit meat, cooked mushrooms, mascarpone and grated pecorino. Season with salt and pepper.

Serve with a few slivers of pecorino, a sneaky drizzle of olive oil and an extra grind of pepper.

One of the mysteries of veg-growing that I've never been able to figure out: rainbow chard versus silverbeet (Swiss chard). I've bought both varieties in seed form, both having these separate names on the seed packet. They may have different names, but both grow in the same season and they end up looking pretty similar, so I'm totally stumped as to what the difference is. I do like to propagate rainbow chard, if only because its mixed colours make the garden look pretty. I like my garden to be functional and to look pretty. It makes life feel nice in a world that's, at times, a bit fucked. The rich colours of rainbow chard in winter sure pick me up, or maybe it's the high iron levels in this leafy green. Whatever the case may be, I love chard, silverbeet, Swiss chard, whatever you want to call it.

You could make a vegetarian version of this dish by omitting the chorizo, but I just love the odd 'sprinkle' of chorizo in a meal.

Chard & Chorizo Pie

SERVES 4

What you need

60 ml (2 fl oz/¼ cup) olive oil	**Shortcrust pastry**
2 onions, sliced	100 g (3½ oz) butter, diced
4 garlic cloves, sliced	200 g (7 oz/1⅓ cups) plain (all-purpose) flour, plus extra for dusting
50 g (1¾ oz) butter	
4 cups chopped rainbow chard	1 small egg, lightly beaten
150 g (5½ oz) chorizo (page 49), chopped	
90 g (3 oz/1 cup) grated pecorino	
4 eggs, lightly beaten	
handful of chives, snipped	
salt and pepper, to taste	
125 g (4½ oz/1 cup) grated cheddar	

How to make it

To make the shortcrust pastry, whizz the butter and flour in a food processor until the mixture resembles breadcrumbs. With the processor still running, slowly pour in the egg and let the processor do all the work for you. The mixture should bind together to form a lump of dough. If it doesn't quite pull together, add small amounts of chilled water until it does. Wrap the dough in plastic wrap and refrigerate for at least 1 hour.

Preheat the oven to 220°C (430°F) and grease a 23 cm pie dish.

Heat half the olive oil in a frying pan over medium heat, then gently cook the onion and garlic for 15 minutes, or until softened. Transfer to a large mixing bowl.

In the same frying pan, melt the knob of butter with the remaining olive oil over medium heat, then add the chard, cooking it until it wilts right down. Remove from the heat and add to the onion and garlic.

In the same pan, fry the chorizo for a few minutes, then add to the mixing bowl.

Roll out the shortcrust pastry on a floured bench and use it to line the prepared pie dish. Trim the edges and poke the bottom of the pastry with a fork. Line the pastry with baking paper, half-fill with dried beans or uncooked rice and blind bake for 10 minutes. Remove the beans and baking paper and bake for a further 10 minutes, or until golden.

Turn the oven down to 180°C (360°F).

Add the pecorino, eggs and two-thirds of the chives to the chard mixture and stir through well. Season with salt and pepper. Pour into the pastry shell and top with the cheddar.

Bake for 30 minutes, or until set, then allow to rest for 10 minutes before serving with a garnish of the remaining chives.

Three-way experimenting

There's nothing worse than the same old drab approach. Sometimes we get in a rut and we do what seems to come most easily. But I've come to the point where I need to mix things up a little bit, and it involves a deer. Well, a deer shoulder blade, to be precise. After I served my darling Kate *another* (apparently) boring stew, she hinted that I have a 'particular' cooking style I rely on *a lot*. I get it. I need to change my cooking approach. But it's winter and I'm not loaded with choice right now. I have meat in the freezer, I have a few leafy greens in the kitchen garden, a row of carrots, some celery, potatoes, some fresh herbs and whatever stores I have hidden in the larder. I've been making a lot of stews with passata, beans, some meat and whatever veg I have. Winter isn't great here for growing veg. That's the whole point of this system. I've prepared for this, so stews it is, darling!

Secretly, I'm a bit over the hearty meals, too. But let's keep that between you and me. So here I am, pulling a shoulder of deer out of the freezer and thinking of anything but a slow-cooked stew. The good thing about the stews this time of year is that they can sit on the stove for a few days and get added to with a splash of wine here, a pinch of salt there, and the flavour improves over time. I like to make a big batch of stuff –

it's just practical and saves time. So this large cut of meat will need to be spread out to make a few different meals. I decide to cover the meat in fresh garden herbs, such as sage, thyme and rosemary. I add a few garlic cloves, some lard and butter for moisture, and a cup or two of shiraz for zing and to further reduce the chance of the meat drying out during cooking. I wrap the whole parcel in foil and cook it super-slow and low on the outdoor hooded barbecue, until the meat is so tender that mastication is optional.

After letting the venison rest, I make meal number one: a warm salad with slow-cooked onions, broad (fava) beans and spring onions (scallions). It needs some wow factor, so I add preserved lemons, sumac and feta. Job done. I like it, the girls like it, and my darling likes it (and there isn't a stew dish to be seen for miles).

I have heaps of this slow-cooked meat remaining, so I store it in the fridge overnight. I soak white beans that night and in the morning make a bean dish simmered in pig's-head stock and fresh rosemary, then add some of the roast venison meat. I grate in some pecorino for character, throw in a knob of butter and add plenty of cracked pepper. Hello, morning! Best bean breakfast I've had in ages.

That afternoon I come up with the last dish to top off the three-way combo: a pasta sauce – a few slow-fried sprigs of rosemary, garlic and onions, a bottle or two of tomato passata, and the last of the roast venison. I don't even try with this dish, and it isn't anything fancy, but you should see the kids wolf it down then ask for more.

Little victories like these bring me true at-home happiness. It's really such a dorky thing, getting excited about a few meals from a roast shoulder, but it's the bigger picture that makes me smile. First, I reckon I've made it. I've got to where I wanted to be, a bloke who's almost self-reliant regarding the food I feed my family. Secondly, I like that this way of living challenges me to try new things, to look for solutions, to be creative. And the best bit is when my girls eat the food I serve them, not necessarily knowing every ingredient or where it's come from, but they're eating my damn food! That's a victory in itself.

I felt a great deal of guilt about my old lifestyle, especially what I used to allow my kids to eat. I now realise that I was setting my kids up for a life fail. I was forming their future eating habits, which no doubt would have made them a bit unhealthy. But now I feel like we might be on the better path. It's never perfect, but it sure is ace just to be here, at this point. Now, stop talking and eat ya stew!

Officially speaking, this isn't a recipe, it's a technique, but I wanted to share it with you for a reason. I'm not a chef, I've never been trained in the culinary arts, and so I consider myself to be a hack DIY cook. There have been moments when I've observed some aspect of cooking and been totally blown away by the simplicity. These experiences break down that wall of fear and intimidation I sometimes have with cooking. And that's why I wanted to share this skill of making farfalle, because truth be told, it's very easy, and it makes cooking with the kids extra fun.

I'd been asked to present a talk about my life story at an event called the Do Lectures in a little country village somewhere in Wales, where we were fortunate enough to be invited to eat dinner at the house of the event organisers. They had also invited a friend to dinner who just happened to be a chef, who just happened to work for some bloke called Jamie Oliver. We made some fresh pasta that night, but instead of making pappardelle, fettuccine or spaghetti, Mr Chef made farfalle (as I watched in amazement). Now farfalle isn't hard to make, and this is why I observed the process in amazement. Why had I thought it was complicated or difficult?

Farfalle

SERVES 4

What you need

500 g (1 lb 2 oz/ 3⅓ cups) 00 farina flour
5 eggs
plain (all-purpose) flour, for dusting

How to make it

Pour the 00 flour into a large mixing bowl and make a well in the centre for the eggs. Crack the eggs into the well then, using your hands, slowly mix the two ingredients together until a hard dough forms. Knead for a few minutes to ensure the dough is smooth. (The trick I use is to try to pull the dough apart. If it resists, it's done. If it breaks apart easily, it still requires some kneading.) Wrap in plastic wrap and rest at room temperature for 1 hour.

Roll the dough into a sausage-shaped log and cut it into small chunks. Run each chunk of pasta dough through a hand-cranked pasta machine, first on a wide-open setting, then slowly progressing to a tighter setting. You might put each piece of pasta dough through six to eight times, until you have one large strip of flat pasta. Lay the pasta on a flour-dusted bench.

Using a knife or a rolling pasta cutter, cut each wide strip of pasta down the centre lengthways to make two long strips. Now cut the strips into small segments 3–5 cm (1¼–2 in) long.

Pinch each segment to form a bow, and voilà! Farfalle.

Use your farfalle to make Blewit and bunny bows (page 270) or any other kind of pasta you want.

Most times I'll just have a go at anything, like changing an engine in a car or learning how to build a house, but in the kitchen, in front of a chef, I'm often happy to take a back seat because I convince myself that I'm not as able as a trained chef and thus I allow myself to be intimidated.

Anyway, every time I make farfalle I'll be reminded of this experience and tell myself not to be intimidated and give things a go in the kitchen. My girls love helping with making food, and this process is one they always put their hands up to help with.

Our little rented farmhouse sits smack bang in the middle of the potato-growing heartland of the Central Highlands. Each summer, massive diesel tractors turn over the rich volcanic soil into neat rows. A few weeks later the rows are planted by another large tractor full of potatoes that are unrecognisable as potatoes. They are covered in some sort of creamy-white powder, and are owned by the factory that will eventually process the crop, turning them into fries for the world's largest takeaway franchise. The fries are part of the system that's making people very sick, and I think they give the humble spud a bad reputation. Potatoes have been a starchy staple for cultures around the world for centuries. They've saved entire generations from famine, and they've been relied on as human fuel in hard times in many countries.

I love potatoes, and like bread, butter, coffee and pasta, I refuse to give them up. I don't care about their carb-loading attributes, because I believe in balance. I wouldn't eat potatoes every day of my life, but on occasion I like to cook this meal and really pig out and fill up on this humble and easy-to-grow food source.

It's probably not traditional to eat this classic Spanish meal with chorizo, but that's the beauty of being the cook – you can cook your family what you like. When I make a new batch of chorizo I often freeze a few sausages for meals like this. If you can't access fresh chorizo, it still works well with the harder, cured variety.

Patatas Bravas with Unnecessary Chorizo

SERVES 4–6

What you need

1–2 tablespoons olive oil, plus extra for drizzling	½ teaspoon chilli powder or cayenne pepper
3 onions, chopped	handful of parsley, chopped
5 garlic cloves, chopped	8–10 potatoes, washed
725 g (1 lb 10 oz/2¾ cups) tomato passata (puréed tomatoes)	300 g (10½ oz) chorizo (fresh, if possible; page 49), chopped
1 tablespoon smoked pimentón (Spanish paprika)	salt and pepper, to taste
	1 jalapeño chilli, chopped

How to make it

Heat a generous glug of olive oil in a frying pan over low–medium heat. Gently cook the onion and garlic for 20 minutes, stirring often (if they start to dry out, add a splash of water).

Add the passata, pimentón, chilli powder and half the parsley. Simmer for 30 minutes, or until reduced and thickened. Allow to cool slightly, then purée with a hand-held blender.

Preheat the oven to 200°C (390°C).

Parboil the potatoes for 10 minutes. Drain, cut into bite-sized pieces and transfer to a roasting tin. Drizzle over some olive oil, toss to coat, then roast for 30–40 minutes, or until crispy and golden.

Fry the chorizo in a small frying pan over medium heat.

Reheat the tomato sauce.

Serve the potatoes topped with chorizo and smothered in the sauce. Season with salt and pepper, then sprinkle over the remaining parsley and the fresh chilli.

Pork & Ginger Pot Stickers

SERVES 6–8

What you need

500 g (1 lb 2 oz) minced (ground) pork (not too lean – fat is good for this recipe)

150 g (5½ oz/2 cups) finely grated cabbage

4 garlic cloves, crushed

3 tablespoons sesame oil

1 tablespoon mirin

50 g (1¾ oz/¼ cup) freshly grated ginger

pinch of salt

round gow gee (egg) dumpling wrappers

3 tablespoons vegetable oil

soy sauce, to serve

Green sriracha (page 199), to serve

chillies (if you have a poly tunnel ;-)), sliced, to serve

I've learned that if you allow your pig to get too old and fat, you'll inadvertently end up with a lot of sausage meat – probably more than you need for making sausages. This is what happened to me this winter, and I can only wish it upon you too, as it's a delicious pork burden to deal with. Here's a tasty approach to using those many bags of minced (ground) pork in the freezer. I could eat pot stickers for every meal. I love to dip them in hot and spicy sriracha (page 199) and soy sauce, and eat until my belly reaches full capacity. Then I'll wash it down with a dry lager. This is better food than from any chain takeaway. Well, out here in the sticks we don't really have that option, so for me this is as good as it gets!

How to make it

Mix the pork, cabbage, garlic, sesame oil, mirin, ginger and salt.

Lay a wrapper on the bench and wet the edge with water. Spoon a small amount of pork filling into the middle of the wrapper and fold it over, pleating the edges to seal. Repeat until you run out of filling or wrappers.

Heat the oil in a deep frying pan (one with a lid) over medium heat and fry the bottoms of the pot stickers for a few minutes. Leave the pot stickers in the pan and add about 5 mm (¼ in) water. Pop on the lid, turn down the heat and cook for 10–15 minutes, or until the bottoms are crispy and the pastry on top is soft.

Serve with soy sauce, sriracha and chilli.

The over-share

I've been debating whether or not to include this bit, as it's quite the over-share. But it's important to me and I think it's worth sharing, even though parts of it are a bit embarrassing and shameful. I'm going to share some information that some people may not like to hear. The truth is often hard to listen to.

In my early adult life, just after I got my driver's licence, I secured a job and moved out of home. I started to change. I got fat, really fat. And it happened really quickly. Over two years I gained a massive amount of weight. I was close to 120 kilograms (265 pounds) and I'm only 180 centimetres (5 feet 10 inches) tall. So yes, I was clinically obese.

How did this happen? On my wedding day, I was just twenty-two years old and I hated myself. I got drunk to suppress my feelings of self-hatred. In fact, I got drunk most days after that for the next decade or so. I got divorced. Most of my friends hated me, my ex-wife's friends hated me, and I hated me. I was a horrible person.

I can look back at my early adult life with a bit of hindsight now. My self-destructive behaviour was a cycle of eating poor food, remaining overweight, then drinking heavily to suppress my depression. I was fuelling a raging fire. I had a few moments in my adult life where I'd go on a diet, lose some weight, then return to my old ways – and sure enough, I wound up overweight, depressed and very drunk. Somehow along the way I got worn out with taking the bandaid-treatment medication for my self-inflicted woes. I got to the point where I said enough is enough. I guess that's what they call 'the lowest point'.

I looked into what was causing my poor health. I held up the honesty mirror, and it sucked. I was the one choosing the food that went into my body, I was the one pouring in the drinks, lighting the smoke.

I had to make changes, and I had to admit that I needed to change my lifestyle. I started with baby steps. I started eating whole foods. I started growing my own veg. I taught myself how to cook. I went all grow, gather, hunt, cook. It's been a long journey over several years, but I think I've reached a much better place. And that's only measurable by the individual.

I've had to work hard at this lifestyle change. I've had to give up the easy choices and make hard ones. It hasn't been an easy ride. There've been so many moments when I've wanted to light a smoke, pour a glass or eat shit food. The hard option has been to lace up my joggers and run. To not drink that night. To eat well.

Today I watched a clip on the internet that had some masters of medicine arguing about whether or not obesity should be categorised as a disease. I don't really have an opinion either way – it won't make a difference to the person who's obese. What really pissed me off was that they kept saying that obesity is purely a genetic problem, which I agree with to a certain extent. I got fat, while people around me ate the same shit but stayed skinny. But from personal experience, I can say the reason most of us Westerners are getting fatter and sicker is that we're lazy and we make bad food choices. You can get all cranky with me for saying that, but I have an ex-fat-man licence, so I can say whatever the hell I want. I've been there. I know why I got obese and sick. That truth hurts me, too.

I also got healthy. So I know what it takes to get fit. I know that our bodies have evolved to be fuelled with real food and they need to be kept in order with some sort of physical activity. So I have a healthy-man licence, too. And let me tell you, being skinny isn't really a sign of inner health. I'm not saying that being fat is healthy either. I've been hunting and hiking up hills with skinny blokes, and they've huffed and puffed all the way up the hill, when I've not even been out of breath.

I guess the point I'm trying to make is that we as a Western culture have a problem with obesity and diet-related health issues. The reason we're here isn't that people just eat too much. It's the food itself. It's rubbish. I cook with lard and butter and I've still lost weight. But when I ate processed foods and chain takeaway food I was horribly unhealthy. The food I was eating was loaded with hidden salt, sugar and fat.

Look at pre–World War II photos. You'll hardly see any fatties. It doesn't take years of research to realise that the things that have changed in the Western world since the 1940s are the types of food we eat and the reduction in the amount of physical work our bodies do. It's as simple as that. Every fad diet, protein shake, protein bar or weight-loss pill is just a money-making scam that's capitalising on people's ignorance. I can't shout this loudly enough: *Eat well and you'll live well.*

At my worst

- I weighed almost 120 kilograms (265 pounds).

- I could drink three bottles of wine a night.

- I would smoke a packet of twenty-five cigarettes a day.

- I ate highly processed supermarket food and chain takeaway.

- I had massive anxiety attacks and suffered from debilitating depression.

- I was an arsehole to live with.

My in-between bandaid was medication: antidepressants and high-blood-pressure pills. This really helped. It gave me stability. It gave me a starting point.

The endgame

By this stage in the book you'd be fairly aware of how I live. I eat well, I'm healthier and thus less depressed, so I drink less and smoking – well, it's gone, except for those rare occasions. If you're an ex-smoker you'll know what I'm talking about.

Over the years of my new, second-chance life I've had some positive results:

- I've lost more than 20 kilograms (44 pounds).

- My depression and anxiety are practically nonexistent, which I think has a lot to do with removing processed foods and large amounts of alcohol from my lifestyle.

- My blood pressure has taken me a few years to control but is now well down to normal levels.

- I'm no longer medicated for anxiety, depression or high blood pressure. I worked with my GP on this one. He monitored my progress and accepted that my lifestyle changes had improved my health enough for me to work on a program to reduce the medications, with the goal of going off them completely.

I guess I can say that even though it's been a hard slog at times, I've managed to 'cure' myself of my self-inflicted preventable Western illness. My second chance at life wasn't a gift, nor was it lucky. It was all about making choices and working bloody hard. And that's not something that's appealing to most of us who are afflicted with diet-related obesity.

I hope you get something useful from my over-share.

I know, baby rabbit sounds mean, doesn't it. In winter, new rabbits pop out of the ground and just happen to be the most tender due to their age. The same can be said for most animals, actually. Think about lamb and veal, young versions of the sheep and cow. Rabbits are no different. The younger mammals are, the tenderer they are.

Here in Australia, rabbit is an introduced pest and an environmental nightmare. Their numbers will never be controlled – two separate releases of biological control agents haven't fixed the problem. Rabbits occupy the same ecological niche as some of our native marsupials, and they cause significant damage to crops. So they're a problem worth eating.

Avocados come into season in winter and, depending on the variety, seem to last all the way to summer. Then they're absent. So while they're in season, we add avocado to everything. Well, not everything. Avocado and coffee don't work well, FYI.

This recipe is a bit fiddly but the effort is rewarded with a really splendid meal.

Baby Rabbit & Avocado Ravioli

SERVES 4

What you need

2 wild baby spring rabbits	pouring (single/light) cream (I use Inglenook Dairy)
300 g (10½ oz/1¼ cups) fresh ricotta	300 g (10½ oz/2 cups) organic plain (all-purpose) flour, plus extra for dusting
90 g (3 oz/1 cup) grated pecorino (Australian-made is really good)	4 large backyard eggs
handful of soft garden-fresh spring thyme	good-quality extra virgin olive oil, for drizzling
2 avocados	Murray River salt, to taste
juice of 2 lemons (from Mum's lemon tree)	foraged mountain pepper berries, to taste
1 teaspoon chilli powder (I blitz my dried backyard chillies to make the powder), plus extra to serve	

How to make it

Poach the rabbits gently in water for 2 hours, or until the meat starts to fall off the bone. Allow to cool, remove the meat from the bones, then blitz the meat in a food processor. Save the bones for stock.

Transfer the processed meat to a large mixing bowl, then add the ricotta and half the pecorino. Pick the thyme leaves, reserving a sprig or two as a garnish, and add to the meat and cheese. Mix well (this is the stuffing for the ravioli, so try not to eat too much of it as you mix).

Remove the flesh from one and a half of the avocados, then mash with a spoon in a large mixing bowl. Add half the lemon juice, the chilli powder, and a generous dollop of cream. For extra love, add the remaining pecorino.

Pour the flour into a large mixing bowl and make a well in the centre. Break three of the eggs into the well. Using an expensive kitchen mixing device (i.e. your hands, with clean fingers), mix and twirl the egg around in the flour until completely mixed, then knead on a floured bench for 5 minutes, or until a smooth dough forms. Wrap the dough in plastic wrap and set aside to rest at room temperature for 1 hour.

Roll out massive strips of flat pasta following the instructions on page 233. Beat the remaining egg in a small bowl and grab a small pastry brush. Arrange a few spoonfuls of the filling at regular intervals on one half of each strip of pasta. Brush the egg over the exposed pasta, then fold over the half without filling to cover the filling. Seal well, pushing any air

out of the pockets of filling. Use a pasta cutter to cut out your ravioli. Repeat with any remaining pasta and filling.

Cook the ravioli in boiling salted water for 5 minutes, or until al dente. Remove from the hot water with a slotted spoon and pop straight into the bowl with the mashed avocado. Toss and flip the ravioli to cover with the creamy mashed avocado sauce.

Slide the ravioli and avocado sauce onto a pretty plate. Drizzle over the best olive oil you have in the house and the remaining lemon juice, crack over the salt and wild pepper berries, and add a sprinkle of beautiful red chilli powder. To remind you that it's okay to have avocado in pasta, slice the remaining avocado half to sit proudly on top. Garnish with the reserved thyme sprigs and serve.

This flatbread is chewy and bendy, perfect for wrapping up a heap of tasty home-grown ingredients for a hearty breakfast. I nabbed this flatbread recipe from Kate, who makes them in large batches, which we'll then use over the next few days, wrapping things up in them or dipping them into things.

A meal like this uses a heap of home-grown ingredients but tastes like something you'd buy on a hot pavement in LA. Breakfast burritos aren't very popular as street food in Australia, and I'm not often near any streets where food is served anyway. Out here in the sticks, I have to make my own, which actually is a good thing because I can fill these beauties with whatever I like. The chickens are still laying plenty of eggs, I have fresh chorizo, and cheese and chilli sauce are always in the house.

Sourdough Breakfast Burrito

SERVES 6–8 (MAKES 12 FLATBREAD)

What you need

Sourdough flatbread

170 ml (5½ fl oz/⅔ cup) Sourdough starter (page 246)

450 g (1 lb/3 cups) organic plain (all-purpose) flour, plus extra for dusting

1½ teaspoons salt

80 ml (2½ fl oz/⅓ cup) olive oil

125 ml (4 fl oz/½ cup) hot water

Burrito filling

1–2 tablespoons olive oil

50 g (1¾ oz) butter

150 g (5½ oz) chorizo (page 49), chopped

6 eggs, lightly beaten

chives, snipped, for sprinkling

1 jalapeño chilli, sliced (if you have a poly tunnel these may still be hanging off your plants)

Chipotle sauce (page 187), to taste

125 g (4½ oz/1 cup) grated cheddar

salt and pepper, to taste

How to make it

To make the flatbread, mix the starter, flour and salt in a large bowl until combined. Mix in the olive oil, then add the hot water and mix until a dough is formed and it becomes elastic. Cover the dough with a tea towel (dish towel) and set aside to rest for about 30 minutes.

Heat a dry cast-iron frying pan over medium–high heat.

On a lightly floured bench, cut the dough into twelve equal pieces (I'm terrible at getting them the same size) and roll each into a ball. Using a rolling pin and starting in the middle, rolling outwards and turning often, roll each ball into a flat round about 5 mm (¼ in) thick.

Cook each flatbread in the hot frying pan for 45–60 seconds on each side, or until the flatbread no longer looks doughy.

To make the filling, heat the olive oil with the butter in a frying pan over medium heat. Once the butter is melted, add the chorizo and fry until the colour of the sausage begins to leach out. Add the eggs and scramble until cooked.

Lay out each cooked flatbread, paddle over some scrambled egg, sprinkle with chives and chilli, add a squirt of chipotle, and top with grated cheddar. Season to taste.

Wrap and feast.

Back to the start

The last days of this winter are upon us. It's been a beautiful winter – it always is. Hell, let's face it, every season we're alive is pretty good, right? The only thing I don't like about winter is the ability of the cold temperature to shrink certain manly body parts. Apart from that, I just love it. Why do I wait until the end of winter to consider investing in thermal undies?

Cosy undergarments aside, I wanted to share something a little bit more classy than disappearing testicles. Ducks. Baby ducks, in fact. They've started popping up in the dams. The adults paired up long ago and now little ducklings appear with their mum and dad, as they waddle out from the long grass and sedge that grows on the banks of the frigid water. They have the cutest walk; their little bums wiggle as they stumble on dry land, but they look far less awkward in the water. I'm the complete opposite. I look like I'm drowning when I'm in the water, but look almost normal on dry land. The point is, these beautiful little ducklings have the ability to make a bearded man turn all schmoopy-whoopy. All at once I revert to the child version of me and appreciate that beauty through childlike eyes.

Today I sat alone on the bank of the big dam and just watched as the duck family swam about happily. Above the dam, circling on the thermals, was a brown hawk. Birds of prey are common where we live, probably because there are so many damn rabbits around. This bird is an absolute machine of nature, built tough, fast and violent. What a bird. I can't help but compare us humans with the hawk, or any bird of prey for that matter. Although these days, let's face it, most of us aren't built for speed. But we do hunt. Well, actually, there's another lie; we mostly get someone else to do the 'hunting' for us. And by hunt, I mean buy meat, mostly farmed meat, which we get someone else to do. Okay meat, whichever way it comes.

Out here I feel privileged to be able to observe an ecosystem. Ducks have babies, predator eats new ducks, feeds baby hawks, some ducks survive and the cycle continues the following year. It's a basic biological formula that's been in existence for aeons. We humans are part of it; we've just been a little 'smarter' by inventing ways to manipulate the system a little – farming is just an advanced form of hunting, for example, a manipulation of nature to our advantage.

We're currently the masters of our food chain, but I can't help wondering how long we'll last at the top. Our system has its weaknesses. The one particular weakness is fossil fuels. I can't imagine how our current modern system would operate without it. But I bet you, regardless of our dwindling fossil fuels, those ducks will continue raising ducklings, and those hawks will continue soaring in the heavens, stalking their prey for many moons to come.

A dirty great black cloud is rolling in from the north. The wind has picked up and the hawk has buggered off, uninterested or distracted. The view here is amazing: one side of the sky is bright with patches of blue, the other side is dark and menacing. It's the end of winter. This is the beginning of the crazy spring weather, marking the approaching end of another year in our cycle. The garden is full of potential food and some of it has already started to flower. Soon I'll be eating fresh broad (fava) beans, peas and broccoli. In a few months the summer veg will get planted in the damp spring soil and our bellies will rejoice in a mostly vegetarian diet for the summer. It's a beautiful system.

Some people have said I've lost everything by pursuing this life of practiculture: my career, my possessions, my financial wealth. But to tell the truth, I've gained everything. I'm content to exist in this ancient cycle, to live with real food, purpose and mindfulness.

I sound more and more like a damn hippie every day.

Basics

Mayo

MAKES ABOUT 250 G (9 OZ/1 CUP)

2 egg yolks

250 ml (8½ fl oz/1 cup) mild-flavoured oil, such as sunflower oil or a really mild olive oil

juice of ½ lemon or 2 tablespoons Red wine vinegar (opposite)

pinch of salt

There are a few kitchen ingredients that I haven't needed to buy for a few years, and mayonnaise is one of them. It's a really simple process to make it, and you know exactly what's in it, which, let's be honest, we can't say for a lot of the sauces and condiments on the supermarket shelves. If you haven't heard of the health implications of preservative sulfites, I recommend looking them up. It's mind-blowing what's in some of our food, and the impacts on our health – wow! I think we'll be finding out more with medical research in the years to come. Enough about nutrition, let's make mayo!

In a small bowl, whisk the egg yolks until broken up.

Continuing to whisk, ever so slowly introduce the oil to the eggs. You can start on a drip-by-drip basis and then work up to about a teaspoon at a time. The trick is not to add the oil too quickly or the mayo will split – meaning the egg yolk and oil won't combine to form one uniform sauce, or emulsion.

Continue introducing the oil and whisking until the mixture has a thick sauce-like consistency reminiscent of mayo from a supermarket ;-).

Add the lemon juice and salt, then stir through.

You've just made mayonnaise. Keep it in the fridge and eat it over the next few days – it won't keep forever.

Chilli and Smoked Pimentón Aioli

MAKES ABOUT 250 G (9 OZ/1 CUP)

2 egg yolks

250 ml (8½ fl oz/1 cup) mild-flavoured oil, such as sunflower oil or a really mild olive oil

juice of ½ lemon

pinch of salt

2 garlic cloves, crushed

1 teaspoon cayenne pepper or home-ground chilli powder or finely chopped fresh jalapeño chilli

1 teaspoon smoked pimentón (Spanish paprika)

This is my go-to when I have a tray of crispy potato chips roasting in the oven, or to eat with fish, or with poached eggs and bacon in the morning. It's a fairly handy sauce to have in the fridge and will last a week there in an airtight container. I like home-made mayo, but the punchy aioli really sparks up the meal with its heat, its smoky and garlicky flavour, and that lemony zing.

In a small bowl, whisk the egg yolks until broken up.

Continuing to whisk, ever so slowly introduce the oil to the eggs. You can start on a drip-by-drip basis and then work up to about a teaspoon at a time. The trick is not to add the oil too quickly or the mayo will split – meaning the egg yolk and oil won't combine to form one uniform sauce, or emulsion.

Continue introducing the oil and whisking until the mixture has a thick sauce-like consistency reminiscent of mayo from a supermarket ;-).

Add the lemon juice, salt, garlic, cayenne and pimentón. Stir through and enjoy!

Keep it in the fridge and eat it over the next few days.

Pickled Jalapeño

MAKES 6 × 600 ML (20½ FL OZ) JARS

What you need

1 kg (2 lb 3 oz/10 cups) sliced jalapeño chillies, seeds in, stems discarded

1 litre (34 fl oz/4 cups) water

1 litre (34 fl oz/4 cups) white vinegar

2 tablespoons salt

For each jar

1 bay leaf

1 garlic clove

1 teaspoon dried mountain pepper berries

In the middle of winter I love to open these jars (see photo pages 290–91), the contents of which remind me of the summer that's just passed. Each jar is loaded with jalapeños I spent a lot of time with. We've hung out a lot, all through the summer and into the autumn. Way back in spring I propagated the plants from seed. As they germinated and grew, I transplanted them into the warm poly tunnel. All summer I ensured they were watered and fed, until they were so loaded with fruit they required staking to prevent them toppling over under their own top-heavy weight. When the lid comes off a jar and I enjoy some of these pickled jalapeños in a pulled pork bun or on a taco, I can't help but get nostalgic about the system to which I've committed my life – of providing for oneself. It's a beautiful thing and so are these jalapeños.

Pop a bay leaf, garlic clove and some pepper berries into each sterilised jar, then add the sliced chilli to the jars, leaving a gap of about 2 cm (¾ in) at the top.

Combine the water, vinegar and salt in a large saucepan and bring to the boil (this dissolves the salt).

Allow the solution to cool for a few minutes, then pour into each jar, ensuring you fill above where the chillies end.

Place the rubber seals, lids and clips (or whatever vacuum-sealing lid you use) on the jars, then place the sealed jars in a large stockpot. Fill with hot tap water and bring to the boil. Boil for 1 hour.

Turn the stove off and leave the jars in the pot until cool.

Store the jars in a cool dark place such as a larder. They will keep for 6 months. Refrigerate after opening.

Red Wine Vinegar

Ever have a half-glass of left-over wine sitting on the table in the morning? That doesn't need to go to waste. It's perfectly good for making vinegar and it's very easy. A friend of mine gave me some of his home-made red wine vinegar in a bottle, and in it sat a small amount of the vinegar starter culture, which he told me would make me vinegar.

The instructions were simple: store the vinegar in a large glass bottle and add left-over red wine whenever it appeared. This will feed the starter and turn the wine into vinegar. When I need some vinegar I simply decant it from the large glass bottle into a smaller bottle, and use it as an excuse to open a bottle of wine. The starter must be fed!

Toasted Sourdough Breadcrumbs

Each night just before I go to bed I finish the last task for the day, which is to bake the daily loaf. We eat most of a loaf in a day as we have six mouths to feed, but inevitably there's a small section of the loaf that isn't consumed that day and ends up left in the bread bin. These bread ends build up over a week and I turn them into beautiful breadcrumbs for use in all sorts of things, from arancini to schnitzel.

To make the breadcrumbs, I break the stale bread up by hand into smaller chunks. I lay these on a roasting tray and bake them in a medium–hot oven (180–220°C/360–430°F) until all the moisture has been baked out of them and they turn crunchy. I allow them to cool then whizz them in the food processor until fine. The roasting step ensures they'll keep in a glass jar without rotting. You must bake all that moisture out, though, without burning the bread. If it still feels at all doughy, the breadcrumbs won't keep.

Home-made Meat Stock

MAKES 2.5–3 LITRES (85–101 FL OZ/10–12 CUPS)

What you need

1–2 tablespoons olive oil
2 onions, chopped
2 carrots, chopped
2 celery stalks, chopped
left-over roast bones (e.g. from a whole goose)
pinch or 2 of salt

I haven't bought stock for years. I just don't see the point. The stuff that's in those pre-made stocks is gross, and it costs money! Stock is all about using leftovers and basic veg. The origins of stock lie in frugality and resourcefulness. It's become an automatic process for me to make a batch of stock the day after I've roasted a cut of meat that has bones remaining. I have a chef friend who once said that if you want a lamb stock that tastes like lamb, boil lamb bones and don't add veg. Well, that might be the case, but I like to make a meat-infused stock with a few basic veg, especially the three magic veg: onion, carrot and celery. You can use this recipe for most cuts. I make this stock with goose, duck, chicken, rabbit, hare, deer, quail, lamb, beef, pig and goat. All of them are made from bones left over from a roast, as I don't think a stock made from poached meat is very rad. Roasting brings out unique flavours, and using them for a stock will infuse your next meal with roasty goodness.

Heat a glug of olive oil in a stockpot over medium heat and sweat the onion, carrot and celery for 10 minutes, stirring occasionally.

Add the bones, salt and 3 litres (101 fl oz/12 cups) cold water. Bring to the boil then reduce the heat and simmer, uncovered, for 2 hours.

Strain into airtight freezer containers and label them with the animal used. It may be useful information when you're searching through the freezer in the future. I use a waterproof marker on masking tape, which peels off plastic containers easily. Also make a note of the date – the stock will keep in the freezer for 6 months.

Home-made Veg Stock

MAKES 2.5–3 LITRES (85–101 FL OZ/10–12 CUPS)

What you need

1–2 tablespoons olive oil
3 onions, chopped
3 carrots, chopped
2 celery stalks, chopped, leaves reserved
handful of parsley
3 bay leaves
1 teaspoon dried mountain pepper berries
pinch of salt

I don't normally make vegetable stock. I only really make it when a vegetarian friend comes over for dinner. It's not that I'm a bad person, I just tend to make a stock after I've roasted an animal of some description. But veg stock is super-easy, and I make it with a medley of the veg I have growing in the patch.

Heat a glug of olive oil in a stockpot over medium heat and sweat the onion, carrot and celery for 10 minutes, stirring occasionally.

Add the parsley, celery leaves, bay leaves, mountain pepper berries, salt and 3 litres (101 fl oz/12 cups) cold water. Bring to the boil then reduce the heat and simmer, uncovered, for 2 hours.

Strain into airtight freezer containers and label them. I use a waterproof marker on masking tape, which peels off plastic containers easily. Also make a note of the date – the stock will keep in the freezer for 6 months.

Pizza bases

MAKES 4–6 BASES

What you need

375 ml (12½ fl oz/1½ cups) lukewarm water

2 tablespoons dried yeast

a few pinches of caster (superfine) sugar

600 g (1 lb 5 oz/4 cups) organic plain (all-purpose) flour, plus extra for dusting

pinch of salt

2 tablespoons olive oil, plus extra for greasing

semolina, for dusting (optional)

Like anything food-related, you can buy pizza bases pre-made at the supermarket. That's okay – you'll feel well fed after eating them – but the reality is that you've probably eaten more than you bargained for. The food will have additives in it. The flour that made it will be cheap and highly processed, minimising its nutritional value. And the bases will come wrapped in plastic and cardboard, adding to their carbon footprint. The alternative isn't perfect, but it minimises some of the negative impacts. You can source better flour – organic, for a start. And making it yourself means you haven't bought packaged food. I know it doesn't sound like much, but it all adds up. There are a lot of us in the world. If we all make small changes in our buying habits, we have the potential to make a significant impact. Or, as I said earlier, you can just buy the pre-made version.

Mix the water, yeast and caster sugar in a bowl and stir. Set aside for 10 minutes, by which time there should be bubbles on the surface.

In a large bowl, mix the flour, salt, olive oil and yeast mixture until a dough forms.

Turn the dough out onto a floured bench and knead for a few minutes.

Transfer to an oil-greased bowl, cover with plastic wrap, and leave in a warm spot for 30 minutes. It should double in size.

Cut into tennis-ball-sized pieces (I know, sounds odd), and roll each one out on a floured bench to 1 cm (½ in) thick and pizza tin/stone size.

If you have a pizza stone, sprinkle semolina flour on it before laying the pizza base down for baking, as it helps to make a crunchy base.

You can wrap any leftover uncooked bases in plastic wrap and freeze them for later use.

Pasta

We make this all the time. The kids love this process, and I'm all for anything that gets my kids interested in real food.

The basis for all the pasta I make relies on the old rule of **1 large egg for each 100 g (3½ oz/⅔ cup) flour**, and I generally allow 100 g pasta per person.

I mix the egg and flour in a mixing bowl with clean hands until a dough forms. I knead the dough on a floured bench until it sticks together and binds well. To test the pasta I pull the dough apart.

If there's a lot of resistance and the dough holds together, it's done. If it breaks apart easily, it requires more kneading. I then wrap the dough in plastic wrap and set it aside on the bench to rest for 1 hour before forming it into whatever pasta I desire (see page 277 for how to make Farfalle; and pages 233 and 285 for ravioli). For pappardelle, cut the rolled pasta into long wide strips.

Index

Thanks

There are people in our lives who make every day worth living. They offer support, share experiences, and they're humans we love. These are my people. My love and everything, Kate Berry. My daughters, Helena and Tia Anderson, and my stepdaughters, Maya and Pepper Berry. My mum and dad and crazy Grandpa Berry.

My extended family and network of people who generally get up to no good with me. Fran Haysey, Raynor and Mel Pierce, Hatto and Katie, Sam and Kitty Speer, Jack Dickinson, Tammi Jonai, Jen Charmstrong, Dillon Seitchik, Matt Wilkinson, Deano, Lou and Stewart Lang, Julia Hearts, Peta Mazy, Rosco, Nick Parkes, Jeff Adair, Tim Sproal, Gem and Henry.

Thank you to my family over the Pacific who always make me feel at home when I'm very far away from home: Max Wastler, Duquette and Morgan, Matt and Shannon, Sam Newman, Matt Hranek, Joe Gannon, Tim Haught, David and Tereasa, James Fox.

Thanks to Paul, Hannah and the team at Hardie Grant, and a special thank you to Nicola for working with my collection of mumbled words.

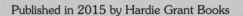

Published in 2015 by Hardie Grant Books

Hardie Grant Books (Australia)
Ground Floor, Building 1
658 Church Street
Richmond, Victoria 3121
www.hardiegrant.com.au

Hardie Grant Books (UK)
5th & 6th Floors
52–54 Southwark Street
London SE1 1UN
www.hardiegrant.co.uk

A Cataloguing-in-Publication entry is available from the catalogue of the National Library of Australia at www.nla.gov.au
A Year of Practiculture
ISBN 9781743790540

Publishing Director: Paul McNally
Project Editor: Hannah Koelmeyer
Editor: Nicola Young
Designer: Mark Campbell
Photographers: Rohan Anderson and Kate Berry
Production Manager: Todd Rechner

Colour reproduction by Splitting Image Colour Studio
Printed in China by 1010 Printing International Limited